German
Verb
HANDBOOK

Joy Saunders

German Verb Handbook

The Author:
Joy Saunders is an experienced teacher, schools inspector and educational consultant.

The Series Editor:
Christopher Wightwick is a former UK representative on the Council of Europe Modern Languages Project and principal Inspector of Modern Languages for England.

Other titles in the Berlitz Language Handbook Series:

French Grammar Handbook	French Vocabulary Handbook ('94)
German Grammar Handbook	German Vocabulary Handbook ('94)
Spanish Grammar Handbook	Spanish Vocabulary Handbook ('94)
French Verb Handbook	
Spanish Verb Handbook	

Published by Berlitz Publishing Co., Ltd.,
Peterley Road, Oxford OX4 2TX

1st printing 1993

Printed in the U.S.A.

CONTENTS

B   The model verbs

C   Subject index

D   Verb index

How to use this Handbook

This handbook aims to provide a full description of the German verb system for all learners and users of the German language. It provides the following information:

• a chapter on the verb system;
• the conjugation in full of ninety-two common verbs, grouped to show the common patterns underlying the system;
• a full subject index;
• a verb index containing over 2,300 verbs with their English meanings.

An important feature of the handbook is that examples, showing many of the verbs in use, are given in the model verb pages.

THE VERB SYSTEM IN GERMAN

This section describes the functions of verbs in general. Information is given on word order, the use of tenses, the way verbs govern different cases and prepositions and the way they are formed.

THE MODEL VERBS

This section gives the conjugation in full of every tense of a verb in the active and the passive. The two reflexive verb forms are also illustrated. Ninety-two common verbs are then set out as models.

A selection of verbs which follow the same pattern as each individual verb is listed underneath. For each model, separable and inseparable verbs are also given. Examples are then provided of these verbs in use, to illustrate different tenses and a wide range of different meanings and idiomatic constructions.

THE SUBJECT INDEX

The subject index gives page references for all the main grammatical terms used.

THE VERB INDEX

For each verb, information is given on whether it is transitive or intransitive, the auxiliary it takes in the past tenses, the case and/or prepositions which it governs and its English meaning. Common secondary meanings are illustrated in a brief phrase. The most important and up-to-date forms of verbs with inseparable prefixes and separable particles are listed.

HOW TO FIND THE INFORMATION YOU WANT

If you want to check on the form, meaning or use of a verb, first look it up in the index. This gives a range of information:

• A hairline in the middle of the verb\shows that the verb is separable. The first part is the separable particle and is stressed;

• Any preposition which normally follows the verb. The preposition takes its normal case, but where there is a choice, this is indicated.

• The case which the verb governs, unless it is the accusative (direct object) or dative (indirect object).

• Whether the verb is transitive, intransitive, reflexive or impersonal, and whether it takes the auxiliary **sein** in the compound past tenses. If no auxiliary is shown, the verb takes **haben**.

• The English meaning of the verb. Only the basic meaning is shown for most verbs.

• A number indicating on which page or pages you will find further information about the verb or others like it.

• A short phrase or sentence following some verbs, giving important subsidiary meanings.

If you want further information on the form or use of the verb, turn to the page reference given. On this page you will find:

• the full conjugation of the present and simple past (imperfect tenses) of each model verb;

• the first person singular form of other tenses, including the **Konjunktiv** (subjunctive);

• a list of other verbs following the same pattern;

• notes indicating any exceptions to this pattern;

• short dialogues and sentences illustrating some of the different tenses and usages of these verbs.

Where two page references are given, the first refers you to a verb with a similar stem. The second indicates a separable or inseparable verb which is similar.

If you want to know the full form of other tenses you should note that they are always regular. They can easily be checked by looking up the full tense of the auxiliary verb indicated, **sein** [➤1] or **haben** [➤2] for the past tenses, and **werden** [➤3] for the future.

For further information on how the verb system works, refer to Part A The Verb System in German.

A
THE VERB SYSTEM IN GERMAN

The verb system

1a Simple and compound verbs

(i) All verbs can either stand alone as a simple verb or be combined with other verbs to form compound tenses. A small group of verbs is commonly used to form the compound tenses. When used like this, they are called auxiliary verbs.

(ii) The main auxiliary verbs are **sein, haben** and **werden. Sein** and **haben** are used to form the past tenses. [➤2i(i)]. **Werden** is used to form the future [➤2h(vii)].

(iii) A group of verbs called *modal auxiliaries* is used to give an indication of a mood. Although some can take a direct object they are more usually followed by an infinitive, without **zu**. They are **können**, (be able, can), **wollen** (want to, will), **mögen** (like, may), **müssen** (must, have to), **dürfen** (may), and **sollen** (shall, am to, be obliged to). **Lassen** (let, have done) can also be included in this group.

Ich will gehen.	I want to go.

[➤model verbs 4-10]

1b Transitive and intransitive verbs

(i) Verbs are said to 'govern' other parts of the sentence. A verb is said to be *transitive* if it governs a direct object, which may be a word or phrase; in German the direct object is in the accusative case.

Wir bauen einen neuen Wohnblock.	We are building a new block of apartments.

(ii) A clause can also be used as direct object.

Er sagte, daß er kommen wollte.	He said he wanted to come.

(iii) A verb is said to be *intransitive* if it stands alone without an object, or is followed by an indirect object or preposition. Although many verbs can be used in both ways, many more cannot, and this must be checked in the index.

Er glaubt *mir.*	He believes *me.*

Note that in this case the English verb governs a direct object and the German verb an indirect object.

Note: that **bitten** (to ask/request), **fragen** (to ask/inquire) and **sprechen** (to speak to) take a direct accusative object.

Ich habe *ihn* gefragt.	I asked *him.*
Ich werde *ihn* sprechen.	I will talk *to him.*

(iv) Some verbs govern two objects, a direct and an indirect: these are still transitive. Verbs of saying, showing, giving and taking from are in this group.

Ich gab *ihm* das Buch.	I gave *him* the book.

The **ihm** here refers to the person *to whom* the book is given and is the indirect object. The indirect object is in the dative case.

(v) The indirect object can also show the person affected by an action. This usage is common in German.

Er hat *mir* das Haus repariert.	He repaired the house *for me.*

(vi) A very few verbs take two objects in the accusative. The most common are **kosten** (to cost), **jehren** (to teach), **nennen/ heißen** (to call/name) and **angehen** (to concern).

Das kostet *mich einen neuen Wagen.*	That is going to cost *me a new car.*

(vii) A very few German verbs, mainly used in formal writing, take an object in the genitive case.

Ich kann mich *seines Namens* nicht entsinnen.	I cannot remember *his name.*

(viii)   A few verbs are used to link two phrases in the nominative, which refer to the same thing. The most common are **sein, werden, heißen** and **bleiben**.

Er *ist/bleibt* mein bester Freund.	He *is/remains* my best friend.

Note   Transitive verbs are indicated in the index by (tr.). Intransitive verbs are indicated by (intr.). Where a verb can be used both transitively and intransitively it is indicated by (tr. & intr.). If a verb is marked as transitive in the index it takes a direct object in the accusative. The normal use of the direct and indirect object is not specially indicated for each verb. The case governed by a verb is only shown where usage is different from what you might expect from the English.

1c   *Reflexive verbs [➤Model verbs sich setzen]*

(i)   Many verbs can be used reflexively as in English, to show:

   • that the action is done by the subject of the verb to him/her/itself.

Ich wasche mich.	I wash myself.

   • that the action is reciprocal, that is, people are doing it to each other.

Wir küßten uns.	We kissed (one another).

(ii)   Some verbs are frequently used reflexively with a change of meaning or an English passive meaning.

Ich interessiere mich für...	I am interested in...

(iii)   A dative reflexive (indirect object) pronoun is often used if the verb already has a direct object, to make it clear that the action is being done to, or affects, the subject.

Ich habe mir den Arm gebrochen.	I have broken my arm.

(iv) A few verbs are always used with a dative reflexive pronoun.

Ich bilde mir etwas ein.	I am imagining something.

Note Reflexive forms are indicated in the index by (refl.) or (dat. refl.). They are only shown if the verb is always used in the reflexive, or if there is a significant change of meaning.

1d Impersonal verbs

(i) A number of verbs are commonly used impersonally, i.e. with **es** as their subject. Some verbs are almost always found in this form.

Es regnet.	It's raining.

(ii) Some verbs have a different meaning when they are used impersonally.

Er kommt an.	He arrives.
Es kommt darauf an, ob ...	It depends whether ...
Er gibt.	He gives.
Es gibt.	There is.

(iii) Verbs are sometimes used impersonally when it is not clear who is performing the action.

Es klopft.	Someone is knocking.

(iv) The **es** subject is commonly used in certain idioms in a caretaker role and not as a true subject. It is omitted when it is not at the beginning of the sentence.

Es tut mir leid.	I am sorry.
Mir ist kalt.	I am cold.

Note Impersonal use is shown in the index as (impers.).

1e   *Verbs governing a preposition*

(i)   Many verbs are commonly followed by a preposition.

Er glaubt an Gott.	He believes in God.

(ii)   The prepositions take the same case as usual. It is worth noting that where the case can be either accusative or dative, the accusative case is most common with **auf** and **über**, and the dative with **an**.

Note   The preposition is only shown in the index where the usage differs from the English. The case is shown where there is a possible choice.

1f   *Separable and inseparable verbs*

(i)   Inseparable prefixes and separable verbal particles are an important feature of the German verb system. They modify the meaning of the simple verb and give greater precision of meaning [➤2I]. All the common simple verbs have a wide range of compounds formed in this way.

The formation of the tenses

2a   *Tenses*

(i)   Verbs are used in tenses, which indicate when the action takes place, i.e. in the past, present or future.

(ii)   Verb tenses can also be said to be either *indicative* or *subjunctive*, which we shall call by its German name **Konjunktiv** [➤2k]. The indicative tenses are the commonest form. For its uses and English meanings see the *Berlitz German Grammar Handbook.*

(iii)   Tenses which are formed of more than one element are called compound tenses.

Ich bin gegangen.	I have gone.

2b   *The stem of the verb*

(i)   The stem is the basic unit of the verb without prefixes, verbal particles or endings. The ending of a verb is determined by the person (first, second, third) and number (singular/plural) of its subject, e.g. **komm** is the stem of **kommen**, and **-en** is the ending.

2c   *The infinitive*

(i)   This is the stem of the verb plus the ending -**en**, e.g. **kommen** (to come). It is the part listed in dictionaries. In English it is usually preceded by 'to'. In German it is sometimes preceded by **zu**.

2d   *The present participle*

(i)   The present participle is the form which corresponds to the English form in '-ing'. All German verbs form it by adding the ending **-d** to the infinitive, e.g. **schreibend** (writing). The only exceptions are **sein** and **tun**, which have the forms **seiend** and **tuend**.

(ii)   German uses its **-end** form far less than English uses its '-ing' form. An infinitive or relative clause is often used instead.

2e   The past participle

(i)   The past participle is the form which combines with auxiliary verbs to form the compound past tenses and the passive.

(ii)   It ends in **-t** or **-et** in weak verbs and **-en** in strong verbs [➤2f]. If the verb is separable the particle is stressed and the past participle is formed with **ge-**, e.g. **umgezogen.**

(iii)   If the verb is inseparable the prefix is unstressed and the past participle is formed without **ge-**, e.g. **erklärt** (explained). A few verbs appear in both forms, but with different meanings.

(iv)   If a modal auxiliary [➤1a (iii)] is followed by an infinitive the past participle is the same as the infinitive; if there is no infinitive it takes the weak form in **ge...t.**

Ich habe ihn nicht sprechen können.	I could not speak to him.
Ich habe es nicht gekonnt.	I could not do it.

2f   The verb endings used to form the tenses

Pronoun	Present tense	Past tense (weak) and Konjunktiv (subjunctive)	Past tense (strong)
ich	-e	-e	-
du	-(e)st	-est	-(e)st
er/sie/es	-(e)t	-e	-
wir	-en	-en	-en
ihr	-(e)t	-et	-(e)t
sie	-en	-en	-en
Sie	-en	-en	-en

Note   The endings are set out in this way to show that the endings of the different tenses are very similar. The simple past of weak verbs also adds -t- or -et- to the stem [➤3a, **machen** 11 and **arbeiten** 12].

2g *The imperative*

(i) The imperative, or command form, is regular in all verbs except **sein** [►**sein** 1]. It is formed as follows:

• **du** form
  – infinitive stem plus **-e**, which is the most common pattern:
    gehe! (go!); **fange an!** (begin!);

  – verbs which change the stem-vowel to **-i-** or **-ie-** in the present also change in the imperative. They take no **-e**:
    gib! (give!); **lies!** (read!).

  – many verbs also drop the **-e**, especially in speech:
    lauf! (run!); **setz dich!** (sit down!).

• **ihr** form
  As in the present tense:
    bittet! (ask!); **setzt euch!** (sit down!).

• **Sie** form
  The **Sie** form, inverted:
    gehen Sie! (go!).

• First person plural
  The **wir** form, inverted:
    gehen wir! (let's go!).

There is an alternative form: **wir wollen gehen!** (let's go!). The **wir** form is not listed in the model verb pages.

2h *The active tenses*

(i) A verb in the active form is a verb in its most usual form, i.e. when the subject performs the action. Active tenses (indicative) are formed as shown below. [For **Konjunktiv** forms ►2k.]

(ii) The present tense is formed from the stem of the verb with present tense endings.

Ich komme.	I come.	**Er geht.**	He goes.

(iii) The simple past imperfect tense of weak verbs is formed from the stem of the verb, plus **-t-** or **-et-** and the weak past tense endings.

Ich kaufte.	I bought.	**Sie holten.**	They fetched.

(iv) The simple past imperfect tense of strong verbs is formed from the stem of the verb, modified as shown in the model verb pages, and the strong past tense endings.

Sie ging.	She went.	**Sie schrieben.**	They wrote.

(v) The present perfect tense is formed from the present of either **sein** or **haben** with the past participle.

Er ist ausgegangen.	He has gone out.
Ich habe geschlafen.	I slept.

(vi) The past perfect (pluperfect) is formed from the simple past of **sein** or **haben** and the past participle.

Sie hatten sich gesetzt.	They had sat down.
Wir waren angekommen.	We had arrived.

(vii) The future tense is formed from the present tense of **werden** and the infinitive.

Sie werden fahren.	You will travel.

(viii) The future perfect is formed from the future of **haben** or **sein** and the past participle.

Er wird ausgegangen sein.	He will have gone out.
Sie werden geschrieben haben.	They will have written.

2i *The auxiliary verbs* sein *and* haben

(i) Compound past tenses are formed from the past participle plus an auxiliary, as in English.

Ich habe geschrieben.	I wrote/I have written.

In German two auxiliaries are used, **haben** and **sein**.

(ii)   If the verb is used transitively or as a reflexive verb it takes **haben**.

(iii)   If the verb is intransitive it may take **sein** or **haben**. It must use **sein** if it indicates a change of place or a change of state.

Ich bin geworden. I became.	**Er ist gegangen.** He went.

(iv)   A few verbs can take either **sein** or **haben** depending on how they are used.

Ich bin nach Frankreich gefahren.   I drove to France (change of place).
Ich habe das neue Auto gefahren.   I drove the new car (transitive use).

(v)   Verbs with prefixes or verbal particles listed as following a certain model do not necessarily take the same auxiliary as the simple verb. Each verb has to be checked separately.

2j   *The passive tenses*

(i)   A verb is used in the passive to show that the action is done to the subject of the sentence.

(ii)   All active tenses are mirrored by passive forms. These are formed from the appropriate tense of the auxiliary **werden** and the past participle of the verb.

Ich wurde geschlagen.   I was struck.

(iii)   The past participle of **werden** is shortened to **worden** in the passive.

Ich bin geschlagen worden.   I was/have been struck.
Er war gesehen worden.   He had been seen.

(iv)　　The future perfect is rarely found and is replaced by a different construction, e.g. using **man**.

Man wird ihn gefunden haben.	He will have been found.

(v)　　Note that an indirect object cannot become the subject when a verb becomes passive: **man sagte mir** (they told me) becomes **es wurde mir gesagt** or **mir wurde gesagt** (I was told) in the passive.

(vi)　　Note the distinction between the true passive, which focuses on an action, and the use of the past participle to describe a state. In this case **sein** is used, not **werden**.

Der Tisch wird gedeckt.	The table is (being) set.
Der Tisch ist gedeckt.	The table is (already) set.

2k　　*Tenses in the* Konjunktiv *(subjunctive) mood*

(i)　　These are the tenses used in indirect speech, in conditional sentences or to indicate uncertainty. All indicative tenses, active and passive, have their 'mirror' **Konjunktiv** tenses. They are formed as shown below. All tenses have the same endings [➤2f].

(ii)　　The names often given to the different tenses can be confusing, since their use and meaning differ from the English. In particular, the terms *present subjunctive, past subjunctive* and *conditional* are misleading. We prefer to use the terms given below, but the terminology used in older grammars is given in parenthesis (brackets).

(iii)　　**Konjunktiv I,** simple, (present subjunctive) is formed from the stem of the verb with **Konjunktiv** endings. The present tense of all verbs (except **sein**) is regular: **er gehe, du laufest, ich sei.**

(iv)　　**Konjunktiv I**, future, (future subjunctive) is formed from the **Konjunktiv I**, simple, of **werden** and the infinitive: **er werde schreiben.**

(v)　　**Konjunktiv I,** perfect, (perfect subjunctive) is formed from the **Konjunktiv I,** simple, of **haben** or **sein** with the past participle: **er sei gegangen, er habe gesehen.**

(vi) **Konjunktiv II**, simple conditional, (past or imperfect subjunctive) of almost all weak verbs is identical with the indicative simple past tense. Strong verbs add the **Konjunktiv** endings to the simple past tense but the vowel is often modified by an *umlaut*. There are several irregular forms and the most common are given. The simple conditional of verbs is often avoided, especially in speech, by using the compound conditional tense instead. This occurs particularly with weak verbs which have no distinct **Konjunktiv** form, and with the irregular strong forms: **er kaufte** or **er würde kaufen**; **er schriebe** or **er würde schreiben.**

(vii) **Konjunktiv II**, compound conditional, (conditional) is formed from the **Konjunktiv II**, simple, of **werden** and the infinitive: **er würde gehen.**

(viii) **Konjunktiv II**, past conditional, (conditional perfect) is formed from the **Konjunktiv II**, simple, of **sein** or **haben** and the past participle: **er hätte gewartet, sie wäre gekommen.**

Note In the model verb pages the terms have been shortened for the sake of simplicity: **Konjunktiv I**, simple, is called **Konjunktiv I**; **Konjunktiv II**, simple, is called **Konjunktiv II**, and the reference to **Konjunktiv I** or **II** has been omitted in the other tenses.

2l   *Inseparable prefixes and separable particles*

(i) Inseparable prefixes are:

• always written as one word with the main verb;
• never stressed.

(ii) Separable particles are:

• semi-independent words which are always placed at or near the end of the clause: **er kommt heute** *an*; **ich fahre** *Ski*;
• attached to the main verb only when this is at the end of a clause: **... wenn ich morgen** *an*komme;
• always attached to the infinitive and the participles: **ich bin** *an*gekommen; **ich werde** *Ski*fahren;
• always stressed: **ich bin** *an*gekommen.

(iii) It is important to check whether verbal prefixes and particles are separable or inseparable.

• **be-, ent-, emp-, er-, ge-, ver-** and **zer-** are always inseparable prefixes. The past participle is formed without **ge-**, e.g. **bestellt.**

• **ab-, an-, auf-, aus-, ein-, mit-** and **zu-** are always separable particles. The past participle is formed with **ge-**, e.g. **abgestellt, ausgegangen.**

• **hin-, her-** and their compounds **hinab-, heraus-** etc. are separable.

• **durch-, hinter-, miß-, über-, unter-, voll-, wider-, wieder-** and **um-** are sometimes separable.

• adverbs, adjectives, nouns or other verbs used as particles are normally separable, e.g. **Rad** in **Radfahren, schlafen** in **schlafengehen.**

(iv)   If there are two prefixes or a combination of prefixes and particles, follow these examples:

• two separables e.g. **ich ging hinaus, ich bin hinausgegangen;**
• two inseparables e.g. **er mißversteht, er hat mißverstanden;**
• separable plus inseparable e.g. **er bestellt ... ab, er hat ... abbestellt;**
• inseparable plus separable e.g. **er beauftragt, er hat beauftragt.**

(v)   There are a large number of double verbal particles formed with **hin-** and **her-**. They are formed fairly freely and added to verbs of movement to show direction. **Hin-** indicates movement away from the speaker or onlooker; **her-** indicates movement away. Most of the commonest forms are given in the index, but not all can be included.

Note   Where there are two forms with a similar meaning e.g. **ausgehen** and **hinausgehen** (to go out), the form with **hin** or **her** has a literal meaning and the form without a more figurative meaning.

Er geht (aus dem Zimmer) hinaus.	He goes (out of the room).
Wir gehen aus.	We are going out (for an outing).

2m   *Word order*

(i)   German word order is often the same as in English, i.e. the verb follows the subject.

***Ich gehe** nach Hause.*	I *am going* home.

(ii)   In main clauses the main verb is always the second idea (although not necessarily the second word). This means that the verb precedes the subject when another word, phrase or clause comes before it.

Heute *gehe ich* nach Hause.	I *am going* home today.
Wenn ich fertig bin, *gehe ich* nach Hause.	When I am ready, I *shall go* home.

(iii)   In compound tenses the past participle and the infinitive always go at the end of the clause. In Part B, which lists model verbs, the words following the three dots are those which go to the end of the clause, e.g. **ich werde ... getan haben** (I will have done …) could be used as follows: **ich werde die Arbeit bis Montag getan haben** (I will have done the work by Monday).

(iv)   In subordinate clauses, the main verb goes to the end. If it is an auxiliary it usually follows the past participle or infinitive.

Er konnte mich nicht sehen, weil ich nach Berlin gefahren *war*.	He could not see me, because I *had* gone to Berlin.

The main categories of verbs

3a   Weak and strong verbs

(i)   There are two main categories of verb, called *weak* and *strong*.

(ii)   *Weak verbs:*

• add **-t-** or **-et-** to the stem in the simple past before the endings;
• add **-t** or **-et** to the stem to form the past participle (with or without the prefix **ge-** [➤2e]).

(iii)   *Strong verbs:*

• change the stem-vowel in the simple past;
• usually change the stem-vowel in the past participle;
• often change the stem-vowel of the **du** and **er/sie/es** forms of the present tense;
• add **-en** to the modified stem to form the past participle (with or without the prefix **ge-** [➤2e]).

(iv)   A few verbs can be either strong or weak. In some of these verbs the strong and weak forms have different meanings, e.g. **schaffen, schaffte, geschafft** (to do, achieve); **schaffen, schuf, geschaffen** (to create) [➤schaffen 74].

(v)   Some verbs have both forms in use, with one form predominating, e.g. **schmelzen** (to melt).

Note   Some verbs have very rare strong forms. These are not given. For further details see the model verb pages.

3b   Classes of verbs

(i)   You can predict the forms of most verbs by knowing which class or group they fall into.

(ii)   Weak verbs are nearly all regular, [for minor spelling changes ➤3c]. For the full conjugation of a weak verb, of a similar verb with an inseparable prefix and for one with a separable verbal particle, see the model verb section. The irregular weak verbs are listed separately.

(iii) Strong verbs fall into seven major classes. Each class has a distinctive pattern of vowel changes, although there are variations of stem-vowel in the infinitive. The main classes are:

Class I

infinitive in **-ei-**,
(occasionally **-e-** or **-au-**),
past stem in **-ie-** or **-i-**,
past participle in **-ie-** or **-i-**;

Class II

infinitive in **-ie-**,
past stem in **-o-**,
past participle in **-o-**;

Class III

infinitive stem in **-ind-**, **-ing-** or **-ink-**,
past stem in **-a-**,
past participle in **-u-**;

Class IV

infinitive in **-e-** or **-i-**,
(except for **kommen**),
past stem in **-a-**,
past participle in **-o-**;

Class V

infinitive in **-e-**,
(occasionally in **-i-/-ie-**),
past stem in **-a-**,
past participle in **-e-**;

Class VI

infinitive in **-a-**
past stem in **-u-**,
past participle in **-a-**;

Class VII

infinitive in **-a-**,
(but also many other vowels),
past stem in **-ie-**,
past participle in **-a-**;

other verbs: **stehen** and **tun**.

For each class, a model is given of a simple verb without a prefix, of a compound verb with an inseparable prefix, and of one with a separable verbal particle. There are some sub-groups, and models of the most important ones are also given in full. A few verbs with small irregularities which could cause problems are given in full.

3c Spelling variations

(i) There are some common spelling changes. These are not shown for every verb if they follow common rules.

(ii) Many verbs add or omit an **-e-** in their different forms, and the rules are set out below. However, a common sense rule is that the **-e-** should be added or omitted when this makes it easier to pronounce the word.

(iii) If the stem of a verb ends in **-d** or **-t** it is always followed by an **-e-**, e.g. **er/sie/es antwortet, du leitest, ich arbeitete, er/sie/es findet.**

There are the following exceptions:

- vowel change in the **du** form of the present tense, e.g. **du hältst, du rätst;**
- vowel change in the **er/sie/es** form of the present tense when the **-t** is not usually added, e.g. **er hält, er rät** (*but* **er lädt**);
- **du** form simple past of strong verbs, e.g. **du fandst, du batst.**

(iv) If the verb ends in **-eln**:

- take off the **-n** of the infinitive before adding endings (not **-en** as with most verbs);
- form the **ich** form of the present tense and the **du** form of the imperative by omitting the **-e** of the stem, e.g. **ich lächle, lächle!**

(v) Verbs ending in **-ern** sometimes drop the **-e-** of the stem in speech, e.g. **ich wandre.**

(vi) The stem of weak verbs ending in a consonant + **m** or **n** usually adds an **-e-** to make it easier to pronounce (not if the consonant is **l** or **r**), e.g. **du atmest, er segnet, ihr rechnet** *but* **es qualmt, er warnt, es wärmt.**

(vii) If the stem of a strong or weak verb ends in: **-s, -ß, -z, -tz, -x:**

- the **du** form of the present ends in **-t** (not **-est**), e.g. **du heißt.** (The full form **heißest** is now archaic.)
- the **du** form of the simple past ends in **-est** (not **-st**), e.g. **du hießest.**

(viii) If the verb stem ends in **-ß** or **-ss**, use **ß** before a **t**, after a long vowel in the middle of a word, and at the end of a word, e.g. **beißen, biß, vergißt, vergaß;** use **-ss** after a short vowel in the middle of a word, e.g. **vergessen, gebissen.**

Personal pronouns

English subject	Nominative	Accusative	Dative	Reflexive accusative/ dative	English object/ reflexive
Singular					
I	ich	mich	mir	mich/mir	me/myself
you	du	dich	dir	dich/dir	you/yourself
he	er	ihn	ihm	sich	him/himself
she	sie	sie	ihr	sich	her/herself
it	es	es	ihm	sich	it/itself
Plural					
we	wir	uns	uns	uns	us/ourselves
you	ihr	euch	euch	euch	you/ yourselves
they	sie	sie	ihnen	sich	them/ themselves
you (formal)	Sie	Sie	Ihnen	sich	you/yourself/ yourselves

Scheme of German tenses and their usual English meanings

Note   Of the **Konjunktiv** tenses, only the **Konjunktiv** II, compound conditional and past conditional, are shown in this scheme. It is misleading to give English meanings for the other **Konjunktiv** tenses because of their range of use and meaning. [See *Berlitz German Grammar Handbook*].

5a   Active

Present
ich werfe

I throw
I am throwing
I do throw

Imperative
wirf!
werft!
werfen Sie!
werfen wir!

throw! (informal, singular)
throw! (informal, plural)
throw! (formal, singular and plural)
let's throw!

Simple past
ich warf

I threw
I was throwing

Present perfect
ich habe geworfen

I threw
I have thrown
I did throw

Past perfect
ich hatte geworfen

I had thrown

Future
ich werde werfen

I shall throw
I shall be throwing

Future perfect
ich werde geworfen haben

I shall have thrown

Konjunktiv II, compound conditional
ich würde werfen   I would throw
                                         (I would be throwing)

Konjunktiv II, past conditional
ich hätte geworfen   I would have thrown

5b   Passive

Present
ich werde gelobt   I am praised
                                         I am being praised

Imperative (rare)
sei gelobt!   be praised!
seid gelobt!   be praised!
seien Sie gelobt!   be praised!

Simple past
ich wurde gelobt   I was praised
                                         I was being praised

Present perfect
ich bin gelobt worden   I was praised
                                         I have been praised

Past perfect
ich war gelobt worden   I had been praised

Future
ich werde gelobt werden   I shall be praised

Future perfect
man wird mich gelobt haben   I shall have been praised

Konjunktiv II, compound conditional
ich würde gelobt (werden)   I would be praised

Konjunktiv II, past conditional
ich wäre gelobt worden   I would have been praised

List of abreviations and conventions used in the index

acc.	accusative	**+s./h.**	the verb takes the auxiliary **sein** or **haben**
dat.	dative		
dat refl.	dative reflexive	**( )**	the verb is normally followed by the case or preposition indicated
gen.	genitive		
impers.	impersonal		
intr.	intransitive	**&**	the verb can be used in both ways with the same meaning
pers.	person		
pl.	plural		
pres.	present	**/**	indicates an alternative e.g. **s/h** – **sein** or **haben**
refl.	reflexive		
sing.	singular		
so.	someone	**|**	a hairline shows that the first part of the verb is a stressed, separable particle.
sth.	something		
tr.	transitive		
+s.	the verb takes the auxiliary **sein**		

Notes

(i)   Parentheses (brackets) in both the German and English columns relate to each other, e.g. '**verhandeln** (**über** + acc.) (tr. & intr.) negotiate (about)' indicates that **verhandeln** may be used with **über** to mean 'negotiate about'.

(ii)   Prepositions govern the same case as usual. The case is only indicated where prepositions govern two possible cases, e.g. **weisen** (**auf** + acc.) shows that **auf** is followed by the accusative.

(iii)   Reflexive use is not indicated where usage is very similar to the English, e.g. **er wäscht sich** (he washes himself) is not shown separately.

Reflexive use is only shown where the verb is used reflexively in German but not in the corresponding English expression, or where the verb has an extended meaning when it is used reflexively, e.g. **vor|stellen** (tr.) (introduce), and (dat. refl.) **ich stelle mir vor** (I imagine).

(iv) Many verbs can be used both transitively and intransitively. Where the meaning is identical this is shown in the parentheses, e.g. **bauen** (tr. & intr.).

Where the meaning changes, it is shown separately, e.g. **halten** (tr.) (hold), (intr.) **er hält** (he stops).

(v) The most important English meanings are listed for each verb. Many German verbs have a great range of shades of meaning and not all these can be shown. For further information a dictionary should be consulted.

B
THE MODEL VERBS

Index of model verbs

Wohnen also serves as an example of a verb with the auxiliary **haben**

PRESENT PARTICIPLE	PAST PARTICIPLE
wohnend	gewohnt

PRESENT PERFECT	SIMPLE PAST
ich wohne	ich wohnte
du wohnst	du wohntest
er/sie/es wohnt	er/sie/es wohnte
wir wohnen	wir wohnten
ihr wohnt	ihr wohntet
sie/Sie wohnen	sie/Sie wohnten

KONJUNKTIV I, SIMPLE CONDITIONAL	KONJUNKTIV II, SIMPLE
ich wohne	ich wohnte
du wohnest	du wohntest
er/sie/es wohne	er/sie/es wohnte
wir wohnen	wir wohnten
ihr wohnet	ihr wohntet
sie/Sie wohnen	sie/Sie wohnten

PRESENT PERFECT	PAST PERFECT (PLUPERFECT)
ich habe ... gewohnt	ich hatte ... gewohnt
du hast ... gewohnt	du hattest ... gewohnt
er/sie/es hat ... gewohnt	er/sie/es hatte ... gewohnt
wir haben ... gewohnt	wir hatten ... gewohnt
ihr habt ... gewohnt	ihr hattet ... gewohnt
sie/Sie haben ... gewohnt	sie/Sie hatten ... gewohnt

IMPERATIVE (rare)

wohne! (du)   wohnen Sie!   (ihr) wohnt!

FUTURE

ich werde ... wohnen
du wirst ... wohnen
er/sie/es wird... wohnen
wir werden ... wohnen
ihr werdet ... wohnen
sie/Sie werden ... wohnen

FUTURE PERFECT

ich werde ... gewohnt haben
du wirst ... gewohnt haben
er/sie/es wird ... gewohnt haben
wir werden ... gewohnt haben
ihr werdet ... gewohnt haben
sie/Sie werden ... gewohnt haben

KONJUNKTIV II, COMPOUND CONDITIONAL

ich würde ... wohnen
du würdest ... wohnen
er/sie/es würde ... wohnen
wir würden ... wohnen
ihr würdet ... wohnen
sie/Sie würden ... wohnen

KONJUNKTIV II, PAST CONDITIONAL

ich hätte ... gewohnt
du hättest ... gewohnt
er/sie/es hätte ... gewohnt
wir hätten ... gewohnt
ihr hättet ... gewohnt
sie/Sie hätten ... gewohnt

KONJUNKTIV I, PERFECT

ich habe ... gewohnt
du habest ... gewohnt
er/sie/es habe ... gewohnt
wir haben ... gewohnt
ihr habet ... gewohnt
sie/Sie haben ... gewohnt

KONJUNKTIV I, FUTURE

ich werde ... wohnen
du werdest ... wohnen
er/sie/es werde ... wohnen
wir werden ... wohnen
ihr werdet ... wohnen
sie/Sie werden ... wohnen

Fallen also serves as an example of a verb with the auxiliary **sein**

PRESENT PARTICIPLE	PAST PARTICIPLE
fallend	gefallen

PRESENT	SIMPLE PAST
ich falle	ich fiel
du fällst	du fielst
er/sie/es fällt	er/sie/es fiel
wir fallen	wir fielen
ihr fallt	ihr fielt
sie/Sie fallen	sie/Sie fielen

KONJUNKTIV I, SIMPLE	KONJUNKTIV II, SIMPLE CONDITIONAL
ich falle	ich fiele
du fallest	du fielest
er/sie/es falle	er/sie/es fiele
wir fallen	wir fielen
ihr fallet	ihr fielet
sie/Sie fallen	sie/Sie fielen

PRESENT PERFECT	PAST PERFECT (PLUPERFECT)
ich bin ... gefallen	ich war ... gefallen
du bist ... gefallen	du warst ... gefallen
er/sie/es ist ... gefallen	er/sie/es war ... gefallen
wir sind ... gefallen	wir waren ... gefallen
ihr seid ... gefallen	ihr wart ... gefallen
sie/Sie sind ... gefallen	sie/Sie waren ... gefallen

IMPERATIVE
falle! (du)   fallen Sie!   fallt! (ihr)

FUTURE
ich werde ... fallen
du wirst ... fallen
er/sie/es wird ... fallen
wir werden ... fallen
ihr werdet ... fallen
sie/Sie werden ... fallen

FUTURE PERFECT
ich werde ... gefallen sein
du wirst ... gefallen sein
er/sie/es wird ... gefallen sein
wir werden ... gefallen sein
ihr werdet ... gefallen sein
sie/Sie werden ... gefallen sein

KONJUNKTIV II, COMPOUND CONDITIONAL
ich würde ... fallen
du würdest ... fallen
er/sie/es würde ... fallen
wir würden ... fallen
ihr würdet ... fallen
sie/Sie würden ... fallen

KONJUNKTIV II, PAST CONDITIONAL
ich wäre ... gefallen
du wärest ... gefallen
er/sie/es wäre ... gefallen
wir wären ... gefallen
ihr wäret ... gefallen
sie/Sie wären ... gefallen

KONJUNKTIV I, PERFECT
ich sei ... gefallen
du seiest ... gefallen
er/sie/es sei ... gefallen
wir seien ... gefallen
ihr seiet ... gefallen
sie/Sie seien ... gefallen

KONJUNKTIV I, FUTURE
ich werde ... fallen
du werdest ... fallen
er/sie/es werde ... fallen
wir werden ... fallen
ihr werdet ... fallen
sie/Sie werden ... fallen

Reflexive pronoun as direct object

PRESENT PARTICIPLE	PAST PARTICIPLE
sich setzend	sich gesetzt

IMPERATIVE

setz(e) dich! (du)　　　setzen Sie sich!　　　setzt euch! (ihr)

PRESENT	SIMPLE PAST
ich setze mich	ich setzte mich
du setzt dich	du setztest dich
er/sie/es setzt sich	er/sie/es setzte sich
wir setzen uns	wir setzten uns
ihr setzt euch	ihr setztet euch
sie/Sie setzen sich	sie/Sie setzten sich

KONJUNKTIV I	KONJUNKTIV II
ich setze mich	ich setzte mich

PRESENT PERFECT	PAST PERFECT (PLUPERFECT)
ich habe mich ... gesetzt	ich hatte mich ... gesetzt

FUTURE	FUTURE PERFECT
ich werde mich ... setzen	ich werde mich ... gesetzt haben

CONDITIONAL	CONDITIONAL PERFECT
ich würde mich ... setzen	ich hätte mich ... gesetzt

Reflexive pronoun as indirect object

PRESENT PARTICIPLE
sich vorstellend

PAST PARTICIPLE
sich vorgestellt

IMPERATIVE
stell(e) dir vor!   stellen Sie sich vor!   stellt euch vor!

PRESENT
ich stelle mir vor
du stellst dir vor
er/sie/es stellt sich vor
wir stellen uns vor
ihr stellt euch vor
sie/Sie stellen sich vor

SIMPLE PAST
ich stellte mir vor
du stelltest dir vor
er/sie/es stellte sich vor
wir stellten uns vor
ihr stelltet euch vor
sie/Sie stellten sich vor

KONJUNKTIV I
ich stelle mir vor

KONJUNKTIV II
ich stellte mir vor

PRESENT PERFECT
ich habe mir ... vorgestellt

PAST PERFECT (PLUPERFECT)
ich hatte mir ... vorgestellt

FUTURE
ich werde mir ... vorstellen

FUTURE PERFECT
ich werde mir ... vorgestellt haben

CONDITIONAL
ich würde mir ... vorstellen

CONDITIONAL PERFECT
ich hätte mir ... vorgestellt

gelobt werden (be praised)

PRESENT PARTICIPLE	**PAST PARTICIPLE**
(gelobt werdend)	gelobt worden

PRESENT

ich werde ... gelobt
du wirst ... gelobt
er/sie/es wird ... gelobt
wir werden ... gelobt
ihr werdet ... gelobt
sie/Sie werden ... gelobt

SIMPLE PAST

ich wurde ... gelobt
du wurdest ... gelobt
er/sie/es wurde ... gelobt
wir wurden ... gelobt
ihr wurdet ... gelobt
sie/Sie wurden ... gelobt

KONJUNKTIV I

ich werde ... gelobt
du werdest ... gelobt
er/sie/es werde ... gelobt
wir werden ... gelobt
ihr werdet ... gelobt
sie/Sie werden ... gelobt

KONJUNKTIV II

ich würde ... gelobt
du würdest ... gelobt
er/sie/es würde ... gelobt
wir würden ... gelobt
ihr würdet ... gelobt
sie/Sie würden ... gelobt

PRESENT PERFECT

ich bin ... gelobt worden
du bist ... gelobt worden
er/sie/es ist ... gelobt worden
wir sind ... gelobt worden
ihr seid ... gelobt worden
sie/Sie sind ... gelobt worden

PAST PERFECT (PLUPERFECT)

ich war ... gelobt worden
du warst ... gelobt worden
er/sie/es war ... gelobt worden
wir waren ... gelobt worden
ihr wart ... gelobt worden
sie/Sie waren ... gelobt worden

Note   The future perfect is rarely used and is normally replaced by an active construction with **man**.

IMPERATIVE

sei gelobt! (du)   seien Sie gelobt!   seid gelobt! (ihr)

FUTURE

ich werde ... gelobt werden
du wirst ... gelobt werden
er/sie/es wird ... gelobt werden
wir werden ... gelobt werden
ihr werdet ... gelobt werden
sie/Sie werden ... gelobt werden

FUTURE PERFECT

(ich werde ... gelobt worden sein)
etc or
(man wird mich/dich etc gelobt haben)

KONJUNKTIV II, COMPOUND CONDITIONAL

ich würde ... gelobt werden
du würdest ... gelobt werden
er/sie/es würde ... gelobt werden
wir würden ... gelobt werden
ihr würdet ... gelobt werden
sie/Sie würden ... gelobt werden

KONJUNKTIV II, PAST CONDITIONAL

ich wäre ... gelobt worden
du wär(e)st ... gelobt worden
er/sie/es wäre ... gelobt worden
wir wären ... gelobt worden
ihr wäret ... gelobt worden
sie/Sie wären ... gelobt worden

KONJUNKTIV I, PERFECT

ich sei ... gelobt worden
du seiest ... gelobt worden
er/sie/es sei ... gelobt worden
wir seien ... gelobt worden
ihr seiet ... gelobt worden
sie/Sie seien ... gelobt worden

KONJUNKTIV I, FUTURE

ich werde ... gelobt werden
du werdest ... gelobt werden
er/sie/es werde ... gelobt werden
wir werden ... gelobt werden
ihr werdet ... gelobt werden
sie/Sie werden ... gelobt werden

Auxiliary verb, irregular strong, stress on stem **sei-**

PRESENT PARTICIPLE	*PAST PARTICIPLE*
seiend (wesend)	gewesen

PRESENT	*SIMPLE PAST*
ich bin	ich war
du bist	du warst
er/sie/es ist	er/sie/es war
wir sind	wir waren
ihr seid	ihr wart
sie/Sie sind	sie/Sie waren

KONJUNKTIV I	*KONJUNKTIV II*
ich sei	ich wäre
du sei(e)st	du wärest
er/sie/es sei	er/sie/es wäre
wir seien	wir wären
ihr seiet	ihr wäret
sie/Sie seien	sie/Sie wären

Similar verbs

- with separable particle

ansein	be on	**aussein**	be out, have finished
aufsein	be up, open		
		lossein	be the matter

Notes - **wesend** is used as the present participle in forms used as adjectives e.g. **anwesend**.

Unser Sohn Jochen *ist* noch *auf* – er *ist* acht Jahre alt. Was *ist* los, Jochen? *Sei* ruhig! — Warum *ist* er so früh zu Hause? — Normalerweise *ist* seine Schule um 1.00 *aus,* und er *ist* in 5 Minuten zu Hause. Heute *ist* er krank *gewesen* – ihm *war* gestern sehr schlecht.	Our son Jochen *is* still up – he *is* 8 years old. What*'s* the matter, Jochen? Be quiet! —Why *is* he home so early? —Usually his school *finishes* at 1:00 and he *is* home in five minutes. Today he *has been* ill – yesterday he *felt* very sick.

IMPERATIVE
sei! (du)   seien Sie!   seid! (ihr)

PRESENT PERFECT
ich bin ... gewesen

PAST PERFECT (PLUPERFECT)
ich war ... gewesen

FUTURE
ich werde ... sein

FUTURE PERFECT
ich werde ... gewesen sein

COMPOUND CONDITIONAL
ich würde ... sein

PAST CONDITIONAL
ich wäre ... gewesen

Hier *ist* unser Freund, Pierre – er *ist* Schweizer. Wir *waren* zusammen auf der Computerausstellung. Die *ist* jetzt zu Ende, du weißt. Unser Kollege Hans *war* auch dabei. Pierre *ist* Programmierer.

Here *is* our friend, Pierre – he *is* Swiss. We *were* together at the computer exhibition. As you know it *is* finished now. Our colleague Hans *was* also there. He *is* a computer programmer.

Das Wetter *war* gestern schrecklich, und mir *war* im Büro sehr kalt. Die Fenster *waren* alle *auf*, und die Heizung *ist* lange nicht *angewesen*.

The weather *was* dreadful yesterday and I *was* very cold in the office. The windows *were* all *open*, and the heating *has* not *been on* for a long time.

Morgen *sind* wir schon um 12 Uhr in Bremen. Ich wollte *sicher sein*, daß wir rechtzeitig ankommen. *Würden* Sie auch *dafür sein*, daß wir im Hotel essen? — Ja, das *wäre* eine gute Idee.

Tomorrow we *will be* in Bremen by 12. I wanted to *ensure* that we get there in good time. *Would* you *be* happy to eat in the hotel? — Yes, that *would be* a good idea.

Auxiliary verb, irregular weak, stress on stem **hab-**

PRESENT PARTICIPLE	*PAST PARTICIPLE*
habend	gehabt

PRESENT	*SIMPLE PAST*
ich habe	ich hatte
du hast	du hattest
er/sie/es hat	er/sie/es hatte
wir haben	wir hatten
ihr habt	ihr hattet
sie/Sie haben	sie/Sie hatten

KONJUNKTIV I	*KONJUNKTIV II*
ich habe	ich hätte

Similar verbs

- with separable particle

anhaben	have on (clothes)
aufhaben	have on (arrangement)
vorhaben	intend

Notes — **wesend** is used as the present participle in forms used as adjectives e.g. **anwesend**

Die Kinder *haben* heute *frei*, und wir *hatten vor*, zusammen in die Stadt zu fahren. *Hätten* Sie vielleicht Zeit, uns hinzufahren? *Werden* Sie Platz im Auto *haben*? Hoffentlich *haben* Sie nichts *dagegen*.

The children *have the day off school* today and we *were planning* to go to town together. *Would* you perhaps *have* time to drive us there? *Will* you *have* room in the car? I hope you *don't mind*.

Was *habt* ihr heute *auf*? – Nur Mathe.

What *homework have* you *got* today? – Only math/maths.

IMPERATIVE
hab(e)! (du)   haben Sie!   habt! (ihr)

PRESENT PERFECT
ich habe ... gehabt

PAST PERFECT (PLUPERFECT)
ich hatte ... gehabt

FUTURE
ich werde ... haben

FUTURE PERFECT
ich werde ... gehabt haben

COMPOUND CONDITIONAL
ich würde ... haben

PAST CONDITIONAL
ich hätte ... gehabt

Haben Sie ein Zimmer frei? Ich *hätte gern* ein Zimmer mit Bad. —Ja, das geht. Zuerst *haben* Sie das Anmeldeformular anzufüllen. —Verzeihung, ich *habe* keinen Kugelschreiber bei mir. —Hier *haben* Sie einen. — Den wievielten *haben* wir heute? — Den 10. März.

Have you a room free? I *would like* a room with a bathroom. —Yes, that's all right. First you *must* fill in the registration form. —I'm sorry, I *have* no ball-point on me. - Here's one. - *What's* the date today? - The 10th March.

Habt ihr all *Spaß gehabt*? Warum seid ihr alle so müde? - Wir *haben* den ganzen Tag nichts zu essen *gehabt*, weil wir kein Geld *hatten*. Nur Frau Meyer *hatte Mitleid* mit uns und gab uns ein Stück Torte.

Have you all *had fun*? Why are you all so tired? - We *have had* nothing to eat all day because we *had* no money. Frau Meyer was the only one who *took pity* on us and gave us a piece of cake.

Kennen Sie Familie Schmidt? Wir *haben* die ganze Familie sehr *gern*. —Nein, ich *habe* bisher keine Gelegenheit *gehabt*, sie kennenzulernen. —Montag gehen wir zusammen ins Kino – *haben* Sie *Lust* mitzukommen?

Do you know the Schmidt family? We really *like* the whole family.— No, I *have* not yet *had* a chance to meet them. —On Monday we are going to the cinema together – *do* you *want* to come too?

Irregular strong verb, stress on stem **werd-**
Auxiliary verb used to form future and passive

PRESENT PARTICIPLE	*PAST PARTICIPLE*
werdend	geworden

PRESENT	*SIMPLE PAST*
ich werde	ich wurde
du wirst	du wurdest
er/sie/es wird	er/sie/es wurde
wir werden	wir wurden
ihr werdet	ihr wurdet
sie/Sie werden	sie/Sie wurden

KONJUNKTIV I	*KONJUNKTIV II*
ich werde	ich würde

Similar verbs

- with separable particle

fertigwerden	cope	**loswerden**	get rid of

Notes   **loswerden** takes a direct object in the accusative.

Die Kinder *sind* wieder gesund *geworden*, aber ich kann meine Erkältung nicht *loswerden*. Mir *ist* gestern wieder *schlecht geworden*, und ich *bin ohnmächtig geworden*.	The children *are* better again, but I can not *get rid of* my cold. *I felt ill* again yesterday, and *I fainted*.
Leider *kann* ich mit meinem neuen Kollegen nicht *fertigwerden*. Die Lage *muß anders werden*. Ich *werde* morgen mit dem Manager *sprechen*.	Unfortunately, I *can* not *get on* with my new colleague. The situation *must change*. *I will speak* with the manager tomorrow.
Ich *würde mich* sehr *freuen*, wenn Sie an dem Projekt *mitwirken würden*. Sie *werden sehen*, es *wird* schon *gehen*. Es *wird* zu einem großen Erfolg *werden*.	I *would be delighted* if you *would work with us* on the project. You *will see*, it *will be* all right. It *will be* a great success.
Es wurde viel *gelacht*.	*There was* a lot of *laughing*.

IMPERATIVE
werde! (du)   werden Sie!   werdet! (ihr)

PRESENT PERFECT   *PAST PERFECT (PLUPERFECT)*
ich bin ... geworden   ich war ... geworden

FUTURE   *FUTURE PERFECT*
ich werde ... werden   ich werde ... geworden sein

COMPOUND CONDITIONAL   *PAST CONDITIONAL*
ich würde ... werden   ich wäre ... geworden

Hans, es *wird* Zeit, daß du schlafen gehst, es *ist* sehr spät *geworden*. *Wird's* bald!

Hans, it *is* time to go to bed, it *is/has got/ten* very late. *Get a move on!*

***Es wird* heute abend im großen Saal *getanzt*. Das ganze Gemeinde *ist eingeladen worden*.**

There is dancing this evening in the big hall. The whole parish *has been invited*.

Der Einbrecher *wurde* von einem Hund *gebissen*. Ich *bin* später von der Polizei *aufgesucht worden*. Mir *wurde gesagt*, ich *werde* von ihm deswegen *angeklagt werden*. Ich *müßte* den Hund *loswerden*, falls er den Briefträger beißt.

The burglar *was bitten* by a dog. I *was visited* later by the police. I *was told* I *am to be sued* by him. I *may have to get rid* of the dog in case he bites the postman.

Wann *wurde* das Schloß *gebaut*? Der Architekt *wurde* 1765 *geboren*. Das Schloß *wurde* 1805 *gebaut*. Jetzt *wird* es *renoviert* - das Dach *war* schon 1978 *repariert worden*, letztes Jahr *ist* der Garten neu *angelegt worden*. Es bleibt aber viel zu tun. Nächstes Jahr *wird* der große Saal *restauriert werden*.

When *was* the castle *built?* The architect *was born* in 1765. The castle *was built* in 1805. Now it *is being restored* - the roof *had been repaired* in 1978, and last year the garden *was replanned*. But a lot remains to be done. Next year the big hall *will be redesigned*.

Modal verb, irregular weak, stress on stem **könn-**

PRESENT PARTICIPLE	*PAST PARTICIPLE*
(könnend)	gekonnt/können

PRESENT	*SIMPLE PAST*
ich kann	ich konnte
du kannst	du konntest
er/sie/es kann	er/sie/es konnte
wir können	wir konnten
ihr könnt	ihr konntet
sie/Sie können	sie/Sie konnten

KONJUNKTIV I	*KONJUNKTIV II*
ich könne	ich könnte

Die Kinder *können* alle *schwimmen* und *radfahren*.

My children *can* all *swim* and *cycle*.

Meine Mutter *kann* das Kreuzworträtsel immer *lösen* – ich *habe* es nie *gekonnt*.

My mother *can* always *solve* the crossword puzzle – I *have* never *been able to do* it.

Er rief, so laut er *konnte*, aber da *konnte* man nichts *machen* - er *konnte* nicht *schwimmen*. Ich *konnte nicht anders*, ich mußte schreien.

He shouted as loud as he *could*, but nothing *could be done* - he *couldn*'t *swim*. I *couldn*'t *help* screaming.

Können Sie italienisch? Es *kann sein*, daß wir einen Vertreter in Rom brauchen. Ich weiß nicht, ob ich dieses Jahr werde hinfahren *können* (hinfahren *kann*).

Do you *know* Italian? It *may be* that we shall need a representative in Rome. I don't know if I *shall be able to go* there this year.

IMPERATIVE

—   —   —

PRESENT PERFECT
ich habe ... gekonnt/können

PAST PERFECT (PLUPERFECT)
ich hatte ... gekonnt/können

FUTURE
ich werde ... können

FUTURE PERFECT
ich werde ... gekonnt haben
ich werde ... haben können

COMPOUND CONDITIONAL
ich würde ... können

PAST CONDITIONAL
ich hätte ... gekonnt/können

Kann ich Ihnen *helfen*? – Danke, *könnten* Sie mir *sagen*, wo man hier *parken kann*? —*Es kann sein*, daß Sie vor dem Bahnhof einen Parkplatz finden.

Can I *help* you? – Thank you, *could* you *tell* me where one *can park* around here? —*Maybe* you will find a parking space in front of the station.

Leider *habe* ich Ihre Waschmaschine nicht *reparieren können. Könnte* ich Sie an unser Sonderangebot *erinnern*?

Unfortunately I *have* not *been able to repair* your washing machine. *Could* I *remind* you of our special offer?

Ich *hätte* es gestern *machen können*, wenn ich rechtzeitig davon gewußt hätte. Jetzt *kann* ich nichts *dafür*.

I *could have done* it yesterday, if I had known in good time about it. No I *can't do* anything *about it*.

Wer *kann* das *gewesen sein*? *Kannst* du es mir sagen?

Who *can* that *have been*? *Can* you tell me?

Modal verb, irregular weak, stress on stem **woll-**

PRESENT PARTICIPLE	*PAST PARTICIPLE*
wollend	gewollt/wollen

PRESENT	*SIMPLE PAST*
ich will	ich wollte
du willst	du wolltest
er/sie/es will	er/sie/es wollte
wir wollen	wir wollten
ihr wollt	ihr wolltet
sie/Sie wollen	sie/Sie wollten

KONJUNKTIV I	*KONJUNKTIV II*
ich wolle	ich wollte

Willst du *schwimmen gehen*?
— Nein, ich *will lieber* zu Hause bleiben.

Do you *want to go swimming*?
— No, I *would rather* stay at home.

Wollen Sie jetzt nach Hause?
Wollen wir *gehen*?

Do you *want to go* home now?
Shall we *go*?

Unsere Freunde *wollen*, daß wir sie nach Spanien *begleiten*. Wir *haben* oft dorthin *fahren wollen*.

Our friends *want* us *to go* to Spain with them. We *have* often *wanted to go* there.

Als Kind *wollte* ich Fußballspieler *werden*.

As a child I *wanted to be* a soccer player.

Ich *wollte*, er wäre schon da, aber er *will* erst morgen *kommen*.

I do *wish* he was already here, but he *does* not *want to come* until tomorrow.

Hans *will* ihn gestern in der Stadt *gesehen haben*.

Hans *claims to have seen* him yesterday in town.

IMPERATIVE

wolle (du)! wollen Sie! wollt! (ihr)

PRESENT PERFECT
ich habe ... gewollt/wollen

PAST PERFECT (PLUPERFECT)
ich hatte ... gewollt/wollen

FUTURE
ich werde ... wollen

FUTURE PERFECT
ich werde ... gewollt haben
ich werde ... haben wollen

COMPOUND CONDITIONAL
ich würde ... wollen

PAST CONDITIONAL
ich hätte ... gewollt/wollen

6 mögen like (may)

Modal verb, irregular weak, stress on stem **mög-**

PRESENT PARTICIPLE	PAST PARTICIPLE
mögend	gemocht/mögen

PRESENT	SIMPLE PAST
ich mag	ich mochte
du magst	du mochtest
er/sie/es mag	er/sie/es mochte
wir mögen	wir mochten
ihr mögt	ihr mochtet
sie/Sie mögen	sie/Sie mochten

KONJUNKTIV I	KONJUNKTIV II
ich möge	ich möchte

Similar verbs

vermögen   be capable of

Ich *mag* das Buch sehr.	*I like* the book very much.
***Mögen* Sie Kaffee oder Tee? – Ich *mag* keinen Kaffee, ich *möchte lieber* Tee.**	*Do* you *like* coffee or tea? – I *do* not *like* coffee, I *would prefer* tea.
Ich *möchte* wissen, was die Kinder *tun möchten*. —Sie *mögen* gern *schwimmengehen*. Aber *es mag* wohl *sein*, daß sie heute *am liebsten radfahren möchten*.	I *would like* to know, what the children *would like to do*. —They *like swimming* a lot. But it *may* well *be* that today they *would like to go for a bike ride* most of all.
Was sie auch *sagen mag*, ich *habe* das Buch nicht *gemocht*.	Whatever she *may say*, I *did* not *like* the book.
Sie *mochte* etwa 18 *sein*.	She *might have been* about 18.

IMPERATIVE

—   —   —

PRESENT PERFECT
ich habe ... gemocht/mögen

PAST PERFECT (PLUPERFECT)
ich hatte ... gemocht/mögen

FUTURE
ich werde ... mögen

FUTURE PERFECT
ich werde ... gemocht haben
ich werde ... haben mögen

COMPOUND CONDITIONAL
ich würde ... mögen

PAST CONDITIONAL
ich hätte ... gemocht/mögen

Was *möchten* Sie bitte? – Ich *möchte* Herrn Schmidt *sprechen.*	What *do* you *want/ would* you *like*? – I *would like to talk* to Mr. Schmidt.
Sie *vermochte* es nicht, die Prüfung zu bestehen.	She *was* not *able* to pass the examination.
Er sagte, er *möchte* nicht kommen.	He said he *did* not *want* to come.
Er *vermag* nur wenig.	He *is* not *capable* of much.
Ich *hätte gern dabei sein mögen.*	I *would very much have liked to have been* there.
Meine Mutter *mag* es *gern*, wenn die ganze Familie da ist.	My mother *likes* it when the whole family is there.

Modal verb, irregular weak, stress on stem **müss-**

PRESENT PARTICIPLE	PAST PARTICIPLE
müssend	gemußt/müssen

PRESENT	SIMPLE PAST
ich muß	ich mußte
du mußt	du mußtest
er/sie/es muß	er/sie/es mußte
wir müssen	wir mußten
ihr müßt	ihr mußtet
sie/Sie müssen	sie/Sie mußten

KONJUNKTIV I	KONJUNKTIV II
ich müsse	ich müßte

Muß ich schon um 6 Uhr *losfahren*? – Sie *müssen* nicht. – Wenn es *sein muß*, so *müssen* die Koffer bis halb fünf *gepackt werden*. Wann *muß* ich auf dem Flughafen *sein*? – Sie *müßten sich* an der Information *erkundigen*.

Ich weiß, Sie *mußten* letztes Jahr nach Washington. Leider *muß* ich Ihnen jetzt *mitteilen*, daß Sie auch dieses Jahr *werden hinfahren müssen*.

Must I *set off* at 6 o'clock? – You don't *have to*. – If I *do have to*, then the suitcases *will have to be packed* by four-thirty. When *must* I *be* at the airport? – You *ought to ask* at the information desk.

I know you *had to go* to Washington last year. I am sorry *to have to tell* you now, that you *will have to go there* this year as well.

IMPERATIVE

—   —   —

PRESENT PERFECT
ich habe ... gemußt/müssen

PAST PERFECT (PLUPERFECT)
ich hatte ... gemußt/müssen

FUTURE
ich werde ... müssen

FUTURE PERFECT
ich werde ... gemußt haben
ich werde ... haben müssen

COMPOUND CONDITIONAL
ich würde ... müssen

PAST CONDITIONAL
ich hätte ... gekonnt/können

Du *mußt* dich *umziehen. – Muß* ich?

You *must get changed. – Must* I?

Ich *muß* mal.

I *must* go to the bathroom/loo.

Er *hat* das Auto heute um sechs Uhr früh *waschen müssen.* Das *muß* man *gesehen haben.* Wir *mußten* alle *lachen,* als er es erzählte. Er *hätte* es gestern *machen müssen.*

He *had to wash* the car today at six in the morning. That *must have been worth seeing.* We *could not help laughing* when he told us. He *should have done* it yesterday.

Es *muß* stark *geregnet haben.* Wir *müßten* eigentlich einen anderen Campingplatz *finden.*

It *must have rained* heavily. We really *ought to find* another campsite.

Modal verb, irregular weak, stress on stem **dürf-**

PRESENT PARTICIPLE	**PAST PARTICIPLE**
dürfend	gedurft/dürfen

PRESENT	**SIMPLE PAST**
ich darf	ich durfte
du darfst	du durftest
er/sie/es darf	er/sie/es durfte
wir dürfen	wir durften
ihr dürft	ihr durftet
sie/Sie dürfen	sie/Sie durften

KONJUNKTIV I	**KONJUNKTIV II**
ich dürfe	ich dürfte

Similar verbs

bedürfen *(gen)*   need

Was *darf* es *sein*? – Ein Glas Bier bitte, aber die Kinder *dürfen* keinen Alkohol *trinken*. *Dürfte* ich Sie um das Brot bitten?

What *is it to be/would you like*? – A glass of beer, please, but the children *are not allowed to drink* alcohol. *Might I ask* you *to pass* the bread?

Die Kinder *durften* im Wasser nicht *spielen*, aber sie haben es trotzdem getan. Sie *dürfen* aber auf dem Rasen *spielen*. Das hätten sie nicht *tun dürfen*.

The children *were* not *allowed to play* in the water, but they did it all the same. They *can play* on the lawn, however. They *should* not *have done* that.

IMPERATIVE

—   —   —

___

PRESENT PERFECT	*PAST PERFECT (PLUPERFECT)*
ich habe ... gedurft/dürfen	ich hatte ... gedurft/dürfen

FUTURE	*FUTURE PERFECT*
ich werde ... dürfen	ich werde ... gedurft haben
	ich werde ... haben dürfen

COMPOUND CONDITIONAL	*PAST CONDITIONAL*
ich würde ... dürfen	ich hätte ... gedurft/dürfen

Darf ich ins Kino?	*May* I *go* to the movies?
Ich *darf* Ihnen *mitteilen*, daß Sie befördert werden.	I *would like to inform* you that you are being promoted.
Darf ich Sie *bitten*, schon am Montag hier zu sein? Wir *bedürfen* dringend eines Buchhalters. Herr Braun, unser Kollege, war letzte Woche nicht hier. Er *dürfte* krank *gewesen sein.*	*May* I *ask* you to be here on Monday? We urgently *need* an accountant. Mr Braun, our colleague was not here last week. He *might have been* sick.

Modal verb, irregular weak, stress on stem **soll-**

PRESENT PARTICIPLE	*PAST PARTICIPLE*
sollend	gesollt/sollen

PRESENT	*SIMPLE PAST*
ich soll	ich sollte
du sollst	du solltest
er/sie/es soll	er/sie/es sollte
wir sollen	wir sollten
ihr sollt	ihr solltet
sie/Sie sollen	sie/Sie sollten

KONJUNKTIV I	*KONJUNKTIV II*
ich solle	ich sollte

Deutschland *sollte* 1991 *wiedervereinigt werden.*	Germany *was to be reunified* in 1991.
Wir *sollen* **nach Frankfurt** *versetzt werden.* **Wenn wir hier** *bleiben sollen,* **werden wir sowieso ein neues Büro** *mieten* *sollen.* **Falls man die Firma nach München verlegen sollte,** *würden* **wir alle umziehen** **müssen.** **– Sie** *hätten* **früher daran** *denken sollen.* **– Der Chef hat mir gesagt, ich** *solle* **nach Frankfurt** *umziehen.*	We *are to be moved* to Frankfurt. If we *are to stay* here we *will have to* rent a new office anyway. If they *were to move* the firm to Munich, we *would* all *have to move* (*house*). – You *should have thought* of that sooner. – The boss told me I *was to move* to Frankfurt.

IMPERATIVE

—   —   —

PRESENT PERFECT	*PAST PERFECT (PLUPERFECT)*
ich habe ... gesollt/sollen	ich hatte ... gesollt/sollen

FUTURE	*FUTURE PERFECT*
ich werde ... sollen	ich werde ... gesollt haben
	ich werde ... haben sollen

COMPOUND CONDITIONAL	*PAST CONDITIONAL*
ich würde ... sollen	ich hätte ... gesollt/sollen

Was *soll* das? Ich weiß nicht, was ich *tun soll*. Ich *soll* weniger rauchen.

What's the matter? I don't know what to do. I am supposed to smoke less.

Das Gerät *soll* nächste Woche *repariert werden*. Der Techniker *sollte* letzte Woche *kommen*. Er *sollte* uns nicht *warten lassen*. Sie *sollten* eine andere Firma anrufen.

The machine is to be repaired next week. The technician was supposed to come last week. He should not keep us waiting. You ought to call another firm.

Was *sollte* ich *tun* - die Reise dauert so lange. – Sie *sollten* lieber *fliegen*.

What should I do - the journey takes so long. – You ought to fly instead.

Class VII strong verb, stress on stem **lass-**

PRESENT PARTICIPLE	*PAST PARTICIPLE*
lassend	gelassen

PRESENT	*SIMPLE PAST*
ich lasse	ich ließ
du läßt	du ließest
er/sie/es läßt	er/sie/es ließ
wir lassen	wir ließen
ihr laßt	ihr ließt
sie/Sie lassen	sie/Sie ließen

KONJUNKTIV I	*KONJUNKTIV II*
ich lasse	ich ließe

Similar verbs

[With an inseparable prefix]

entlassen	dismiss	**hinterlassen**	bequeath, leave
erlassen	pass (law)	**verlassen**	leave, desert

[With a separable particle]

ablassen	let out	**laufenlassen**	let go
anlassen	start	**loslassen**	let loose
auslassen	omit, leave out	**nachlassen**	decrease
durchlassen	let in, leak	**sich niederlassen**	settle (somewhere)
fallenlassen	drop	**sitzenlassen**	abandon
freilassen	free, release	**zulassen**	allow, authorize
herablassen	lower, deign to	**zurücklassen**	leave behind
hereinlassen	admit, let in		

Notes   This verb is included with the modal auxiliaries, as it functions in a very similar way. It belongs strictly with the Class VII group of verbs.

Er *verläßt* das Büro um sechs. Gestern *ließ* er mich *warten*, da er seine Aktentasche im Büro *hatte liegenlassen*.	He *leaves* the office at six. He *kept* me *waiting* yesterday as he *had left* his briefcase in the office.
Er *ließ* den Brief *fallen*.	He *dropped* the letter.
Laß das!	*Stop* that!

IMPERATIVE
laß(e)! (du) lassen Sie! laßt! (ihr)

PRESENT PERFECT	PAST PERFECT (PLUPERFECT)
ich habe ... gelassen/lassen	ich hatte ... gelassen/lassen

FUTURE	FUTURE PERFECT
ich werde ... lassen	ich werde ... gelassen haben
	ich werde ... haben lassen

COMPOUND CONDITIONAL	PAST CONDITIONAL
ich würde ... lassen	ich hätte ... gelassen/lassen

Wir *ließen* uns letztes Jahr ein neues Haus *bauen*. Das *läßt sich* nicht leicht *machen*. Und dann *hat sich* meine Frau *operieren lassen*.

We *had* a new house *built* last year. That's not easily *done*. And then my wife *had an operation*.

Das Fenster *läßt sich* nicht leicht *öffnen*, so zerbrach der Einbrecher das Glas. Aber wir *hatten* unseren Hund Maxi zu Hause *gelassen*. Man *kann sich* auf ihn *verlassen*. Maxi *wollte* seinen Arm nicht *loslassen*. Wir *haben* die Polizei kommen *lassen*. Und jetzt *läßt* das Fenster *Wasser durch*.

The window *can't be opened* easily, so the burglar broke the glass. However, we *had left* our dog Maxi at home. You *can rely* on him. Maxi *would* not *let go* of his arm. We *sent for* the police. And now the window *is leaking*.

Ich *würde* den Hund jetzt *hereinlassen*, aber er ist sehr aufgeregt.

I *would let* the dog *in* now, but he is very excited.

Die Großmutter *hinterließ* ein Vermögen. Sie *ließ* mich das Haus *behalten*. Nur *hat* sie das Haus nie *reparieren lassen*.

Grandmother *left* a fortune. She *let* me keep the house. Only she never *had* the house *repaired*.

Ich *kann* das Rauchen nicht *lassen*.

I *can* not *stop* smoking.

Regular weak verb, stress on stem **mach-**

PRESENT PARTICIPLE	PAST PARTICIPLE
machend	gemacht

PRESENT	SIMPLE PAST
ich mache	ich machte
du machst	du machtest
er/sie/es macht	er/sie/es machte
wir machen	wir machten
ihr macht	ihr machtet
sie/Sie machen	sie/Sie machten

KONJUNKTIV I	KONJUNKTIV II
ich mache	ich machte

Notes   Regular weak verbs of this type form a large group.

Ich *koche*, du *putzt* und Mutter *bastelt* in der Garage. Sie *macht* einen neuen Schrank. Ich *wundere mich* darüber, daß wir so fleißig sind. *Wollen* wir jetzt *Schluß machen?* Ich *will mich frisch machen*, bevor wir *uns auf den Weg machen.*

I *am cooking*, you *are cleaning*, and mother *is doing DIY* in the garage. She *is making* a new cabinet/cupboard. I *am surprised* that we are all working so hard. *Shall* we *(make a) stop* now? I *want to freshen up* before we *set out.*

Machen wir jetzt *Feierabend?* Hoffentlich *hast* du gute *Fortschritte gemacht.*

Shall we *stop work* now? I hope you *have made* good *progress.*

Die Arbeit *drängt*, und wir *hoffen* auf eine schnelle Antwort auf unsere Frage. Bitte *fassen* Sie sich *kurz*. Es *wird* sicher nicht lange *dauern.*

The work *is pressing* and we *are hoping* for a quick answer to our query. Please *be brief*. It *will* surely not *take* long.

Er *blickte* auf die Pläne und *dankte* mir aufs herzlichste für meine Arbeit. Er *sagte*, er *hätte* mir nicht *geglaubt*, als ich *sagte*, daß ich es rechtzeitig *schaffen würde.*

He *looked* at the plans and *thanked* me warmly for my work. He *said* he *had* not *believed* me, when I *said* I *would get* it *done* in time.

IMPERATIVE
mach(e)! (du)   machen Sie!   macht! (ihr)

PRESENT PERFECT
ich habe ... gemacht

PAST PERFECT (PLUPERFECT)
ich hatte ... gemacht

FUTURE
ich werde ... machen

FUTURE PERFECT
ich werde ... gemacht haben

COMPOUND CONDITIONAL
ich würde ... machen

PAST CONDITIONAL
ich hätte ... gemacht

Jochen *hat gefehlt*. Er *hat sich* krank *gefühlt*; er *hat* über Bauchschmerzen *geklagt*. Und dann *ist* Peter *gestürzt*.

Jochen *wasn't there*. He *felt* ill; he *complained* of a stomach ache. And then Peter *fell down*.

Gestern *haben* wir *uns* sehr *gelangweilt*.

Yesterday we *were/got* very *bored*.

Haben Sie die Fahrscheine schon *gelöst*? Wir *reisen* morgen früh in die Schweiz. Ich *freue mich* schon darauf.

Have you already *bought* the tickets? We *are travelling* early tomorrow morning to Switzerland. I *am looking forward* to it.

Ich *kann* es nicht *fassen*. Mein Kollege *hat* schon wieder *Schwierigkeiten gemacht*, als ich ihm *sagte*, daß wir *uns geirrt hätten*. Leider *mangelte* es mir an Mut, ihm die Wahrheit zu *sagen*. Ich *muß mich* jetzt darum *kümmern*, wie ich das Problem *lösen* soll.

I *can* not *understand* it. My colleague *made difficulties* again when I *told* him that we *had made a mistake*. Unfortunately, I *lacked* the courage to *tell* him the truth. I *must* now *see* how I *am going to solve* the problem.

Schmeckt es? – Ja, ausgezeichnet. Es *schmeckt* nach Zitrone. *Zeigen* Sie mir bitte, wie es *gemacht wird*.

Does it *taste* good? – Yes, excellent. It *tastes* of lemon. Please *show* me how it *is made*.

Wir *hätten* Tennis *gespielt*, wenn es nicht *geregnet hätte*.

We *would have played* tennis if it *had* not *rained*.

Regular weak verb, stress on stem **arbeit-**, stem ending in **-t**

PRESENT PARTICIPLE	*PAST PARTICIPLE*
arbeitend	gearbeitet

PRESENT	*SIMPLE PAST*
ich arbeite	ich arbeitete
du arbeitest	du arbeitetest
er/sie/es arbeitet	er/sie/es arbeitete
wir arbeiten	wir arbeiteten
ihr arbeitet	ihr arbeitetet
sie/Sie arbeiten	sie/Sie arbeiteten

KONJUNKTIV I	*KONJUNKTIV II*
ich arbeite	ich arbeitete

Notes   Regular weak verbs of this type form a large group.

Er *antwortete* auf meine Frage, daß der Film um 23 Uhr *ende/enden würde*.	He *answered* my question, saying that the movie *would finish* at 11 o'clock.
Das Flugzeug *startete* um zehn Uhr und wir *werden* um zwölf *landen*.	The plane *took off* at 10 o'clock, and we *will land* at 12.
Die Wohnung *hat* zu viel *gekostet*. Wir *schulden* dem Vermieter immer noch Geld. Wir *mieten* jetzt eine kleinere Wohnung. Und wir *brauchen* auch nicht *im Garten zu arbeiten*.	The apartment *cost* too much money. We still *owe* the landlord rent. We *are renting* a smaller apartment now. And we *do* not *need to do* any gardening.
Wer *hat* die Tür *geöffnet?* Es *regnet*.	Who *opened* the door? It *is raining*.

IMPERATIVE
arbeite! (du)   arbeiten Sie!   arbeitet! (ihr)

PRESENT PERFECT   *PAST PERFECT (PLUPERFECT)*
ich habe ... gearbeitet   ich hatte ... gearbeitet

FUTURE   *FUTURE PERFECT*
ich werde ... arbeiten   ich werde ... gearbeitet haben

COMPOUND CONDITIONAL   *PAST CONDITIONAL*
ich würde ... arbeiten   ich hätte ... gearbeitet

Wir *hätten* die Arbeit früher *geleistet*, aber die Papiere *mußten* zuerst alle *geordnet werden*.

We *would have finished* the work sooner, but the papers all *had to be arranged* first.

Ich *habe mir* ein neues Auto *geleistet*.

I *have purchased/managed to afford* a new car.

Als wir auf dem Land *zelteten*, *badeten* wir jeden Tag im Fluß.

When we *were camping* in the country we *used to bathe* every day in the river.

Wir *müssen* mit meinem Vater *rechnen* - du *mußt* zuerst mit ihm *reden*.

We *must reckon* with my father - you *must talk* to him first.

Wir *können* immer auf meinen Kollegen *rechnen*. Die Produkte *werden* immer sorgfältig *getestet*.

We *can* always *rely* on my colleague. The products *are* always carefully *tested*.

Regular weak verb ending in **-ieren**, stress on **-ier-**

PRESENT PARTICIPLE	*PAST PARTICIPLE*
probierend	probiert

PRESENT	*SIMPLE PAST*
ich probiere	ich probierte
du probierst	du probiertest
er/sie/es probiert	er/sie/es probierte
wir probieren	wir probierten
ihr probiert	ihr probiertet
sie/Sie probieren	sie/Sie probierten

KONJUNKTIV I	*KONJUNKTIV II*
ich probiere	ich probierte

Notes   Regular weak verbs of this type form a large group.

Können wir darüber **diskutieren, wie wir die Ausstellung organisieren werden?** —Gerne - **ist** das Videogerät schon **repariert worden?** —Ja, ich **habe** es **ausprobiert.**

Can we *talk* about how we *are going to organize* the exhibition? —Gladly - *has* the video *been repaired* yet? —Yes, I*'ve tried* it out.

Wie *ist* das *passiert?* Ich *hätte* früher mit dem Techniker *telefoniert,* wenn ich gewußt hätte, daß es nicht *funktioniert.* Jetzt sagt der Direktor, ich *müsse* die Konferenz *stornieren.*

How *did* that *happen?* I *would have called* the technician sooner if I had known that it *wasn't working.* Now the director says I *must cancel* the conference.

IMPERATIVE
probier(e)! (du)   probieren Sie!   probiert! (ihr)

PRESENT PERFECT	*PAST PERFECT (PLUPERFECT)*
ich habe ... probiert	ich hatte ... probiert

FUTURE	*FUTURE PERFECT*
ich werde ... probieren	ich werde ... probiert haben

COMPOUND CONDITIONAL	*PAST CONDITIONAL*
ich würde ... probieren	ich hätte ... probiert

Wofür *interessieren* Sie *sich?* Für einen neuen Computer? Wie *wollen* Sie das *finanzieren?* Wir *werden* das neue Modell im Januar *produziert haben.*

What *are* you *interested* in? A new computer? How *will* you *finance* it? We *shall have brought out* the new model in January.

Wir *haben uns* in München gut *amüsiert.* Das Hotel *ist* letztes Jahr *modernisiert worden.*

We *had a good time* in Munich. The hotel *was modernized* last year.

Ich weiß nicht, wie man so was *arrangiert* - ich *werde mich informieren müssen.*

I don't know how you *go about arranging* something like that - I *will have to find out.*

Regular inseparable weak verb, stress on stem **-kauf-**

PRESENT PARTICIPLE	PAST PARTICIPLE
verkaufend	verkauft

PRESENT	SIMPLE PAST
ich verkaufe	ich verkaufte
du verkaufst	du verkauftest
er/sie/es verkauft	er/sie/es verkaufte
wir verkaufen	wir verkauften
ihr verkauft	ihr verkauftet
sie/Sie verkaufen	sie/Sie verkauften

KONJUNKTIV I	KONJUNKTIV II
ich verkaufe	ich verkaufte

Notes   Regular inseperable weak verbs of this type form a large group. **Interviewen** is included in this group as it takes no **ge-** in the past participle.

Ich *besuchte* meinen alten Freund, als ich die Altstadt *besichtigte*. Ich *erzählte* ihm von meinem Leben in den USA. Ich *versuchte*, ihn zu *beruhigen*.	I *visited* my old friend when I *visited/went round* the old part of the city. I *told* him about my life in the USA. I *tried* to *calm* him.
Ich *wiederhole*: Bitte *beantworten Sie* meine Frage, sonst *werde* ich *mich* bei der Aufsicht *beklagen*.	I *repeat:* please *answer* my question, or I *shall complain* to the management.
Ich *bin* ihm zufällig vor dem Rathaus *begegnet*. Er *hat* mich sehr freundlich *begrüßt*, und *hat* mich zu meiner neuen Stellung *beglückwünscht*.	I *met* him by chance outside the Town Hall. He *greeted* me very warmly and *congratulated* me on my new job.
Ich dachte, ich *würde* den Zug *verpassen*. Aber er *hatte sich verspätet*.	I thought I *would miss* the train. But it *had been delayed*.

IMPERATIVE
verkauf(e)! (du)   verkaufen Sie!   verkauft! (ihr)

PRESENT PERFECT
ich habe ... verkauft

PAST PERFECT (PLUPERFECT)
ich hatte ... verkauft

FUTURE
ich werde ... verkaufen

FUTURE PERFECT
ich werde ... verkauft haben

COMPOUND CONDITIONAL
ich würde ... verkaufen

PAST CONDITIONAL
ich hätte ... verkauft

Ich *habe mich erkältet.* Wenn du *dich erholt hast, werde* ich dir *erlauben,* mich nach Stuttgart zu *begleiten.*

I *have caught cold.* When you *have recovered,* I *will allow* you to *accompany* me to Stuttgart.

Erinnern Sie *sich* an das Hotel in Stuttgart? Was ist dort passiert? Wir *hatten uns* dort *versammelt,* um den Minister zu *interviewen.* Im letzten Augenblick *hat* er *sich entschuldigt.* Der Bericht *wurde* ohne das Interview *veröffentlicht.*

Do you *remember* the hotel in Stuttgart? What happened? We *had assembled* there to *interview* the minister. At the last moment he *sent his apologies.* The report *was published* without the interview.

Sie *verliebte sich* in den jungen Mann auf den ersten Blick, *verlobte sich* einen Monat später, und *wird sich* im Frühjahr *verheiraten.*

She *fell in love* with the young man at first sight, *got engaged* a month later, and *will get married* in the spring.

Regular separable weak verb, stress on particle **ab-**

PRESENT PARTICIPLE	*PAST PARTICIPLE*
abstellend	abgestellt

PRESENT	*SIMPLE PAST*
ich stelle ab	ich stellte ab
du stellst ab	du stelltest ab
er/sie/es stellt ab	er/sie/es stellte ab
wir stellen ab	wir stellten ab
ihr stellt ab	ihr stelltet ab
sie/Sie stellen ab	sie/Sie stellten ab

KONJUNKTIV I	*KONJUNKTIV II*
ich stelle ab	ich stellte ab

Notes Regular seperable weak verbs of this type form a large group.

Wir *machen* das Haus zuerst sauber, und *hören* mit der Arbeit um 16.00 Uhr *auf*. Dann *können* wir *uns ausruhen*.	We *will clean* the house first and *stop* work at 4:00 pm. Then we *can rest*.
Ich *werde* auf die Kinder *aufpassen*, und Sie *können einkaufen gehen. Wollen* wir morgen *abwechseln*?	I *will look after* the children and you *can go shopping. Shall we change around* tomorrow?
Er *machte halt* und *stellte sich vor*. Dann *setzte* er *sich hin*.	He *stood still* and i*ntroduced himself*. Then he *sat down*.
Das alte Schulsystem *wurde* 1945 *abgeschafft*.	The old school system *was abolished* in 1945.
Als ich *aufblickte*, sah ich, daß alle Mauern *eingestürzt waren*.	When I *looked up*, I saw that all the walls *had fallen in*.

IMPERATIVE
stell(e) ab! (du)   stellen Sie ab!   stellt ab! (ihr)

PRESENT PERFECT
ich habe ... abgestellt

PAST PERFECT (PLUPERFECT)
ich hatte ... abgestellt

FUTURE
ich werde ... abstellen

FUTURE PERFECT
ich werde ... abgestellt haben

COMPOUND CONDITIONAL
ich würde ... abstellen

PAST CONDITIONAL
ich hätte ... abgestellt

Wir *haben* die Theaterkarten *abbestellt*. Das Stück *stellt* das Leben Galileos *dar*. Ich *kann mir vorstellen*, daß es sehr interessant ist, aber es *hat sich herausgestellt*, daß wir keine Zeit haben. Es *macht mir* nichts *aus*. Ich *kann* mir morgen ein anderes Stück *aussuchen*.

We *have cancelled* the theater tickets. The play *describes* the life of Galileo. I *can imagine* that it is very interesting, but as it *turns out* we have no time. I *don't mind*. I *can choose* another play to go to tomorrow.

Er *hat* mir *mitgeteilt*, daß sie sich vor zwei Jahren *kennengelernt hätten*. Er *fügte hinzu*, daß sie zusammen nach Deutschland *zurückkehren wollen*.

He *told* me that they (had) *got to know* each other two years ago. He *added* that they *wanted to return* to Germany together.

Irregular weak verb, stress on stem **kenn-**

PRESENT PARTICIPLE	PAST PARTICIPLE
kennend	gekannt

PRESENT	SIMPLE PAST
ich kenne	ich kannte
du kennst	du kanntest
er/sie/es kennt	er/sie/es kannte
wir kennen	wir kannten
ihr kennt	ihr kanntet
sie/Sie kennen	sie/Sie kannten

KONJUNKTIV I	KONJUNKTIV II
ich kenne	ich kennte

Similar verbs

brennen	burn
nennen	name, call
rennen	run

Es *brennt!*	The house *is on fire*.
Wir *brennen* **Holz im Kamin. Es** *brennt* **besser.**	We *burn* wood in the chimney. It *burns* better.
Die Sonne *brannte* **über dem Meer.**	The sun *burnt* over the sea.
Das Licht *wird* **die ganze Nacht** *brennen.*	The light *will burn* all night.
Ich *habe mich* **am Ofen** *verbrannt.*	I *burned myself* on the stove.
Er *wird* **vor Neugierde** *gebrannt haben.*	He *will have been burning* with curiosity.

IMPERATIVE

kenn(e)! (du)   kennen Sie!   kennt! (ihr)

PRESENT PERFECT	**PAST PERFECT (PLUPERFECT)**
ich habe ... gekannt	ich hatte ... gekannt
FUTURE	**FUTURE PERFECT**
ich werde ... kennen	ich werde ... gekannt haben
COMPOUND CONDITIONAL	**PAST CONDITIONAL**
ich würde ... kennen	ich hätte ... gekannt

Kennen Sie Frau Freising? Ja, wir kennen uns schon seit langem. Sie nannte ihren Sohn nach meinem Bruder. Ihr Mann nennt sich Paul.	*Do you know* Frau Freising? Yes, we *have known each other* for a long time. She *named* her son after my brother. Her husband is *called* Paul.
Herr Topolski nennt sich Maler.	Mr. Topolski *calls himself* a painter.
Mein Sohn hätte die Städte genannt, wenn er sie gewußt hätte.	My son *would have named* the towns if he *had known* them.
Wir rennen heute um die Wette.	We *are having a race* today.
Er ist mit dem Kopf gegen die Mauer gerannt.	He *ran* head first against the wall.
Er rannte ihr das Messer durch den Leib.	He *ran* the knife through her body.

Irregular inseparable weak verb, stress on stem **kenn-**

PRESENT PARTICIPLE	PAST PARTICIPLE
erkennend	erkannt

PRESENT	SIMPLE PAST
ich erkenne	ich erkannte
du erkennst	du erkanntest
er/sie/es erkennt	er/sie/es erkannte
wir erkennen	wir erkannten
ihr erkennt	ihr erkanntet
sie/Sie erkennen	sie/Sie erkannten

KONJUNKTIV I	KONJUNKTIV II
ich erkenne	ich erkennte

Similar verbs

bekennen	confess
ernennen *(zu)*	appoint (to)
verbrennen *(+sein/haben)*	burn up
verkennen	misjudge

IMPERATIVE
erkenn(e)! (du)   erkennen Sie!   erkennt! (ihr)

PRESENT PERFECT	*PAST PERFECT (PLUPERFECT)*
ich habe ... erkannt	ich hatte ... erkannt

FUTURE	*FUTURE PERFECT*
ich werde ... erkennen	ich werde ... erkannt haben

COMPOUND CONDITIONAL	*PAST CONDITIONAL*
ich würde ... erkennen	ich hätte ... erkannt

Er *wurde* zum Minister *ernannt.* Ich *erkannte* ihn sofort, aber meine Mutter *hätte* ihn nie *erkannt.*	He *was appointed* minister. I *recognized* him at once, but my mother *would* never *have known* him.
Sie *verkannte* den Ernst der Sache - unser Haus *ist* völlig *verbrannt.*	She *misjudged* the seriousness of the situation - our house *has been burned* to the ground.
Es ist nicht *wiederzuerkennen.*	It *is unrecognizable.*
Er *hatte* die Wahrheit *bekannt,* bevor ich kam.	He *had confessed* the truth before I came.
Wir *werden* die Briefe sofort *verbrennen.*	We *will burn* the letters at once.
Er *gab* seine Absichten deutlich *zu erkennen.*	He *made* his intentions *clear.*
Sein Gesicht *war von der Sonne verbrannt.*	His face *was sunburned.*
Ich *habe* mir den Mund mit der heißen Kartoffel *verbrannt.*	I *burned* my mouth on the hot potato.

Irregular separable weak verb, stress on particle **nieder-**

PRESENT PARTICIPLE	*PAST PARTICIPLE*
niederbrennend	niedergebrannt

PRESENT	*SIMPLE PAST*
ich brenne nieder	ich brannte nieder
du brennst nieder	du branntest nieder
er/sie/es brennt nieder	er/sie/es brannte nieder
wir brennen nieder	wir brannten nieder
ihr brennt nieder	ihr branntet nieder
sie/Sie brennen nieder	sie/Sie brannten nieder

KONJUNKTIV I	*KONJUNKTIV II*
ich brenne nieder	ich brennte nieder

Similar verbs

anerkennen	acknowledge, respect
sich auskennen *(auf/in+dat)*	know a lot about
durchbrennen *(+sein/haben)*	blow (fuse)
herrennen *(+sein) (hinter+dat)*	chase

IMPERATIVE
brenn(e) nieder! (du)   brennen Sie nieder!   brennt nieder! (ihr)

PRESENT PERFECT ich habe/bin ... niedergebrannt	**PAST PERFECT (PLUPERFECT)** ich hatte/war ... niedergebrannt
FUTURE ich werde ... niederbrennen	**FUTURE PERFECT** ich werde ... niedergebrannt haben/sein
COMPOUND CONDITIONAL ich würde ... niederbrennen	**PAST CONDITIONAL** ich hätte/wäre ... niedergebrannt

Das wiedervereinigte Deutschland *wurde* von allen Ländern *anerkannt*.	The reunified Germany *was recognized* by all countries.
Er *erkannte* das Kind *an*.	He *acknowledged* the child as his own.
Ich *würde* seine Leistungen *anerkennen*, wenn ich *mich* hier *gut auskannte*.	I *would recognize* his achievements if I *were a specialist* in the field.
In dieser Sache *kenne* ich *mich* gut *aus*.	I *know a lot* about this matter.
Ich *kannte mich* in der Stadt nicht gut *aus*.	I *did* not *know* the town very well/*did* not *know my way around* the town.
Wenn die Sicherung nur nicht *durchgebrannt wäre*!	If only the fuse *had* not *burned through*.
Er *ist* hinter mir *hergerannt*.	He *ran along* behind me.

Irregular weak verb, stress on stem **wend-**

PRESENT PARTICIPLE	PAST PARTICIPLE
wendend	gewendet (gewandt)

PRESENT	SIMPLE PAST
ich wende	ich wendete (wandte)
du wendest	du wendetest (wandtest)
er/sie/es wendet	er/sie/es wendete (wandte)
wir wenden	wir wendeten (wandten)
ihr wendet	ihr wendetet (wandtet)
sie/Sie wenden	sie/Sie wendeten (wandten)

KONJUNKTIV I	KONJUNKTIV II
ich wende	ich wendete

Similar verbs

senden *(nach)*   send (for)

Notes   **wenden** (regular weak) [➤arbeiten12] has the literal meaning 'to turn' or 'change direction'. The irregular strong form (refl.) has the figurative meaning of turning to someone for support.

senden (regular weak) [➤arbeiten12] has the literal meaning 'to broadcast'. It is sometimes used to mean 'to send'. The irregular form always means 'to send'.

***Wenden Sie** das Auto!*	*Turn the car, please!*
Er *wandte sich (um).*	He *turned around.*
Sie *wandte sich* **an mich mit einer Bitte.**	She *turned* to me with a request.
Alles *hatte sich* **zum Guten** *gewendet.*	Everything *had changed* for the good.

IMPERATIVE
wend(e)! (du)   wenden Sie!   wendet! (ihr)

PRESENT PERFECT
ich habe ... gewandt (gewendet)

PAST PERFECT (PLUPERFECT)
ich hatte ... gewandt (gewendet)

FUTURE
ich werde ... wenden

FUTURE PERFECT
ich werde ... gewandt (gewendet) haben

COMPOUND CONDITIONAL
ich würde ... wenden

PAST CONDITIONAL
ich hätte ... gewandt (gewendet)

Der Wind *hat sich gewendet*.	The wind *has changed*.
Ich *werde* **den Fisch in der Pfanne** *wenden*.	I *will turn* the fish in the pan.
Ich *wandte mich* **an meinen Bruder um Rat.**	I *turned* to my brother for advice.
Ich *würde* **nach dem Arzt** *senden*, **wenn du wirklich krank wärest.**	I *would send* for the doctor if you were really sick.
Der Rundfunk *sendete* **eine Durchsage.**	The radio *broadcast* an announcement.
Das Paket *wurde* **mit der Post** *gesandt/gesendet*.	The parcel *was sent* by post.
Wir *werden* **alle Karten bis zum 20 Dezember** *gesandt haben*.	We *shall have sent* all the cards by the 20th of December.

Irregular inseparable weak verb, stress on stem **-wend-**

PRESENT PARTICIPLE	PAST PARTICIPLE
verwendend	verwendet (verwandt)

PRESENT	SIMPLE PAST
ich verwende	ich verwendete (verwandte)
du verwendest	du verwendetest (verwandtest)
er/sie/es verwendet	er/sie/es verwendete (verwandte)
wir verwenden	wir verwendeten (verwandten)
ihr verwendet	ihr verwendetet (verwandtet)
sie/Sie verwenden	sie/Sie verwendeten (verwandten)

KONJUNKTIV I	KONJUNKTIV II
ich verwende	ich verwendete

Similar verbs

entsenden	dispatch
entwenden	purloin, steal
versenden	send out

Notes The past simple and past participle forms in **-andt** are rarely found.

Wir *verwenden* diesen Stoff für die Kleider.	We *use* this material for the dresses.
Viel Mühe *wurde* darauf *verwendet*. Ein Bote *wurde* *entsendet*.	A lot of trouble *was taken* over it. A messenger *was dispatched*.
Sie *verwendete* die besten Zutaten, um die Torte zu backen.	She *used* the best ingredients to make the cake.
Ich *werde* meine Kenntnisse gut *verwenden müssen*.	I *shall have to make* good *use of* my knowledge.

IMPERATIVE
verwend(e)! (du)   verwenden Sie!   verwendet! (ihr)

PRESENT PERFECT
ich habe ... verwendet (verwandt)

PAST PERFECT (PLUPERFECT)
ich hatte ... verwendet (verwandt)

FUTURE
ich werde ... verwenden
haben

FUTURE PERFECT
ich werde ... verwendet (verwandt)

COMPOUND CONDITIONAL
ich würde ... verwenden

PAST CONDITIONAL
ich hätte ... verwendet (verwandt)

Ich *würde* dieses Holz nie *verwenden* – wir *haben* immer nur das beste *verwendet*.

I *would* never *use* this wood – we *have* always *used* only the best.

Ich *bin* mit ihm *verwandt*.

I *am related* to him.

Die neuen Computer *sind* der Firma *entwendet worden*, gerade als wir die Kataloge *versenden wollten*.

The new computers have been *stolen* from the firm just when we *wanted to send out* the catalogues.

Irregular weak verb, stress on particle **ab-**

PRESENT PARTICIPLE	PAST PARTICIPLE
absendend	abgesandt (abgesendet)

PRESENT	SIMPLE PAST
ich sende ab	ich sandte (sendete) ab
du sendest ab	du sandtest (sendetest) ab
er/sie/es sendet ab	er/sie/es sandte (sendete) ab
sir senden ab	wir sandten (sendeten) ab
ihr sendet ab	ihr sandtet (sendetet) ab
sie/Sie senden ab	sie/Sie sandten (sendeten) ab

KONJUNKTIV I	KONJUNKTIV II
ich sende	ich sendete

Similar verbs

abwenden	turn away
anwenden	apply, use
einwenden	object

Note　The weak form of **senden (ich sendete), (ich habe gesendet)** etc. is found when it means 'broadcast'. The weak form is more common in the compound form **absenden** and in compounds of **wenden**.

Wir *senden* unsere Weihnachtsgrüße schon Anfang Dezember *ab*.	We *send off* our at Christmas cards at the beginning of December.
Ich *werde* das Paket nächste Woche *absenden*. Ich *würde* es früher *absenden*, aber es ist noch nicht fertig. Wenn ich es *abgesandt habe*, werden Sie es in ein paar Tagen *erhalten*.	I *will send off* the parcel next week. I *would send* it *off* sooner, but it is not yet ready. You *will get* it a few days after I *have sent* it *off*.

IMPERATIVE
send(e) ab! (du)   senden Sie ab!   sendet ab! (ihr)

PRESENT PERFECT
ich habe ... abgesandt
(abgesendet)

PAST PERFECT (PLUPERFECT)
ich hatte ... abgesandt
(abgesendet)

FUTURE
ich werde ... absenden
haben

FUTURE PERFECT
ich werde ... abgesandt (abgesendet)

COMPOUND CONDITIONAL
ich würde ... absenden

PAST CONDITIONAL
ich hätte ... abgesandt (abgesendet)

Die Jacke hat einen Flecken, ich **werde** dieses Reinigungsmittel **anwenden**.

The jacket has a mark, I *will use* this spot remover.

Er **wandte** den Blick von mir **ab**, als er sah, wie ich reagierte.

He *turned* his gaze *away* from me when he saw how I reacted.

Er **hätte** das falsche Heilmittel **angewendet**, wenn ich nicht gesagt hätte, daß er den Arzt um Rat bitten sollte.

He *would have used* the wrong medicine if I had not objected that he should ask the doctor for advice first.

Irregular weak verb, stress on stem **denk-**

PRESENT PARTICIPLE	PAST PARTICIPLE
denkend	gedacht

PRESENT	SIMPLE PAST
ich denke	ich dachte
du denkst	du dachtest
er/sie/es denkt	er/sie/es dachte
wir denken	wir dachten
ihr denkt	ihr dachtet
sie/Sie denken	sie/Sie dachten

KONJUNKTIV I	KONJUNKTIV II
ich denke	ich dächte

Similar verbs

bringen   bring, take

Ich *denke*, er wird sein Studium in einem Jahr abschließen. Er *wird* es sicher bis zum Facharzt *bringen*. Leider *denkt* er nicht daran, hier in Bonn zu bleiben.	I *think* he will finish his studies in a year. He *will* certainly *get* a consultancy. Unfortunately he *is* not *thinking* of staying here in Bonn.
Ich *bringe* Sie zum Bahnhof. *Denken* Sie daran, wie Sie nach Berlin weiterkommen werden.	I *will take* you to the station. Work out how you will get to Berlin.
Ich *muß* die Kinder ins Bett *bringen*.	I *must put* the children to bed.
Was *denken* Sie von diesem Film?	What *do* you *think* of this movie?
Ich *denke mir* den Garten, wir er vor Jahren war.	I *imagine* the garden as it was years ago.
Er *dachte* lange, bevor er antwortete.	He *thought* for a long time before answering.

IMPERATIVE
denk(e)! (du)   denken Sie!   denkt! (ihr)

PRESENT PERFECT   *PAST PERFECT (PLUPERFECT)*
ich habe ... gedacht   ich hatte ... gedacht

FUTURE   *FUTURE PERFECT*
ich werde ... denken   ich werde ... gedacht haben

COMPOUND CONDITIONAL   *PAST CONDITIONAL*
ich würde ... denken   ich hätte ... gedacht

Die Zeitung *brachte* einen langen Artikel über die Schule. Das *wird* uns viel Ärger *bringen.* Das *hätte* ich nicht von dem Redakteur *gedacht.*

The paper *printed* a long article about the school. It *will give* us a lot of trouble. I *would* never *have expected* that of the editor.

Der Briefträger *hat* ein Paket *gebracht.* Meine Mutter *hat* wieder an die Kinder *gedacht.*

The mailman/postman *has brought* a parcel. My mother *has been thinking* of the children again.

Wir *haben* das Schauspielhaus *auf den neuesten Stand gebracht.* Es *hat* eine neue Oper *bringen können.* Sie gefiel mir aber nicht – ich *hatte* es *mir* anders *gedacht.*

We *have modernized* the theater. It *has been able to perform* a new opera. But I did not like it – I *had imagined* it differently.

Er *hat* sie um ihre Ersparnisse *gebracht.* Das *hätte* ich *mir denken können.* Ich *wurde* durch sein Benehmen in *die größte Verlegenheit gebracht.*

He *has robbed* her of her savings. I *might have guessed* that would happen. I *was greatly embarrassed* by his behavior.

Irregular inseparable weak verb, stress on stem **-bring-**

PRESENT PARTICIPLE	PAST PARTICIPLE
verbringend	verbracht

PRESENT	SIMPLE PAST
ich verbringe	ich verbrachte
du verbringst	du verbrachtest
er/sie/es verbringt	er/sie/es verbrachte
wir verbringen	wir verbrachten
ihr verbringt	ihr verbrachtet
sie/Sie verbringen	sie/Sie verbrachten

KONJUNKTIV I	KONJUNKTIV II
ich verbringe	ich verbrächte

Similar verbs

bedenken	consider, think (about)
gedenken *(gen)*	commemorate
vollbringen	accomplish

Wir *gedenken* immer unseres Vaters, wenn wir unsere Heimatstadt besuchen. Er *hat* die ganze Familie in seinem Testament *bedacht.*	We always *think* of our father when we visit our home town. He *remembered* the whole family in his will.
Wir *hatten gedacht*, morgen wieder abzureisen, aber unser Freund *wurde* gestern in die Klinik *gebracht.* Wir *müssen bedenken*, daß er lange liegen wird. *Bedenke dich* gut, ehe du wegreist.	We *had intended* to set off again tomorrow, but our friend *was taken* to the hospital yesterday. We *must take into consideration* the fact that he will be in bed a long time. *Think* carefully before you go away.

IMPERATIVE
verbring(e)! (du)   verbringen Sie!   verbringt! (ihr)

PRESENT PERFECT
ich habe ... verbracht

PAST PERFECT (PLUPERFECT)
ich hatte ... verbracht

FUTURE
ich werde ... verbringen

FUTURE PERFECT
ich werde ... verbracht haben

COMPOUND CONDITIONAL
ich würde ... verbringen

PAST CONDITIONAL
ich hätte ... verbracht

Ich *verbringe* die Sommermonaten immer in den USA. Letztes Jahr *verbrachte* ich drei Monate da. Wir *verbringen* unsere Zeit damit, Verwandte zu besuchen. Ich *hättegern* längere Zeit da *verbracht*, wenn ich mehr Zeit gehabt hätte.

I always *spend* the summer months in the USA. Last year I *spent* three months there. We spend our time visiting relatives. I *would have liked to spend* longer there, if I had had more time.

Er *hat* viele Wunder *vollbracht.*

He *performed* many miracles.

Irregular separable weak verb, stress on particle **nach-**

PRESENT PARTICIPLE	PAST PARTICIPLE
nachdenkend	nachgedacht

PRESENT	SIMPLE PAST
ich denke nach	ich dachte nach
du denkst nach	du dachtest nach
er/sie/es denkt nach	er/sie/es dachte nach
wir denken nach	wir dachten nach
ihr denkt nach	ihr dachtet nach
sie/Sie denken nach	sie/Sie dachten nach

KONJUNKTIV I	KONJUNKTIV II
ich denke nach	ich dächte nach

Similar verbs

abbringen (*von*)	dissuade (from)	**hervorbringen**	produce
ausdenken	think out/up	**mitbringen**	bring along
beibringen	tell, teach	**nahebringen**	bring home to
durchdenken	reason	**umbringen**	kill
durcheinan-derbringen	confuse, disorganize	**unterbringen**	house, accommodate
herausbringen	bring out	**zurückbringen**	bring back

***Bring** noch einige Stühle **heraus**! Sie **haben** alle Kinder **mitgebracht**.*	*Bring out some more chairs. They have brought all the children with them.*
Ein neuer Krieg *ist* **letztes Jahr ausgebrochen**. **Hans** *brachte* **vor Schreck kein Wort** *heraus*.	A new war *broke out* last year. Hans *could* not *utter* a word in horror.
Ich *wurde* **im Hotel gut untergebracht**.	*The accommodation* in the hotel *was* good.

IMPERATIVE

denk(e) nach! (du)   denken Sie nach!   denkt nach! (ihr)

PRESENT PERFECT

ich habe ... nachgedacht

PAST PERFECT (PLUPERFECT)

ich hatte ... nachgedacht

FUTURE

ich werde ... nachdenken

FUTURE PERFECT

ich werde ... nachgedacht haben

COMPOUND CONDITIONAL

ich würde ... nachdenken

PAST CONDITIONAL

ich hätte ... nachgedacht

Die Kinder *bringen* das ganze Haus *durcheinander*. Sie *müssen* ihnen besseres Benehmen *beibringen*.

The children *make a mess* of the whole house. You *must teach* them better behavior.

Ich *habe* mir einen besseren Plan *ausgedacht*. Leider sind die Folgen nicht leicht *auszudenken*.

I *have thought* of a better plan. Unfortunately the consequences *can* not *be* easily *thought out*.

Das Buch *wurde* letztes Jahr *herausgebracht*. Der Verfasser *hat* schon viele Bücher *hervorgebracht*.

The book *was published* last year. The author *has* already *produced* many books.

Irregular weak verb, stress on stem **wiss-**

PRESENT PARTICIPLE	PAST PARTICIPLE
wissend	gewußt

PRESENT	SIMPLE PAST
ich weiß	ich wußte
du weißt	du wußtest
er/sie/es weiß	er/sie/es wußte
wir wissen	wir wußten
ihr wißt	ihr wußtet
sie/Sie wissen	sie/Sie wußten

KONJUNKTIV I	KONJUNKTIV II
ich wisse	ich wüßte

Notes   **wissen** is the only verb of this type.

IMPERATIVE
(du) wisse! wissen Sie! wißt! (ihr)

PRESENT PERFECT
ich habe ... gewußt

PAST PERFECT (PLUPERFECT)
ich hatte ... gewußt

FUTURE
ich werde ... wissen

FUTURE PERFECT
ich werde ... gewußt haben

COMPOUND CONDITIONAL
ich würde ... wissen

PAST CONDITIONAL
ich hätte ... gewußt

Wissen Sie vielleicht, wann er kommt? Ich *würde es gerne wissen*.	*Do* you *know* when he is coming? I *would like to know.*
Ich *weiß* nichts davon. Wenn ich es *wüßte*, würde ich es Ihnen sofort sagen.	I *have* no *idea.* If I *knew*, I would tell you at once.
Wissen Sie etwas von der Geschichte Jugoslawiens?	*Do* you *know* anything about the history of Yugoslavia?
Da *weiß* ich gar nicht Bescheid.	I *do* not *know* much about that.

Class I strong verb, stress on stem **schreib-**

PRESENT PARTICIPLE	PAST PARTICIPLE
schreibend	geschrieben

PRESENT	SIMPLE PAST
ich schreibe	ich schrieb
du schreibst	du schriebst
er/sie/es schreibt	er/sie/es schrieb
wir schreiben	wir schrieben
ihr schreibt	ihr schriebt
sie/Sie schreiben	sie/Sie schrieben

KONJUNKTIV I	KONJUNKTIV II
ich schreibe	ich schriebe

Similar verbs

bleiben (+*sein*)	remain
leihen	lend, borrow
meiden	avoid
preisen	praise
reiben	rub, grate
scheiden (+*sein/haben*)	separate, part
scheinen	shine
schreien	scream, call out
schweigen (+*sein*)	be silent
steigen (+*sein*)	climb, go up
treiben	drive
weisen (*auf+acc*)	point (to)

Er *hat* mir *geschrieben*, er *wolle sich scheiden lassen*. Es *scheint*, daß seine Frau ihn zur Verzweiflung *getrieben hat*.	He *wrote* to me explaining that he *wanted to get divorced*. It *seems* that his wife *has driven* him to the point of despair.

IMPERATIVE
schreib(e)! (du)   schreiben Sie!   schreibt! (ihr)

PRESENT PERFECT
ich habe ... geschrieben

PAST PERFECT (PLUPERFECT)
ich hatte ... geschrieben

FUTURE
ich werde ... schreiben

FUTURE PERFECT
ich werde ... geschrieben haben

COMPOUND CONDITIONAL
ich würde ... schreiben

PAST CONDITIONAL
ich hätte ... geschrieben

Bleiben Sie alle ruhig!	Please *be* quiet!
Er *ist* aus dem Dienst *geschieden*.	He *has retired* from the service.
Die Sonne *hat* den ganzen Tag lang *geschienen*. Die Temperatur *ist* bis auf 24 Grad *gestiegen*.	The sun *shone* all day. The temperature *rose* to 24 degrees.
Wir *sind* auf den Berg *gestiegen* und *blieben* zwei Stunden dort oben.	We *climbed* the mountain and *stayed* at the top for two hours.
Er *wies* auf das Plakat und *schwieg*. Dann fing er an *zu schreien*.	He *pointed* to the notice and *said nothing*. Then he began *to scream*.
An Ihrer Stelle *würde* ich ihn *meiden*. Er *scheint* krank zu sein.	If I were you I *would avoid* him. He *seems* to be sick.

Class I inseparable verb, stress on stem **-schein-**

PRESENT PARTICIPLE	**PAST PARTICIPLE**
erscheinend	erschienen

PRESENT
ich erscheine
du erscheinst
er/sie/es erscheint
wir erscheinen
ihr erscheint
sie/Sie erscheinen

SIMPLE PAST
ich erschien
du erschienst
er/sie/es erschien
wir erschienen
ihr erschient
sie/Sie erschienen

KONJUNKTIV I
ich erscheine

KONJUNKTIV II
ich erschiene

Similar verbs

beschreiben	describe, characterize	**verbleiben** (+*sein*)	remain
besteigen	climb, mount	**verleihen**	lend
beweisen	prove, show	**vermeiden**	avoid
entscheiden	decide	**verschreiben**	prescribe
gedeihen (+*sein*)	flourish	**verschweigen**	keep quiet about
übersteigen	exceed	**vertreiben**	drive away
übertreiben	exaggerate	**verweisen**	expel
unterscheiden	distinguish	**verzeihen** (dat)	forgive (someone)
unterschreiben	sign		

Der Chef *erschien* pünktlich um 8 Uhr. Der Buchhalter *wird offenbar entlassen.* Er *wird* nur so lange in seiner Stellung *verbleiben*, bis die Sache *entschieden ist.* Zuerst *muß* das Verbrechen *bewiesen werden.*

The boss *appeared* punctually at 8 o'clock. The accountant *is apparently being sacked.* He *will* only *stay* in his post until the matter *is decided.* First of all the crime *must be proved.*

IMPERATIVE
erschein(e)! (du)   erscheinen Sie!   erscheint! (ihr)

PRESENT PERFECT   *PAST PERFECT (PLUPERFECT)*
ich bin ... erschienen   ich war ... erschienen

FUTURE   *FUTURE PERFECT*
ich werde ... erscheinen   ich werde ... erschienen sein

COMPOUND CONDITIONAL   *PAST CONDITIONAL*
ich würde ... erscheinen   ich wäre ... erschienen

Der Arzt *verschrieb* mir ein neues Mittel; er *hat* mir aber die möglichen Folgen *verschwiegen*. Das *werde* ich ihm nicht *verzeihen*. Jetzt *muß* ich jede Aufregung *vermeiden*.

The doctor *prescribed* a new medicine for me; however, he *kept quiet* about the possible consequences. I *will* never *forgive* him for it. Now I *must avoid* any excitement.

Es *ist entschieden worden*, daß die Firma nach Berlin ziehen wird. Ich *werde mich* erst morgen *entscheiden*, ob ich mitgehe oder nicht.

It *has been decided* that the firm will move to Berlin. I *will* not *decide* until tomorrow if I will go too or not.

Verzeihen Sie! Aus dieser Entfernung *kann* ich die Farben nicht *unterscheiden*. Sie *sind* sehr *verblichen*.

I'm sorry, from this distance I *can* not *distinguish* the colors. They *have faded* badly.

Bitte *verzeihen Sie* mir! Ich *verbleibe* Ihr sehr ergebener ...

Please *forgive* me! I *remain*, yours sincerely,...

28 aussteigen

Class I separable verb, stress on particle **aus-**

PRESENT PARTICIPLE	PAST PARTICIPLE
aussteigend	ausgestiegen

PRESENT	SIMPLE PAST
ich steige aus	ich stieg aus
du steigst aus	du stiegst aus
er/sie/es steigt aus	er/sie/es stieg aus
wir steigen aus	wir stiegen aus
ihr steigt aus	ihr stiegt aus
sie/Sie steigen aus	sie/Sie stiegen aus

KONJUNKTIV I	KONJUNKTIV II
ich steige aus	ich stiege aus

Similar verbs

abschreiben	copy	**hinweisen**	point (out)
absteigen (+*sein*)	get off, go down	(*auf+acc*)	
ansteigen (+*sein*)	rise, increase	**nachweisen**	prove
aufschreiben	list, note down	**niederschreiben**	write down
aufschreien	exclaim	**steckenbleiben**	get stuck
ausleihen	lend, borrow	(+*sein*)	
ausscheiden	eliminate	**stehenbleiben**	stop, pause
ausschreiben	write out	(+*sein*)	
aussteigen (+*sein*)	get down	**umsteigen** (+*sein*)	change (trains)
einschreiben	enter	**vorschreiben**	specify
einsteigen (+*sein*)	get in/on, board	**zurückweisen**	turn down,
gleichbleiben	remain		refuse
(+*sein*)	unchanged	**zuschreiben** (*dat*)	credit,
gutschreiben (*dat*)	credit (to)		ascribe (to)
sich herumtreiben	hang around	**zuweisen**	assign
hinscheiden (+*sein*)	pass away		

IMPERATIVE

steig aus! (du)   steigen Sie aus!   steigt aus! (ihr)

PRESENT PERFECT	**PAST PERFECT (PLUPERFECT)**
ich bin ... ausgestiegen	ich war ... ausgestiegen

FUTURE	**FUTURE PERFECT**
ich werde ... aussteigen	ich werde ... ausgestiegen sein

COMPOUND CONDITIONAL	**PAST CONDITIONAL**
ich würde ... aussteigen	ich wäre ... ausgestiegen

Bitte *schreiben Sie* die Uhrzeiten *auf!* Wir *steigen* in Köln *um*, und dann in Bremen *aus*. Ich *habe mir* ein gutes Buch für die Reise *ausgeliehen*. Alles einsteigen!

Please *write down* the times! We *are changing trains* in Cologne, and then *getting out* at Bremen. I *have borrowed* a good book for the journey. *All aboard*, please!

Du *mußt* hier vom Fahrrad *absteigen*. Sonst *bleibst* du im Tunnel *stecken*.

You *must dismount* from your bike here. Otherwise you *will get stuck* in the tunnel.

Er *wies* auf den Stadtplan *hin*. Hier *sind* wir gestern im Stau *stehengeblieben*.

He *pointed* to the town map. We *came to a halt* in the traffic jam here yesterday.

Der Wasser im Fluß *ist* sehr *angestiegen*.

The river *rose* very high.

Ich *weise* Sie auf die Gefahren *hin*. Seine Schuld *ist* nie *nachgewiesen worden*. Ich *würde* sein Angebot *zurückweisen*, wenn ich irgend einen Zweifel hätte.

I *am indicating* the dangers. His guilt *was never proved*. I *would turn down* his offer if I had any doubts at all.

Mein Vater *war* vor zwei Jahren *hingeschieden*.

My father *had passed away* two years ago.

Class I verb, stress on stem **leid-**

PRESENT PARTICIPLE	PAST PARTICIPLE
leidend	gelitten

PRESENT	SIMPLE PAST
ich leide	ich litt
du leidest	du littest
er/sie/es leidet	er/sie/es litt
wir leiden	wir litten
ihr leidet	ihr littet
sie/Sie leiden	sie/Sie litten

KONJUNKTIV I	KONJUNKTIV II
ich leide	ich litte

Similar verbs

beißen	bite	**schleichen**	creep, slip, steal
bleichen	bleach	(+sein)	
gleichen (dat)	resemble	**schleifen**	sharpen, drag
gleiten (+sein)	glide, slide	**schmeißen**	throw, chuck
greifen (nach)	grasp, reach (for)	**schneiden**	cut, slice
kneifen	pinch	**schreiten**	stride
pfeifen	whistle	**streichen**	stroke, paint
reißen	tear	**streiten**	argue, quarrel
eiten	ride	**weichen**	yield (to)
(+sein/haben)		(+sein) (dat)	
scheißen	defecate, excrete		

Er *gleicht* seinem Vater sowohl im Ausssehen als auch in Charakter. Sie *stritten* sich oft.	He *resembles* his father both in appearance and character. They often *used to quarrel.*
Unser Hund *beißt!* Sehen Sie, wie er um die Ecke *schleicht.* Letzte Woche *hat* er mich ins Bein *gebissen* und mir den Mantel *zerrissen.*	Our dog *bites!* Look how he sneaks around the corner. Last week he *bit* my leg and *tore* my coat.

IMPERATIVE
leide! (du)   leiden Sie!   leidet! (ihr)

PRESENT PERFECT
ich habe ... gelitten

PAST PERFECT (PLUPERFECT)
ich hatte ... gelitten

FUTURE
ich werde ... leiden

FUTURE PERFECT
ich werde ... gelitten haben

COMPOUND CONDITIONAL
ich würde ... leiden

PAST CONDITIONAL
ich hätte ... gelitten

Er kann jetzt *reiten*. Sein Vater *ist* früher oft *geritten*. Wenn er seines Vaters Pferd *reiten kann*, freut er sich immer.

He can *ride* now. In the past his father *rode* often. He is always pleased *to ride* his father's horse.

Wenn ich sicher wäre, daß er Recht hat, *würde* ich seinem Argument *weichen*.

If I were sure he were right I *would give in to* his argument.

Die Gäste *haben* die Gläser in den Garten *geschmissen*.

The guests *flung* the glasses into the yard/garden.

Die neu *gestrichene* Wände sehen gut aus.

The newly *painted* walls look good.

Ich *bin* auf der glatten Straße *geglitten* aus und ich bin hingefallen.

I *slipped* on the smooth road and I fell down.

Sie *griff* nach dem Messer und *schnitt* das Fleisch in kleine Stücke.

She *grasped* the knife and *cut* the meat into small pieces.

Class I inseparable verb, stress on stem **-reiß-**

PRESENT PARTICIPLE	PAST PARTICIPLE
zerreißend	zerrissen

PRESENT	SIMPLE PAST
ich zerreiße	ich zerriß
du zerreißt	du zerrissest
er/sie/es zerreißt	er/sie/es zerriß
wir zerreißen	wir zerrissen
ihr zerreißt	ihr zerrißt
sie/Sie zerreißen	sie/Sie zerrissen

KONJUNKTIV I	KONJUNKTIV II
ich zerreiße	ich zerrisse

Similar verbs

begreifen	realize
bestreichen	spread
bestreiten	dispute
ergreifen	grasp, seize
umreißen	outline
unterschreiben	sign
unterstreichen	underline
verbleichen (+sein)	fade
vergleichen	compare

IMPERATIVE
zerreiße! (du)   zerreißen Sie!   zerreißt! (ihr)

PRESENT PERFECT
ich habe ... zerrissen

PAST PERFECT (PLUPERFECT)
ich hatte ... zerrissen

FUTURE
ich werde ... zerreißen

FUTURE PERFECT
ich werde ... zerrissen haben

COMPOUND CONDITIONAL
ich würde ... zerreißen

PAST CONDITIONAL
ich hätte ... zerrissen

Ich *begreife* nicht, warum Sie nicht *unterschreiben*. Ich *würde unterschreiben*, wenn er mich nicht geärgert hätte. Ich *bestreite*, daß die Tatsachen hier stimmen.

I *don't understand* why you *don't sign*. I *would sign* if he hadn't annoyed me. I *dispute* the notion that the facts are right.

Er *ergriff* das Blatt und *zerriß* es. Er sagte mir, er *begreife* nicht, warum er es *zerrissen habe*.

He *seized* the paper and *tore* it to pieces. He told me he *did* not *understand,* why he *had torn* it up.

Wer *wird* die Kosten jetzt *bestreiten?*

Who *will pay* the costs now?

Sie *müssen* die Produkte *vergleichen.*

You *must compare* the products.

Wir *haben* die beiden Bilder *verglichen* - sie sind nicht *zu unterscheiden.* Leider *sind* die Farben *verblichen.* Aber die Figuren *sind* immer noch scharf *umrissen.*

We *have compared* the two pictures - they *can* not *be told apart.* Unfortunately, the colors *have faded.* But the figures *are* still sharply *outlined.*

Nehmen Sie ein beliegtes Brot *mit!* Das Brot ist mit Butter und Käse *bestrichen worden.*

Take a sandwich *with you!* The bread *has been spread* with butter and cheese.

Class I separable verb, stress on particle **an-**

PRESENT PARTICIPLE	PAST PARTICIPLE
angreifend	angegriffen

PRESENT	SIMPLE PAST
ich greife an	ich griff an
du greifst an	du griffst an
er/sie/es greift an	er/sie/es griff an
wir greifen an	wir griffen an
ihr greift an	ihr grifft an
sie/Sie greifen an	sie/Sie griffen an

KONJUNKTIV I	KONJUNKTIV II
ich greife an	ich griffe an

Similar verbs

abreißen	tear off, demolish	**ausweichen** (+sein) (dat)	avoid
abschneiden	cut off	**einschneiden** (in+acc)	cut, carve into
abweichen (+sein) (von)	deviate, diverge (from)	**einschreiten**	intervene
anstreichen	decorate, paint	**glattstreichen**	smooth
ausgleichen	even out, equalize	**rausschmeißen**	throw out
ausschneiden	cut out	**zugreifen**	help oneself

Bitte *greifen* Sie *zu!* Keine Umstände!

Please *help yourself!* Don't stand on ceremony.

Die Torte sieht gut aus - Oma *hat* den Guß *glattgestrichen.*

The cake looks good - Grandma *has made* the icing *smooth*.

Es *gleicht sich aus*. Er arbeitet im Garten und ich im Haus.

It *is fair*. He works in the garden and I work in the house.

Wir wohnen jetzt auf dem Lande und fühlen uns von unserem alten Leben in der Stadt ziemlich *abgeschnitten*.

We are now living in the country and feel fairly *cut off* from our old life in the town.

IMPERATIVE

greif(e) an! (du)   greifen Sie an!   greift an! (ihr)

PRESENT PERFECT ich habe ... angegriffen	*PAST PERFECT (PLUPERFECT)* ich hatte ... angegriffen
FUTURE ich werde ... angreifen	*FUTURE PERFECT* ich werde ... angegriffen haben
COMPOUND CONDITIONAL ich würde ... angreifen	*PAST CONDITIONAL* ich hätte ... angegriffen

Das Haus *wurde* letzte Woche frisch *angestrichen*. Die alte Garage *wurde abgerissen,* und jetzt fangen wir mit dem Garten an.	The house *has been* freshly *painted* last week. The old garage *was pulled down* and now we are beginning on the garden.
Euer Vater *wird* mir nicht mehr *ausweichen können*. Es muß jetzt fertiggemacht werden.	Your father *will* not *be able to avoid* me any longer. It must be finished now.
Bei der Sitzung *sind* wir vom Thema *abgewichen*. Der Vorsitzende *hat einschreiten müssen*. Ein paar Leute *haben* ihn fast *angegriffen* und *sind rausgeschmissen worden*.	We *got off* the subject at the meeting. The chairman *had to intervene*. A few people almost *attacked* him and *were thrown out*.

Class II verb, stress on stem **bieg-**

PRESENT PARTICIPLE	PAST PARTICIPLE
biegend	gebogen

PRESENT	SIMPLE PAST
ich biege	ich bog
du biegst	du bogst
er/sie/es biegt	er/sie/es bog
wir biegen	wir bogen
ihr biegt	ihr bogt
sie/Sie biegen	sie/Sie bogen

KONJUNKTIV I	KONJUNKTIV II
ich biege	ich böge

Similar verbs

biegen *(+sein/haben)*	bend, curve
bieten	offer, bid
fliegen *(+sein/haben)*	fly
fliehen *(+sein)*	flee
frieren *(+sein/haben)*	freeze
schieben	push, shove
wiegen	weigh

Notes   **wiegen** meaning 'rock' is weak [**➤machen**].

Die Flüchtlinge *wurden* nach Frankfurt *geflogen.*	The refugees *were flown* to Frankfurt.
Wir *fliegen* morgen nach Südamerika. Bis Rio *fliegt* man zwölf Stunden. *Sind* Sie schon *geflogen?*	We *are flying* to South America tomorrow. *The flight* to Rio *lasts* 12 hours. *Have* you *flown* before?

IMPERATIVE

bieg(e)! (du)   biegen Sie!   biegt! (ihr)

PRESENT PERFECT	**PAST PERFECT (PLUPERFECT)**
ich habe/bin ... gebogen	ich hatte/war ... gebogen

FUTURE	**FUTURE PERFECT**
ich werde ... biegen	ich werde ... gebogen haben/sein

COMPOUND CONDITIONAL	**PAST CONDITIONAL**
ich würde ... biegen	ich hätte/wäre ... gebogen

Das ganze Haus *ist* in die Luft *geflogen*. Die Möbel *wurden* in einen Lastkraftwagen *geschoben* und wegtransportiert. Die Frauen und Kinder *haben gefroren*. Sie *sind* später ins Ausland *geflohen*.

The whole house *blew up*. The furniture *was pushed* into a truck and taken away. The women and children *were very cold*. They *fled* abroad later.

Es *hat* in der Nacht *gefroren*. Als wir aufwachten, *war* der Fluß *zugefroren*.

It *froze* in the night. When we woke up the river *was frozen over*.

Das Fleisch *wog* drei Kilo; ich *habe* ihm 40DM dafür *geboten*.

The meat *weighed* three kilos; I *offered* him 40 Marks for it.

Ich *hätte* Ihnen schon früher eine neue Stellung *geboten*, aber leider *hat sich* bisher keine Gelegenheit dazu *geboten*.

I *would have offered* you a new job sooner, but unfortunately there *has been* no opportunity up to now.

Class II irregular verb with -g- in stem of past tenses, stress on stem
zieh-

PRESENT PARTICIPLE	PAST PARTICIPLE
ziehend	gezogen

PRESENT	SIMPLE PAST
ich ziehe	ich zog
du ziehst	du zogst
er/sie/es zieht	er/sie/es zog
wir ziehen	wir zogen
ihr zieht	ihr zogt
sie/Sie ziehen	sie/Sie zogen

KONJUNKTIV I	KONJUNKTIV II
ich ziehe	ich zöge

Similar verbs

[For inseparable verbs ➤**verlieren** 34]
beziehen   cover

[For separable verbs ➤**anbieten** 35]

abziehen	take off,	**hinausziehen**	draw out
(+sein/haben)	make a copy	*(+sein/haben)*	
anziehen	attract, put on	**umziehen** *(+sein)*	move house
aufziehen	bring up	**vollziehen**	carry out
ausziehen	take off	**vorziehen** *(dat)*	prefer (to)
(+sein/haben)		**zurückziehen**	draw back,
einziehen	draft, enlist	*(+sein/haben)*	move back
(+sein/haben)		**zusammenziehen**	move together
erziehen	bring up	*(+sein/haben)*	
großziehen	bring up, rear	**zuziehen**	close
herausziehen	pull out, extract		

IMPERATIVE
zieh(e)! (du)   ziehen Sie!   zieht! (ihr)

PRESENT PERFECT ich habe/bin ... gezogen	**PAST PERFECT (PLUPERFECT)** ich hatte/war ... gezogen
FUTURE ich werde ... ziehen	**FUTURE PERFECT** ich werde ... gezogen haben/sein
COMPOUND CONDITIONAL ich würde ... ziehen	**PAST CONDITIONAL** ich hätte/wäre ... gezogen

Wir *sind* von Bremen nach Hamburg, zu meinem Vater, *gezogen.* —Welche Stadt *ziehen* Sie *vor?* —Zuerst, als wir in das neue Haus *eingezogen waren,* fühlte ich mich von der ganzen Kultur der Großstadt *angezogen.* Aber es ist schwer *umzuziehen.* —Sie müssen auch daran denken, wie Sie die Kinder *erziehen werden*.

We *have moved* from Bremen to Hamburg, to my father's. —Which town *do* you *prefer?* —At first, when we *moved* into the new house, I felt *attracted* by the city culture. But *moving* is difficult. —You must also think about how you *are going to educate* the children.

Zieh dich jetzt *an! Es zieht* hier im Haus. Mach schnell! — Aber Mutti, gestern *habe* ich *beim Ausziehen* den Verschluß zu stark *gezogen,* und er ist kaputt gegangen.

Get dressed now! *There is a draft* in the house. Be quick! — But Mom/Mum, yesterday I *pulled* the zipper too hard *when getting undressed* and it broke.

Ich *werde* Ihnen 20 Kopien des Dokument *abziehen*. Es *bezieht sich* auf die Zukunft der Firma. Ich *habe* die finanzielle Lage auch in *Betracht gezogen.*

I *will duplicate* 20 copies of the paper for you. The document *deals with* the future of the firm. I *have* also *taken* the financial situation *into account.*

Class II inseparable verb, stress on stem **-lier-**

PRESENT PARTICIPLE	**PAST PARTICIPLE**
verlierend	verloren

PRESENT	**SIMPLE PAST**
ich verliere	ich verlor
du verlierst	du verlorst
er/sie/es verliert	er/sie/es verlor
wir verlieren	wir verloren
ihr verliert	ihr verlort
sie/Sie verlieren	sie/Sie verloren

KONJUNKTIV I	**KONJUNKTIV II**
ich verliere	ich verlöre

Similar verbs

entfliehen *(+sein) (dat)*	escape (from)
überwiegen	outweigh, predominate
verbieten	forbid
verschieben	postpone

Du *solltest* die Abreise nicht *verschieben*. Die Vorteile eines Urlaubs im Frühling *überwiegen* die Nachteile, weil das Wetter dann *überwiegend* heiter ist. Wir *wollen* dem Lärm der Stadt *entfliehen*.	You *should* not *postpone* the departure. The advantages of a spring holiday *outweigh* the disadvantages, because the weather is *generally* good. We *want* to *escape from* the noise of the city.
Ich *habe* meinen Schirm *verloren*. Wir *haben* den Schrank in die Ecke *geschoben*, aber er ist nicht zu finden.	I *have lost* my umbrella. We *pushed* the cabinet/cupboard into the corner, but it can't be found.

IMPERATIVE
verlier(e)! (du)   verlieren Sie!   verliert! (ihr)

PRESENT PERFECT	*PAST PERFECT (PLUPERFECT)*
ich habe ... verloren	ich hatte ... verloren

FUTURE	*FUTURE PERFECT*
ich werde ... verlieren	ich werde ... verloren haben

COMPOUND CONDITIONAL	*PAST CONDITIONAL*
ich würde ... verlieren	ich hätte ... verloren

Der Verbrecher *ist* aus dem Gefängnis *entflohen.*	The criminal *has escaped* from prison.
Wir *hätten* viel Zeit *verloren,* wenn ich den Kindern nicht *verboten hätte,* Garten zu spielen.	We *would have wasted* a lot of time if I *had* not *forbidden* the children to play in the yard/garden.
Wir *hatten* den Termin auf einen späteren Zeitpunkt *verschoben* – leider *ist* viel Zeit dabei *verlorengegangen.*	We *had postponed* the date – unfortunately a lot of time *was wasted.*

Class II separable verb, stress on particle **an-**

PRESENT PARTICIPLE	PAST PARTICIPLE
anbietend	angeboten

PRESENT	SIMPLE PAST
ich biete an	ich bot an
du bietest an	du botst an
er/sie/es bietet an	er/sie/es bot an
wir bieten an	wir boten an
ihr bietet an	ihr botet an
sie/Sie bieten an	sie/Sie boten an

KONJUNKTIV I	KONJUNKTIV II
ich biete an	ich böte an

Similar verbs

abbiegen	turn off
einbiegen *(+sein/haben) (in+acc)*	turn in
einfrieren *(+sein/haben)*	freeze

Biete unseren Gästen eine Tasse Kaffee *an!*	*Offer* our guests a cup of coffee.
Biegen Sie an der Ampel *ab!* Dann *müssen* Sie nach rechts in die Hauptstraße *einbiegen.*	*Turn off* at the street lights. Then *turn right* onto the Main Street.
Wenn wir nach links *eingebogen wären,* wären wir schneller zum Bahnhof gekommen.	If we *had turned* left, we would have got to the station quicker.
Er *bot* mir *an,* mich im Wagen mitzunehmen.	He *offered* me a lift in the car.

IMPERATIVE

biet(e) an! (du)　　　bieten Sie an!　　　bietet an! (ihr)

PRESENT PERFECT
ich habe ... angeboten

PAST PERFECT (PLUPERFECT)
ich hatte ... angeboten

FUTURE
ich werde ... anbieten

FUTURE PERFECT
ich werde ... angeboten haben

COMPOUND CONDITIONAL
ich würde ... anbieten

PAST CONDITIONAL
ich hätte ... angeboten

Ich *würde* ihm ein Glas Wein *anbieten,* aber er darf keinen Alkohol zu sich nehmen.

I *would like* to *offer* him a glass of wine, but he is not allowed to take any alcohol.

Wir *werden* das Gemüse für den Winter *einfrieren.*

We *will freeze* the vegetables for the winter.

Das Dach *hat sich* unter dem Schnee *eingebogen,* und die *eingefrorenen* Wasserrohre sind geplatzt.

The roof *bent* under the snow, and the *frozen* water pipes burst.

Class II verb, stress on stem **heb-**

PRESENT PARTICIPLE	PAST PARTICIPLE
hebend	gehoben

PRESENT	SIMPLE PAST
ich hebe	ich hob
du hebst	du hobst
er/sie/es hebt	er/sie/es hob
wir heben	wir hoben
ihr hebet	ihr hobt
sie/Sie heben	sie/Sie hoben

KONJUNKTIV I	KONJUNKTIV II
ich hebe	ich höbe

Similar verbs

gären (+sein/haben)	ferment	**schwören**	swear
lügen	lie	**trügen**	deceive
saugen	suck	**wägen**	weigh
scheren	shear, clip	**weben**	weave

Notes There are no vowel changes in the present tense in this sub-group. **wägen** is sometimes used in a weak form; **saugen** and **weben** generally are; **gären** is used figuratively in a weak form; **scheren** is used in a weak form when it means 'to concern' or 'clear off'; **schwören** has a simple past **schwur** with alternative **schwor**; it also occurs regionally in a weak form [➤**machen** 11].

Hebt das Glas und laßt unseren lieben Vater hochleben!	*Lift* your glasses and drink to the health of our dear father.
Heb den Finger, wenn du die Antwort weißt!	*Put* your hand *up* if you know the answer.
Er *hob* den Arm und *schwur* auf die Bibel, daß es die Wahrheit sei.	He *lifted* his arm and *swore* on the Bible that it was true.
Er sprach in *gehobener* Sprache und *hat* jedes seiner Worte *gewogen.*	He expressed himself in formal language and *weighed* every word.

IMPERATIVE
heb(e)! (du)   heben Sie!   hebt! (ihr)

PRESENT PERFECT   *PAST PERFECT (PLUPERFECT)*
ich habe ... gehoben   ich hatte ... gehoben

FUTURE   *FUTURE PERFECT*
ich werde ... heben   ich werde ... gehoben haben

COMPOUND CONDITIONAL   *PAST CONDITIONAL*
ich würde ... heben   ich hätte ... gehoben

Ich *könnte schwören,* daß ich ihn gestern gesehen habe. Er *hat* seinen Bart kurz *geschoren.*

I *could swear* I saw him yesterday. He *has cut* his beard short.

Was *schert* mich das! Ich *schere mich* nicht darum, was er auch machen will.

What *do I care* about that! I *don't care* what he does.

Erst *wägen,* dann wagen!

Look before you leap!

Hast du schon gut *Staub gesaugt?*

Have you *vacuumed* thoroughly?

Die Teppiche *wurden* im Osten *gewoben.* Man *muß* sie nur sorgfältig *saugen.*

The carpets *were woven* in the East. You *have to clean* them carefully.

Wenn mich meine Erinnerung *nicht trügt, hatten* sie dem König ewige Treue *geschworen.*

If my memory *serves me right,* they *had sworn* eternal loyalty to the king.

Der Wein *gärt* in großen Fässen.

The wine *ferments* in large barrels.

Class II inseparable verb, stress on stem **-wäg-**

PRESENT PARTICIPLE	PAST PARTICIPLE
erwägend	erwogen

PRESENT	SIMPLE PAST
ich erwäge	ich erwog
du erwägst	du erwogst
er/sie/es erwägt	er/sie/es erwog
wir erwägen	wir erwogen
ihr erwägt	ihr erwogt
sie/Sie erwägen	sie/Sie erwogen

KONJUNKTIV I	KONJUNKTIV II
ich erwäge	ich erwöge

Similar verbs

beschwören	conjure up
betrügen	deceive
bewegen	persuade
erheben	raise
sich verschwören	conspire

Notes   There are no vowel changes in the present tense in this sub-group. **erwägen** is sometimes used in a weak form [➤**verkaufen** 14]. **sich bewegen** (to move) is always weak [➤**verkaufen** 14].

Der Berg *erhebt sich* bis zu 2500 Meter über den Meeresspiegel.	The mountain *rises* to 2500 meters above sea level.
Ich *habe* den Plan schon gründlich *erwogen*.	I *have weighed (up)* the plan thoroughly.
Die Kranke *erhob sich* halb vom Bett und *beschwor* ihn, sie nicht zu verlassen.	The sick woman *raised herself up* in bed and *implored* him not to leave her.

IMPERATIVE
erwäg(e)! (du)   erwägen Sie!   erwägt! (ihr)

PRESENT PERFECT
ich habe ... erwägen

PAST PERFECT (PLUPERFECT)
ich hatte ... erwogen

FUTURE
ich werde ... erwägen

FUTURE PERFECT
ich werde ... erwogen haben

COMPOUND CONDITIONAL
ich würde ... erwägen

PAST CONDITIONAL
ich hätte ... erwogen

Don Giovanni *hat* Tausende von Frauen *betrogen.* Er *beschwor* den Geist des Ermordeten, *erhob* sein Glas und trank auf sein Wohl.

Don Giovanni *deceived* thousands of women. He *conjured* up the ghost of the murdered man, *raised* his glass and drank his health.

Das Volk *hätte sich* gegen den Kaiser *erhoben,* wenn *sich* nicht ein großer Sturm *erhoben hätte.*

The people *would have risen* against the emperor, if a great storm *had not arisen.*

Es *erhebt sich* die Frage, ob wir uns einer anderen Partei anschließen sollten. Der Minister *betrügt* uns alle.

The question *arises* of whether we should join another party. The minister *is deceiving* us all.

An Ihrer Stelle *würde* ich jede Möglichkeit *erwägen.*

In your place I *would weigh (up)* every possibility.

Class II separable verb, stress on particle **auf-**

PRESENT PARTICIPLE	PAST PARTICIPLE
aufhebend	aufgehoben

PRESENT	SIMPLE PAST
ich hebe auf	ich hob auf
du hebst auf	du hobst auf
er/sie/es hebt auf	er/sie/es hob auf
wir heben auf	wir hoben auf
ihr hebt auf	ihr hobt auf
sie/Sie heben auf	sie/Sie hoben auf

KONJUNKTIV I	KONJUNKTIV II
ich hebe auf	ich höbe auf

Similar verbs

abheben	abolish
abwägen	weigh (up)
hervorheben	highlight
hochheben	hoist

Notes   There are no vowel changes in the present tense in this sub-group.

Er *wägt* seine Worte gut *ab.*	He *weighs* his words well.
Das Flugzeug *ist* schließlich um zwei Uhr *abgehoben.*	The plane finally *took off* at 2 o'clock.
Das Geld *ist* bei der Bank *gut aufgehoben.*	The money *is safe* at the bank.
Er ging zur Bank und *hob* das Geld *ab.* Er *hätte* mehr Geld *abgehoben,* aber seine Strafe *ist aufgehoben worden.*	He went to the bank and *withdrew* the money. He *would have taken out* more money, but his fine *was cancelled.*

IMPERATIVE
heb(e) auf! (du)   heben Sie auf!   hebt auf! (ihr)

PRESENT PERFECT
ich habe ... aufgehoben

PAST PERFECT (PLUPERFECT)
ich hatte ... aufgehoben

FUTURE
ich werde ... aufheben

FUTURE PERFECT
ich werde ... aufgehoben haben

COMPOUND CONDITIONAL
ich würde ... aufheben

PAST CONDITIONAL
ich hätte ... aufgehoben

Man muß die Vorteile gegen die Nachteile gut *abwägen.*	You must *weigh (up)* the advantages well against the disadvantages.
Sehen Sie sich die neueste Mode an – die Farben *heben sich* gut voneinander *ab.*	Look at the latest fashion – the colors *contrast* well.
Hebt die Fahne *hoch!*	*Lift* the flag *high!*

Class II verb, stress on stem **schieß-**

PRESENT PARTICIPLE	PAST PARTICIPLE
schießend	geschossen

PRESENT	SIMPLE PAST
ich schieße	ich schoß
du schießt	du schossest
er/sie/es schießt	er/sie/es schoß
wir schießen	wir schossen
ihr schießt	ihr schoßt
sie/Sie schießen	sie/Sie schossen

KONJUNKTIV I	KONJUNKTIV II
ich schieße	ich schösse

Similar verbs

dreschen	thresh	**saufen**	drink (of
fechten	fence		animals),
flechten	twine		booze
fließen *(+sein)*	flow	**schießen** *(+sein/haben)*	shoot,
gießen	cast,		fire
	pour	**schließen**	close,
glimmen	glow		conclude
kriechen *(+sein)*	crawl	**schmelzen** *(+sein/haben)*	melt
melken	milk	**schwellen** *(+sein/haben)*	swell
quellen *(+sein)*	well up	**sprießen** *(+sein)*	sprout
riechen *(nach)*	smell (of)		

Notes Vowel changes in the second and third person singular present tense
are as follows: **-e-** to **-i-** and **-au-** to **-äu-**, with the exception of
melken. **saufen** and **triefen** double the **f** in the simple past and past
participle **soff**, **gesoffen**.

***Schließ** die Tür! Es **gießt**!*	*Shut* the door. *It's pouring.*
Die Tür *schließt sich* **von selbst.**	The door *shuts* automatically.
Er *säuft* **wie ein Loch. Er** *wird* **sich zu Tode** *saufen*. **Das ganze Haus** *riecht* **nach Schnaps.**	He *drinks* like a fish. He *will drink* himself to death. The whole house *smells* of brandy.

IMPERATIVE
schieß(e)! (du)   schießen Sie!   schießt! (ihr)

PRESENT PERFECT
ich habe ... geschossen

PAST PERFECT (PLUPERFECT)
ich hatte ... geschossen

FUTURE
ich werde ... schießen

FUTURE PERFECT
ich werde ... geschossen haben

COMPOUND CONDITIONAL
ich würde ... schießen

PAST CONDITIONAL
ich hätte ... geschossen

Das Eis *ist* vor Millionen von Jahren *geschmolzen*. Aus unseren Forschungen *haben* wir *geschlossen*, daß der Fluß früher in die andere Richtung *floß*.

The ice *melted* millions of years ago. We *concluded* from our research that the river *used to flow* in the other direction.

Eine lebhafte Diskussion *schloß sich* an den Vortrag an.

A lively discussion *followed* the lecture.

Ich *bin beschossen worden*. Man *hat* mich ins Bein *geschossen*. Der Mann *hat* mehrere Male nach mir *geschossen*.

I *have been shot*. I *have been shot* in the leg. The man *shot* at me several times.

Das Boot *ist* durch das Wasser *geschossen*.

The boat *shot* through the water.

Er *hat* sich eine Kugel durch den Kopf *geschossen*.

He *has shot* himself through the head.

Wir *müssen* das Geld in das Fach *schließen*.

We *must lock* the money in the drawer.

Class II inseparable verb, stress on stem **-nieß-**

PRESENT PARTICIPLE	PAST PARTICIPLE
genießend	genossen

PRESENT	SIMPLE PAST
ich genieße	ich genoß
du genießt	du genossest
er/sie/es genießt	er/sie/es genoß
wir genießen	wir genossen
ihr genießt	ihr genoßt
sie/Sie genießen	sie/Sie genossen

KONJUNKTIV I	KONJUNKTIV II
ich genieße	ich genösse

Similar verbs

begießen	water	**erschießen**	shoot dead
beschießen	shoot dead, shell	**erschließen**	open up
		umschließen	border
beschließen	decide	**verdrießen**	annoy
sich entschließen	make up one's mind	**vergießen**	spill
		verschließen	lock, seal
erlöschen *(+sein)*	go out (fire)		

Notes   **erlöschen** changes the vowel in the second and third person singular present tense to **-i-**.

Haben Sie *sich entschlossen* **abzureisen?** – Ja, wir *haben beschlossen*, **nach Frankreich zu fahren.** Bitte *gießen* Sie die **Blumen, während ich in Urlaub bin.**	*Have* you *made up your mind* to go away? – Yes, we *have decided* to go to France. Please *water* the flowers while I'm on vacation/on holiday.

IMPERATIVE
genieß(e)! (du)   genießen Sie!   genießt! (ihr)

PRESENT PERFECT ich habe ... genossen	**PAST PERFECT (PLUPERFECT)** ich hatte ... genossen
FUTURE ich werde ... genießen	**FUTURE PERFECT** ich werde ... genossen haben
COMPOUND CONDITIONAL ich würde ... genießen	**PAST CONDITIONAL** ich hätte ... genossen

---

Was mich *verdrießt,* ist die Tatsache, daß unsere Eltern *sich nur schwer entschließen können.*

What *annoys* me is the fact that our parents have such difficulty *making up their minds.*

Die Verhandlungen wurden hinter *verschlossenen* Türen geführt.

The negotiations were carried out behind *locked* doors.

Das Essen *war nicht zu genießen;* wir *beschlossen,* in ein anderes Restaurant zu gehen.

The meal *was inedible;* we *decided* to go to another restaurant.

Er *verschloß* die Tür und *erschoß sich.*

He *locked* the door and *shot himself.*

Wir *werden* nächstes Jahr neue Märkte *erschließen.*

We *will open up* new markets next year.

Es *wurde beschlossen,* die Gegend als Reisegebiet *zu erschließen.* Hier *kann* man die schöne Berglandschaft *genießen.*

It *was decided to open up* the region as a tourist area. You *can enjoy* the beautiful mountain landscape here.

Class II separable verb, stress on particle **ab-**

PRESENT PARTICIPLE	**PAST PARTICIPLE**
abschließend	abgeschlossen

PRESENT	**SIMPLE PAST**
ich schließe ab	ich schloß ab
du schließt ab	du schlossest ab
er/sie/es schließt ab	er/sie/es schloß ab
wir schließen ab	wir schlossen ab
ihr schließt ab	ihr schloßt ab
sie/Sie schließen ab	sie/Sie schlossen ab

KONJUNKTIV I	**KONJUNKTIV II**
ich schließe ab	ich schlösse ab

Similar verbs

anschließen	connect
aufschließen	unlock
ausschließen	bar, exclude
einschließen	enclose, include
kurzschließen	short-circuit
sich zusammenschließen	join together

Mutti *hat sich ausgeschlossen.* *Schließ* die Tür *auf!* Hier ist der Schlüssel.	Mother *has locked herself out.* *Unlock* the door! Here is the key.
Kannst du bitte die Lampe *anschließen?*	Please *can* you *plug* in the lamp?
Die ganze Stadt *ist* vom See *eingeschlossen,* und unser Garten *schließt sich* an den Wald an.	The whole town *is surrounded* by the lake and our yard/garden *adjoins* the woods.

IMPERATIVE

schließ(e) ab! (du)   schließen Sie ab!   schließt ab! (ihr)

PRESENT PERFECT ich habe ... abgeschlossen	*PAST PERFECT (PLUPERFECT)* ich hatte ... abgeschlossen
FUTURE ich werde ... abschließen	*FUTURE PERFECT* ich werde ... abgeschlossen haben
COMPOUND CONDITIONAL ich würde ... abschließen	*PAST CONDITIONAL* ich hätte ... abgeschlossen

Wir *müssen* **den Hund** *einschließen,* **sonst folgt er uns.**	We *must shut* the dog in, otherwise he will follow us.
Ist **die Bedienung** *eingeschlossen?*	*Is* service *included?*
Alle, mich *eingeschlossen,* **haben sich der sozialistischen Partei** *angeschlossen.* **Wir** *hätten* **uns vielleicht zu einer neuen Partei** *zusammengeschlossen.* **Man** *kann* **diese Möglichkeit nicht** *ausschließen.*	We *have* all, *joined* the Socialist Party, *including* me. We *might have formed* a new party. One *can* not *exclude* the possibility.
Er sagte, er *habe sich* **der konservativen Partei** *angeschlossen.*	He said he *had joined* the Conservatives.

Class III verb, stress on stem **trink-**

PRESENT PARTICIPLE	PAST PARTICIPLE
trinkend	getrunken

PRESENT	SIMPLE PAST
ich trinke	ich trank
du trinkst	du trankst
er/sie/es trinkt	er/sie/es trank
wir trinken	wir tranken
ihr trinkt	ihr trankt
sie/Sie trinken	sie/Sie tranken

KONJUNKTIV I	KONJUNKTIV II
ich trinke	ich tränke

Similar verbs

dringen *(+sein)*	penetrate
klingen	sound
ringen	ring, wrestle
schwingen	swing, oscillate
singen	sing
sinken *(+sein)*	sink, fall
springen *(+sein)*	jump
stinken	stink
wringen	wring
zwingen	force, compel

Trinken Sie **ein Glas Wein!**

Have a glass of wine!

Der Wechselkurs *ist* **wieder** *gesunken.* **Das** *hat* **uns (dazu)** *gezwungen,* **das Haus zu verkaufen.**

The rate of exchange *has gone down* again. It *has forced* us to sell the house.

IMPERATIVE
trink(e)! (du)　　　　　trinken Sie!　　　　　trinkt! (ihr)

PRESENT PERFECT
ich habe ... getrunken

PAST PERFECT (PLUPERFECT)
ich hatte ... getrunken

FUTURE
ich werde ... trinken

FUTURE PERFECT
ich werde ... getrunken haben

COMPOUND CONDITIONAL
ich würde ... trinken

PAST CONDITIONAL
ich hätte ... getrunken

Leider hat er damals angefangen zu trinken. Es *stank* nach Alkohol im Haus. Er *hat* auch dabei *gesungen.* Der Lärm *ist* durch die Wand zu uns *gedrungen.* Eines Tages *ist* er sogar ins Schwimmbad *gesprungen,* ohne sich auszuziehen.

Unfortunately he began *to drink* at that time. The house *stank* of alcohol. He *sang* at the same time. We *could hear the noise* through the wall. One day, he even *jumped* fully clothed into the swimming pool.

Wer *trinkt* noch was? *Wollen wir* auf das Wohl unseres lieben Paul *trinken!*

Who *wants* another *drink? Let's drink* to the health of our dear Paul.

Er *wäre* viel weiter *gesprungen,* wenn er sich den Fuß nicht verstaucht hätte.

He *would have jumped* much further if he had not twisted his foot.

Class III inseparable verb, stress on stem **-dring-**

PRESENT PARTICIPLE	PAST PARTICIPLE
durchdringend	durchdrungen

PRESENT	SIMPLE PAST
ich durchdringe	ich durchdrang
du durchdringst	du durchdrangst
er/sie/es durchdringt	er/sie/es durchdrang
wir durchdringen	wir durchdrangen
ihr durchdringt	ihr durchdrangt
sie/Sie durchdringen	sie/Sie durchdrangen

KONJUNKTIV I	KONJUNKTIV II
ich durchdringe	ich durchdränge

Similar verbs

sich betrinken	get drunk
entspringen *(+sein) (dat)*	rise (from)
ertrinken *(+sein)*	drown
gelingen *(+sein) (dat)*	succeed
mißlingen *(+sein) (dat)*	fail
überspringen	jump over
verklingen *(+sein)*	fade
verschlingen	devour, gobble

Notes   **durchdringen** can also be used intransitively as a separable verb with the auxiliary **sein**.

Er *betrinkt sich* jeden Abend. Es *ist* mir bisher *mißlungen*, ihn davon *abzubringen*.	He *gets drunk* every evening. Up until now, I *have failed to stop* him.
Der Rhein *entspringt* in den Alpen.	The Rhine *rises* in the Alps.

IMPERATIVE
durchdringe! (du)   durchdringen Sie!   durchdringet! (ihr)

PRESENT PERFECT
ich habe ... durchdrungen

PAST PERFECT (PLUPERFECT)
ich hatte ... durchdrungen

FUTURE
ich werde ... durchdringen

FUTURE PERFECT
ich werde ... durchdrungen haben

COMPOUND CONDITIONAL
ich würde ... durchdringen

PAST CONDITIONAL
ich hätte ... durchdrungen

Zuerst *gelang es uns* ihm zu helfen, aber dann ist er in den Fluß gestürzt und *ist ertrunken.*

At first *we succeeded* in helping him, but then he fell in the river and *drowned.*

Er *verschlingt* jedes Buch in ein paar Tagen. Ich denke, er *überspringt* viele Seiten.

He *consumes* each book in a few days. I think he *skips* many pages.

Die Oper *ist gut gelungen.* Allmählich *durchdringt* das Licht die Dunkelheit und der Hort schimmert mitten auf der Bühne. Wenn die Musik am Ende *verklingt,* steht die ganze Bühne in Flammen.

The opera *was a great success.* Gradually light *penetrates* the darkness and the treasure gleams on the stage. When the music *dies away* at the end, the whole stage is in flames.

Die Kinder *haben* die ganze Torte *verschlungen.*

The children *have wolfed down* the whole cake.

Das Haus *wird* Millionen *verschlingen.*

The house *will cost* millions.

Class III separable verb, stress on particle **auf-**

PRESENT PARTICIPLE	PAST PARTICIPLE
aufspringend	aufgesprungen

PRESENT	SIMPLE PAST
ich springe auf	ich sprang auf
du springst auf	du sprangst auf
er/sie/es springt auf	er/sie/es sprang auf
wir springen auf	wir sprangen auf
ihr springt auf	ihr sprangt auf
sie/Sie springen auf	sie/Sie sprangen auf

KONJUNKTIV I	KONJUNKTIV II
ich springe auf	ich spränge auf

Similar verbs

absingen	sight-read
absinken *(+sein)*	sink, subside
abspringen *(+sein)*	jump down, come off
anspringen *(+sein)*	jump, start
antrinken	start drinking
austrinken	drink up
einspringen *(+sein) (für)*	stand in (for)
zutrinken	toast

Er hat das Glas *beim Aufspringen* fallen lassen. Er *hatte* den Wein nur *angetrunken*. Er *wollte* seinem Freund *zutrinken*.	He dropped the glass *when he jumped up*. He *had* only *sipped* some of the wine. He *wanted to toast* his friend.
Wenn du nicht so schnell *aufgesprungen wärst*, so wäre es nicht passiert.	If you *had* not *jumped up* so fast, it would not have happened.

IMPERATIVE
spring(e) auf! (du)   springen Sie auf!   springt auf! (ihr)

PRESENT PERFECT
ich bin ... aufgesprungen

PAST PERFECT (PLUPERFECT)
ich war ... aufgesprungen

FUTURE
ich werde ... aufspringen

FUTURE PERFECT
ich werde ... aufgesprungen sein

COMPOUND CONDITIONAL
ich würde ... aufspringen

PAST CONDITIONAL
ich wäre ... aufgesprungen

Er *springt* immer *ein*, wenn jemand fehlt.	He always *steps in* when someone is absent.
***Könnten* Sie heute mal *einspringen*?**	*Could* you please *help out* today?
Er *ist* gestern für mich *eingesprungen*.	He *stood in* for me yesterday.
Er *sprang auf*, sobald wir von der Mauer *absprangen*.	He *jumped up* as soon as we *leaped down* from the wall.
Der Motor *ist* nicht *angesprungen*. Das Boot *ist* gesunken.	The engine *would*n't *start*. The boat *sank*.

Class III verb, stress on stem **bind-**

PRESENT PARTICIPLE	PAST PARTICIPLE
bindend	gebunden

PRESENT	SIMPLE PAST
ich binde	ich band
du bindest	du bandst
er/sie/es bindet	er/sie/es band
wir binden	wir banden
ihr bindet	ihr bandet
sie/Sie binden	sie/Sie banden

KONJUNKTIV I	KONJUNKTIV II
ich binde	ich bände

Similar verbs

finden	find
schwinden *(+sein)*	dwindle, fade
winden	curl, wind

Jede Hoffnung *schwindet*, sie noch am Leben *zu finden*.	Hopes *are fading of finding* them alive.
Ich *kann* meine Brille nicht finden. Sie *wird sich* wieder finden.	I *can*'t *find* my glasses. They *will turn up* again.

IMPERATIVE

binde! (du)   binden Sie!   bindet! (ihr)

PRESENT PERFECT   *PAST PERFECT (PLUPERFECT)*

ich habe ... gebunden   ich hatte ... gebunden

FUTURE   *FUTURE PERFECT*

ich werde ... binden   ich werde ... gebunden haben

COMPOUND CONDITIONAL   *PAST CONDITIONAL*

ich würde ... binden   ich hätte ... gebunden

Binde die Schnur um das Paket.	*Tie* the string around the parcel.
Er *band sich* einen Schal um den Hals und *wand sich* vor Schmerz.	He *tied* a scarf around his neck and *curled up* in pain.
Viele junge Menschen *hatten* im Weltkrieg den Tod *gefunden*.	Many young people *had met* their deaths in the world war.
Sie *findet* ihn immer bereit, ihr bei der Hausarbeit zu helfen.	She always *finds* him ready to help her with the housework.
Ich *finde*, daß die Sache sich nicht leicht klären läßt. Wir dachten, wir *hätten* die Lösung *gefunden*.	I *find* the matter cannot be settled easily. We thought we *had found* the solution.

Class III inseparable verb, stress on stem **-schwind-**

PRESENT PARTICIPLE	*PAST PARTICIPLE*
verschwindend	verschwunden

PRESENT	*SIMPLE PAST*
ich verschwinde	ich verschwand
du verschwindest	du verschwandst
er/sie/es verschwindet	er/sie/es verschwand
wir verschwinden	wir verschwanden
ihr verschwindet	ihr verschwandet
sie/Sie verschwinden	sie/Sie verschwanden

KONJUNKTIV I	*KONJUNKTIV II*
ich verschwinde	ich verschwände

Similar verbs

sich befinden	be located
erfinden	invent, make up
überwinden	overcome
verbinden *(mit)*	bind, connect (with)

Verschwinde!	*Get lost!*
Ich *muß* **mal** *verschwinden.*	I *must go* to the bathroom/loo.
Wie befinden Sie sich? (Wie geht es Ihnen?) – Der Arm tut mir weh. – Wir *müssen* **die Wunde** *verbinden.*	How *are you?* – My arm hurts. – We *must bandage* the wound.
Die Stadt *befindet sich* **in einer schönen Gegend.**	The town *lies* in a beautiful area.
Die Bahn *verbindet* **das Dorf mit der Stadt.**	The railroad *links* the village with the town.

IMPERATIVE
verschwinde! (du) verschwinden Sie! verschwindet! (ihr)

PRESENT PERFECT	*PAST PERFECT (PLUPERFECT)*
ich bin ... verschwunden	ich war ... verschwunden

FUTURE	*FUTURE PERFECT*
ich werde ... binden	ich werde ... verschwunden sein

COMPOUND CONDITIONAL	*PAST CONDITIONAL*
ich würde ... verschwinden	ich wäre ... verschwunden

Ich *bin* falsch *verbunden.* Bitte *verbinden Sie* mich mit London.	I *have a wrong number.* Please *will you connect* me with London.
Wer *hat* die erste Nähmaschine *erfunden?* – Ich weiß nicht.	Who *invented* the first sewing machine? – I don't know.
Die ganze Geschichte *ist* frei *erfunden.*	The whole story *is a* complete *invention.*
Wir *befanden uns* in einer schwierigen Lage. Die Mannschaft hat sich für *überwunden* erklärt.	We *found ourselves* in a difficult situation. The team declared itself *beaten.*
Die Krise *ist überwunden worden.*	The crisis *has been overcome.*

Class III separable verb, stress on particle **heraus-**

PRESENT PARTICIPLE	*PAST PARTICIPLE*
herausfindend	herausgefunden

PRESENT
ich finde heraus
du findest heraus
er/sie/es findet heraus
wir finden heraus
ihr findet heraus
sie/Sie finden heraus

SIMPLE PAST
ich fand heraus
du fandst heraus
er/sie/es fand heraus
wir fanden heraus
ihr fandet heraus
sie/Sie fanden heraus

KONJUNKTIV I
ich finde heraus

KONJUNKTIV II
ich fände heraus

Similar verbs

sich abfinden *(mit)*	put up (with)
festbinden	tie up
losbinden	untie, loosen
stattfinden	take place
wiederfinden	find again
sich zurechtfinden	find one's way

IMPERATIVE
finde heraus! (du)   finden Sie heraus!   findet heraus! (ihr)

PRESENT PERFECT
ich habe ... herausgefunden

PAST PERFECT (PLUPERFECT)
ich hatte ... herausgefunden

FUTURE
ich werde ... herausfinden

FUTURE PERFECT
ich werde ... herausgefunden haben

COMPOUND CONDITIONAL
ich würde ... herausfinden

PAST CONDITIONAL
ich hätte ... herausgefunden

Ich *habe mich* in Berlin nicht *zurechtfinden können.* Endlich *haben* wir *uns wiedergefunden.*

I *could* not *find my way* around Berlin. At last we *found one another.*

Vater *hatte* den Hund an den Zaun *festgebunden*, aber jemand *hatte* ihn *losgebunden.*

Father *had tied* the dog to the fence, but somebody *had untied* him.

Das Musikfest *findet* jedes Jahr in Salzburg *statt.*

The music festival *takes place* every year in Salzburg.

Was hoffen Sie *herauszufinden?*

What are you hoping *to find out?*

Sie *müssen sich* damit *abfinden.*

You *will have to put up* with it.

Haben Sie schon alle Fehler *herausgefunden?*

Have you already *found* all the errors?

Class IV verb, stress on stem **sprech-**

PRESENT PARTICIPLE	PAST PARTICIPLE
sprechend	gesprochen

PRESENT	SIMPLE PAST
ich spreche	ich sprach
du sprichst	du sprachst
er/sie/es spricht	er/sie/es sprach
wir sprechen	wir sprachen
ihr sprecht	ihr spracht
sie/Sie sprechen	sie/Sie sprachen

KONJUNKTIV I	KONJUNKTIV II
ich spreche	ich spräche

Similar verbs

bergen	rescue, salvage	**sinnen**	ponder
bersten *(+sein)*	burst	**spinnen**	spin
brechen	break, beat	**stechen**	sting, stab, bite
gelten	be worth	**sterben** *(+sein)*	die
helfen *(dat) (bei)*	help, aid (with)	**werben**	recruit, advertize
rinnen *(+sein)*	run, trickle	**werfen**	throw, cast
schwimmen	swim, float		
(+sein/haben)			

Notes   **werden** also belongs to this group [➤**werden** 3].
bersten (burst) present tense: **du birst, er/sie/es birst**.

Die Kinder *haben* noch einmal mit Sand und Wasser *geworfen*. Du *mußt* mit ihnen *sprechen*.	The children *have been throwing* sand and water *about* again. You *must talk* to them.
Unser jüngster Sohn *kann* noch nicht *schwimmen*, aber unser Ältester *ist* gestern über den Fluß *geschwommen*.	Our youngest son *can* not yet *swim*, but our eldest *swam* across the river yesterday.
Er *hat* die 100m in neuer Bestzeit *geschwommen*. Er *hat* beinahe den Weltrekord *gebrochen*.	He *has swum* a new best time in the 100 metres. He almost *broke* the world record.

IMPERATIVE
sprich! (du)   sprechen Sie!   sprecht! (ihr)

PRESENT PERFECT	**PAST PERFECT (PLUPERFECT)**
ich habe ... gesprochen	ich hatte ... gesprochen

FUTURE	**FUTURE PERFECT**
ich werde ... sprechen	ich werde ... gesprochen haben

COMPOUND CONDITIONAL	**PAST CONDITIONAL**
ich würde ... sprechen	ich hätte ... gesprochen

Darf ich den Arzt heute *sprechen?*	*May* I *see* the doctor today?
Helft mir bitte beim Abwaschen! Kinder, *das gilt* euch! —Ich *würde gerne helfen.*	Please *help* me with the dishwashing! Children, *I'm speaking* to you! —I *would be only too glad to help.*
Das Kind *konnte* mit einem Jahr schon *sprechen. Es gilt* als sehr begabt.	The child *could talk* when only one year old. *It is said to be* very gifted.
Herr Smith *spricht* fließend Deutsch und *das gilt* auch *von* seinem französischen Kollegen. Wir *haben* lange miteinander über die politische Situation *gesprochen.*	Mr. Smith *speaks* German fluently and *that is* also *true of* his French colleague. We *discussed* the political situation for a long time.
Er *spricht* nie von sich selbst.	He never *talks* of himself.
Sein Vater *ist* vor einem Jahr an einer Lungenentzündung *gestorben.*	His father *died* a year ago of pneumonia.
Wir *werben* für die Partei. Wir *müssen* neue Mitglieder *werben.*	We *are canvassing* for the party. We *must recruit* new members.

Class IV verb, stress on stem **stehl-**

PRESENT PARTICIPLE	PAST PARTICIPLE
stehlend	gestohlen

PRESENT	SIMPLE PAST
ich stehle	ich stahl
du stiehlst	du stahlst
er/sie/es stiehlt	er/sie/es stahl
wir stehlen	wir stahlen
ihr stehlt	ihr stahlt
sie/Sie stehlen	sie/Sie stahlen

KONJUNKTIV I	KONJUNKTIV II
ich stehle	ich stähle

Similar verbs

[With inseparable prefix ➤**gewinnen** 50]

befehlen *(dat)*	order, tell (someone)
bestehlen	rob
empfehlen	recommend
gebären	give birth (to)

[With separable particle ➤**zusammenbrechen** 51]

sich hinausstehlen	steal out

**Heutzutage *wird viel gestohlen.*
Mir *ist* letzte Woche wieder das
Portemonnaie *gestohlen
worden.***

Nowadays, *there is a lot of
stealing.* My purse *was stolen*
again last week.

**Das sind *gestohlene*
Schmuckwaren. Sie *wird* sie
*gestohlen haben.***

That is *stolen* jewelry. She *must
have stolen* it.

Hier habe ich *zu befehlen*!

I'm the one *in charge* here!

IMPERATIVE
stiehl! (du)   stehlen Sie!   stehlt! (ihr)

PRESENT PERFECT
ich habe ... gestohlen

PAST PERFECT (PLUPERFECT)
ich hatte ... gestohlen

FUTURE
ich werde ... stehlen

FUTURE PERFECT
ich werde ... gestohlen haben

COMPOUND CONDITIONAL
ich würde ... stehlen

PAST CONDITIONAL
ich hätte ... gestohlen

Der arme Mann *stahl* nur, um seine Kinder zu ernähren.

The poor man only *stole* to feed his children.

Er *stahl sich* aus dem Haus *hinaus*, wenn er seinen Schwager kommen sah.

He *sneaked out* of the house whenever he saw his brother-in-law coming.

Er *befahl*, und ich gehorchte.

He *commanded* and I obeyed.

Uns *wurde befohlen*, sofort nach Berlin zu fliegen.

We *were ordered* to fly to Berlin at once.

Sie *hat* mir *befohlen*, ihr zu helfen.

She *ordered* me to help her.

Was *würden* Sie *empfehlen*?

What *would* you *recommend*?

Es *empfiehlt sich*, den besten zu kaufen, den Sie sich leisten können.

It *is recommended* that you should buy the best you can afford.

Ich *hätte* diesen Fotoapparat *empfohlen*, aber ich weiß nicht, wieviel Geld Sie ausgeben wollen.

I *would have recommended* this camera, but I do not know how much money you want to spend.

Class IV inseparable verb, stress on stem **-winn-**

PRESENT PARTICIPLE	PAST PARTICIPLE
gewinnend	gewonnen

PRESENT	SIMPLE PAST
ich gewinne	ich gewann
du gewinnst	du gewannst
er/sie/es gewinnt	er/sie/es gewann
wir gewinnen	wir gewannen
ihr gewinnt	ihr gewannt
sie/Sie gewinnen	sie/Sie gewannen

KONJUNKTIV I	KONJUNKTIV II
ich gewinne	ich gewönne (gewänne)

Similar verbs

beginnen *(mit)*	begin (on)	**erwerben**	acquire
sich behelfen	manage,	**gewinnen**	win, obtain
	cope	**übertreffen**	surpass
sich besinnen	reflect	**unterbrechen**	break off,
besprechen	discuss		interrupt
bestechen	corrupt, bribe	**unterwerfen**	subject
sich bewerben *(um)*	apply (for)	**verbergen** *(vor+dat)*	conceal
durchstechen	pierce		(from)
sich entsinnen *(gen)*	recall	**verderben**	spoil
entsprechen *(dat)*	correspond	**verschwimmen**	become
	(to)	*(+sein)*	blurred
entwerfen	sketch,	**versprechen**	promise
	design	**widersprechen** *(dat)*	contradict
erbrechen	break open	**zerbrechen**	break,
erschrecken	be frightened	*(+sein/haben)*	smash

Notes   **erschrecken** has simple past **erschrak**. Used tr. (frighten) it is weak [➤**verkaufen** 14].

Du *mußt dich* **vor der Polizei** *verbergen.* **Du** *wirst dich* **jetzt ohne meine Hilfe** *behelfen müssen.*	You *must hide* from the police. You *will* now *have to manage* without my help.

IMPERATIVE
gewinne! (du)   gewinnen Sie!   gewinnt! (ihr)

PRESENT PERFECT	*PAST PERFECT (PLUPERFECT)*
ich habe ... gewonnen	ich hatte ... gewonnen

FUTURE	*FUTURE PERFECT*
ich werde ... gewinnen	ich werde ... gewonnen haben

COMPOUND CONDITIONAL	*PAST CONDITIONAL*
ich würde ... gewinnen	ich hätte ... gewonnen

Widersprich (mir) nicht!	Don't *answer back!* /Don't *contradict* me!
Er *erschrak*, *unterbrach* mich und *begann* zu schreien.	He *jumped in surprise, interrupted* me and *began* to scream.
Wer *hat* das große Los gewonnen? Es *entspricht* meinem Jahresgehalt.	Who *has won* first prize in the lottery? It equals my yearly salary.
***Wollen wir* die Lage erst einmal besprechen? Sie *müssen sich* um eine neue Stellung *bewerben*.**	*Let's discuss* the situation first. You *must apply* for a new job.
Ich *verspreche* es Ihnen. Ich *werde* sofort mit der Arbeit beginnen.	I *promise* you. I *will start* on the work at once.
Ich *hätte* die Feier *gern* mit ihr *besprochen*, aber das *hätte* den ganzen Spaß *verdorben*. Die Feier *hat* all unsere Erwartungen *übertroffen*.	I *would have liked to discuss* the party with her but that *would have spoiled* the fun. The party *exceeded* all our expectations.
Die Scheibe *ist zerbrochen*. Die Kinder *haben* sie mit dem Ball *zerbrochen*.	The window is *smashed*. The children *smashed* it with the ball.

Class IV separable verb, stress on particle **zusammen-**

PRESENT PARTICIPLE	**PAST PARTICIPLE**
zusammenbrechend	zusammengebrochen

PRESENT	**SIMPLE PAST**
ich breche zusammen	ich brach zusammen
du brichst zusammen	du brachst zusammen
er/sie/es bricht zusammen	er/sie/es brach zusammen
wir brechen zusammen	wir brachen zusammen
ihr brecht zusammen	ihr bracht zusammen
sie/Sie brechen zusammen	sie/Sie brachen zusammen

KONJUNKTIV I	**KONJUNKTIV II**
ich breche zusammen	ich bräche zusammen

Similar verbs

abbrechen	break off	**einbrechen** *(+sein)*	burglarize/
absterben *(+sein)*	die out		burgle,
anbrechen	open, break		break in
(+sein/haben)	into	**einwerfen**	post, mail
ansprechen	address	**freisprechen**	acquit
aufbrechen	break	**hervorbrechen** *(+sein)*	burst out
(+sein/haben)	open/up/out	**umwerfen**	knock over,
ausbrechen *(+sein)*	burst out,		down
	erupt	**vorwerfen** *(dat)*	reproach
aussprechen	speak out,	**wegwerfen**	throw away
	pronounce	**zurückwerfen**	reflect,
aussterben *(+sein)*	die		throw back
		zusprechen	award

Wirf die Abfälle **weg.**	*Throw* the garbage *away.*
Ich **werde** die Briefe **einwerfen.**	I *will mail* the letters.
Sie **sind** vor einer Stunde **aufgebrochen.**	They *set off* an hour ago.
Der Wald **ist** allmählich **abgestorben,** und das Wild **stirbt** jetzt **aus.**	The forest *has* gradually *died off* and the wild animals *are dying out* now.

IMPERATIVE
brich zusammen! (du)   brechen Sie zusammen!   brecht zusammen! (ihr)

PRESENT PERFECT   *PAST PERFECT (PLUPERFECT)*
ich bin ... zusammengebrochen   ich war ... zusammengebrochen

FUTURE   *FUTURE PERFECT*
ich werde ... zusammenbrechen   ich werde ... zusammengebrochen sein

COMPOUND CONDITIONAL   *PAST CONDITIONAL*
ich würde ... zusammenbrechen   ich wäre ... zusammengebrochen

---

Bei uns *ist eingebrochen worden*. Das Schloß *wurde aufgebrochen*.

We *have been burglarized*. The lock *was broken open*.

Wenn es taut, *bricht* das Eis *auf*, und im Frühling *brechen* die Knospen *auf*.

When it thaws the ice *breaks up* and in spring the buds *burst*.

Die Verbrecher *sind* aus dem Gefängnis *ausgebrochen*.

The criminals *have broken out* of prison.

Als der Angeklagte *freigesprochen wurde*, *ist* er *zusammengebrochen*.

When the accused man *was acquitted*, he *collapsed*.

Das Kind *war* der Mutter *zugesprochen worden*, als die Eltern sich scheiden ließen. Man *hat* dem Vater *vorgeworfen*, er habe sich zu wenig um seine Familie gekümmert.

The mother *was given custody* of the child when the parents divorced. The father *was accused* of paying too little attention to his family.

Class IV irregular verb, stress on stem **nehm-**

PRESENT PARTICIPLE	PAST PARTICIPLE
nehmend	genommen

PRESENT	SIMPLE PAST
ich nehme	ich nahm
du nimmst	du nahmst
er/sie/es nimmt	er/sie/es nahm
wir nehmen	wir nahmen
ihr nehmt	ihr nahmt
sie/Sie nehmen	sie/Sie nahmen

KONJUNKTIV I	KONJUNKTIV II
ich nehme	ich nähme

Notes   **nehmen** is the only verb of this type. However, note the compound
verbs ➤**sich benehemen** 53; **annehmen** 54.

Du *mußt* das Ergebnis hoch drei *nehmen.*	You *must raise* the result to the power of three.
Bitte *nehmen Sie Platz! Möchten Sie etwas zu sich nehmen?*	*Do sit down! Would you like to take some refreshment?*
Wir *werden* ein Glas Wein zusammen *nehmen.*	We *will take* a glass of wine together.
Nimm die Butter aus dem Kühlschrank!	*Take* the butter out of the refrigerator!
Nehmen wir ein Taxi!	*Let's take* a taxi!
Woher *soll* ich das Geld *nehmen?*	Where *shall I get* the money from?

IMPERATIVE
nimm! (du)   nehmen Sie!   nehmt! (ihr)

PRESENT PERFECT
ich habe ... genommen

PAST PERFECT (PLUPERFECT)
ich hatte ... genommen

FUTURE
ich werde ... nehmen

FUTURE PERFECT
ich werde ... genommen haben

COMPOUND CONDITIONAL
ich würde ... nehmen

PAST CONDITIONAL
ich hätte ... genommen

Sie *haben Abschied* voneinander *genommen*.	They *said goodbye* to each other.
Unser Sohn *wird* Musikunterricht bei ihr *nehmen*.	Our son *will take* music lessons from her.
Man *nehme* einen Vierteler Liter Sahne und drei Eier.	*Take* a quarter of a liter of cream and three eggs.
Ich *werde* mir Zeit *nehmen müssen*.	I *will have to give myself* time.
Das Unglück *hat* ihm jede Hoffnung auf die Zukunft *genommen*. Er *hat sich* das Leben genommen.	The accident *took away* all his hopes for the future. He *took his own life*.

Class IV inseparable irregular verb, reflexive, stress on stem **-nehm-**

PRESENT PARTICIPLE	**PAST PARTICIPLE**
sich benehmend	sich benommen

PRESENT	**SIMPLE PAST**
ich benehme mich	ich benahm mich
du benimmst dich	du benahmst dich
er/sie/es benimmt sich	er/sie/es benahm sich
wir benehmen uns	wir benahmen uns
ihr benehmt euch	ihr benahmt euch
sie/Sie benehmen sich	sie/Sie benahmen sich

KONJUNKTIV I	**KONJUNKTIV II**
ich benehme mich	ich benähme mich

Similar verbs

entnehmen *(dat)*	withdraw (from)
übernehmen	take over
vernehmen	hear, perceive

Kinder, *benehmt euch!*	Children, *behave yourselves!*
Ihr Sohn *benahm sich* immer schlecht, als wir da waren. In der Schule *benimmt* er *sich* besser.	Her son *always used to behave* badly when we were there. At school he *behaves* better.
Er *hätte sich* besser *benommen,* wenn du nicht dabei gewesen wärest.	He *would have behaved* better if you had not been there.
Ich *habe* unten ein leises Geräusch *vernommen.*	I *heard* a small noise downstairs.
Von hier aus *vernimmt* man den Verkehr auf der Autobahn.	From here you *hear* the traffic on the highway/motorway.

IMPERATIVE

benimm dich (du)!   benehmen Sie sich!   benehmt euch (ihr)!

PRESENT PERFECT

ich habe mich ... benommen

PAST PERFECT (PLUPERFECT)

ich hatte mich ... benommen

FUTURE

ich werde mich ... benehmen

FUTURE PERFECT

ich werde mich ... benommen haben

COMPOUND CONDITIONAL

ich würde mich ... benehmen

PAST CONDITIONAL

ich hätte mich ... benommen

Die Polizei *vernahm* den Verbrecher. Der Zeuge *war* schon *vernommen worden*.

The police *interrogated* the criminal. The witness *had* already *been questioned*.

Ich *entnahm* seinem Brief, daß der Chef die Firma verlassen hatte. Wer *hat* jetzt die Führung *übernommen?*

I *gathered* from his letter, that the boss had left the firm. Who *has taken over* as boss?

Ich *habe* der Kasse 200DM *entnommen*.

I *have taken* 200 Marks from the petty cashbox.

Würden Sie es *übernehmen*, die Blumen zu besorgen?

Would you *take charge* of getting the flowers?

Class IV separable irregular verb, stress on particle **an-**

PRESENT PARTICIPLE	PAST PARTICIPLE
annehmend	angenommen

PRESENT	SIMPLE PAST
ich nehme an	ich nahm an
du nimmst an	du nahmst an
er/sie/es nimmt an	er/sie/es nahm an
wir nehmen an	wir nahmen an
ihr nehmt an	ihr nahmt an
sie/Sie nehmen an	sie/Sie nahmen an

KONJUNKTIV I	KONJUNKTIV II
ich nehme an	ich nähme an

Similar verbs

abnehmen	take off	**teilnehmen** (an+dat)	take part (in)
aufnehmen	receive, absorb	**übelnehmen**	take amiss
		sich (dat) **vornehmen**	make up one's mind to
auseinandernehmen	dismantle		
ausnehmen	make exceptions	**wahrnehmen**	perceive
		wegnehmen (dat)	take away (from)
einnehmen	earn		
festnehmen	arrest	**zunehmen**	increase, grow
gefangennehmen	take prisoner		
malnehmen (mit)	multiply (by)	**sich**	pull oneself
mitnehmen	take along	**zusammennehmen**	together

Ich *nehme an*, Sie wollen den ganzen Tag hier bleiben. – Nein, wir sind bei unserem Onkel zum Kaffee eingeladen. Wir *werden* die Kinder *mitnehmen*.

I *assume* you want to stay here all day. – No, we *have been invited* to our uncle's for coffee. We *will take* the children with us.

Ich *hatte* mir *vorgenommen*, am Sportfest *teilzunehmen*.

I *had intended to take part* in the sports festival.

Er *hat* die Einladung *angenommen*.

He *has accepted* the invitation.

IMPERATIVE
nimm an! (du)   nehmen Sie an!   nehmt an! (ihr)

PRESENT PERFECT   *PAST PERFECT (PLUPERFECT)*
ich habe ... angenommen   ich hatte ... angenommen

FUTURE   *FUTURE PERFECT*
ich werde ... annehmen   ich werde ... angenommen haben

COMPOUND CONDITIONAL   *PAST CONDITIONAL*
ich würde ... annehmen   ich hätte ... angenommen

Er *hat* ihr *übelgenommen*, daß sie ihm das Buch *weggenommen hat*.	He *was cross* with her for *taking* the book *away* from him.
Der Verbrecher *wurde* gestern *festgenommen*.	The criminal *was arrested* yesterday.
***Nehmen* Sie den Motor *auseinander*, dann können wir sehen, was damit los ist.**	*Take* the engine *to pieces*, then we can see what's the matter with it.
Diese Fernsehsendung *werden* wir auf Video *aufnehmen*.	We *will video tape* this TV program.
***Nimm* dich *zusammen*!**	*Pull* yourself *together*.
Man *hat* uns sehr freundlich *aufgenommen*.	We *were* warmly *welcomed*.
Im Oktober *wird* er sein Studium auf der Uni *aufnehmen*.	In October, he *will start* his studies at the university.
Bitte *nehmen* Sie mich davon *aus*. Ich kann nicht mitmachen.	Please *count* me *out*. I cannot join you.

Class IV irregular verb, stress on stem **komm-**

PRESENT PARTICIPLE	PAST PARTICIPLE
kommend	gekommen

PRESENT	SIMPLE PAST
ich komme	ich kam
du kommst	du kamst
er/sie/es kommt	er/sie/es kam
wir kommen	wir kamen
ihr kommt	ihr kamt
sie/Sie kommen	sie/Sie kamen

KONJUNKTIV I	KONJUNKTIV II
ich komme	ich käme

Notes   **kommen** is the only verb of this type.   However, note the compound verbs ➤**bekommen** 57; **ankommen** 58.

Kommen Sie doch zum Essen zu uns!	*Come* and have a meal with us!
Er *kommt* erst um acht Uhr.	He *is* not *coming* until 8 o'clock.
Ich freue mich sehr, daß Sie *gekommen sind*. Stimmt es, daß Sie aus Australien *kommen*?	I am very glad you've *come*. Is it right that you *come* from Australia?
Wie *sind* Sie *gekommen*? – Wir *wären am liebsten* mit dem Flugzeug *gekommen*, aber es dauert zu lange, zum Flughafen *zu kommen*.	How *did* you *get here*? – We *would have preferred to come* by plane, but it takes too long *to get* to the airport.
Der Hund *kommt* immer *angelaufen*, wenn *Besuch kommt*.	The dog always *comes running* when *we have visitors*.

IMPERATIVE
komme! (du)　　　　kommen Sie!　　　　kommt! (ihr)

PRESENT PERFECT
ich bin ... gekommen

PAST PERFECT (PLUPERFECT)
ich war ... gekommen

FUTURE
ich werde ... kommen

FUTURE PERFECT
ich werde ... gekommen sein

COMPOUND CONDITIONAL
ich würde ... kommen

PAST CONDITIONAL
ich wäre ... gekommen

Unsere Tochter *kommt* im *kommenden* Monat in *die Schule.*

Our daughter *starts school next* month.

Wie *ist* das *gekommen?* Ich *habe* es *kommen sehen.* Das *kommt* davon, wenn man nicht aufpaßt. Man sagt, er *sei* fast *ums Leben gekommen.* Der Nachbar hat den Arzt *kommen lassen.* Er *ist* erst zwei Tage später wieder *zu sich gekommen.*

How *did* that *happen?* I *saw it coming.* It *comes* from not paying attention. They say he nearly *died.* Our neighbor *sent for* the doctor. He only *regained consciousness* two days later.

Ist Post für mich *gekommen?*

Has any mail *come* for me?

Ich *würde* früher *kommen,* wenn ich könnte.

I *would come* sooner if I could.

Class IV irregular verb, stress on stem **treff-**

PRESENT PARTICIPLE	PAST PARTICIPLE
treffend	getroffen

PRESENT	SIMPLE PAST
ich treffe	ich traf
du triffst	du trafst
er/sie/es trifft	er/sie/es traf
wir treffen	wir trafen
ihr trefft	ihr traft
sie/Sie treffen	sie/Sie trafen

KONJUNKTIV I	KONJUNKTIV II
ich treffe	ich träfe

Similar verbs

[With an inseparable prefix ➤**bekommen** 57]

| **betreffen** | concern, affect |
| **übertreffen** | surpass |

[With a separable particle ➤**ankommen** 58]

| **eintreffen** (+sein) | arrive |
| **zutreffen** | apply |

Was mich betrifft, ist es egal, ob wir **uns** hier oder da **treffen**. Wir **treffen uns** seit Jahren im selben Restaurant.

As for me, I do not mind whether we *meet* here or there. We *have been meeting* for years in the same restaurant.

Ich **traf** ihn öfters im Turnverein. Er **übertrifft** alle an Energie. Diese Woche *habe* ich ihn wieder *getroffen*.

I *used to meet* him frequently at the gym club. He *has more* energy than anyone. I *met* him again this week.

IMPERATIVE
triff! (du)　　　　　　treffen Sie!　　　　　　trefft! (ihr)

PRESENT PERFECT
ich habe ... getroffen

PAST PERFECT (PLUPERFECT)
ich hatte ... getroffen

FUTURE
ich werde ... treffen

FUTURE PERFECT
ich werde ... getroffen haben

COMPOUND CONDITIONAL
ich würde ... treffen

PAST CONDITIONAL
ich hätte ... getroffen

Er *ist* pünktlich bei uns *eingetroffen*.

He *arrived* punctually at our house.

Die Kugel *hat* ihn im Arm *getroffen*.

The bullet *hit* him in the arm.

Das Unglück *hat* ihn schwer *getroffen*. Alle seine Befürchtungen *sind* *eingetroffen*.

The disaster *hit* him hard. All his fears *were realized*.

***Es trifft zu*, daß alle Leute weniger Geld bekommen werden. Das *wird* viele Familien *betreffen*.**

It is true that everyone will get less money. That *will affect* many families.

Class IV inseparable irregular verb, stress on stem **-komm-**

PRESENT PARTICIPLE	PAST PARTICIPLE
bekommend	bekommen

PRESENT	SIMPLE PAST
ich bekomme	ich bekam
du bekommst	du bekamst
er/sie/es bekommt	er/sie/es bekam
wir bekommen	wir bekamen
ihr bekommt	ihr bekamt
sie/Sie bekommen	sie/Sie bekamen

KONJUNKTIV I	KONJUNKTIV II
ich bekomme	ich bekäme

Similar verbs

entkommen *(+sein) (dat)*	escape (from)
verkommen *(+sein)*	go to pieces

Notes   **bekommen,** meaning 'to agree with' (of food), is intransitive and takes **sein**.

Sie *bekommt* ein Kind im Herbst.	She *is having* a baby in the fall/autumn.
Er *wird* dieses Jahr mehr Geld *bekommen.* Er *bekäme* noch mehr, wenn er fleißiger wäre.	He *will get* more money this year. He *would get* even more if he worked harder.
Was *bekommen* Sie bitte? –Zwei Glas Wein, bitte.	What *can* I *get* you? –Two glasses of wine, please.
Sie *bekommen* noch drei DM von mir.	*Here are* three Marks change.

IMPERATIVE
bekomme! (du)　　　　bekommen Sie!　　　　bekommt! (ihr)

PRESENT PERFECT	*PAST PERFECT (PLUPERFECT)*
ich habe ... bekommen	ich hatte ... bekommen

FUTURE	*FUTURE PERFECT*
ich werde ... bekommen	ich werde ... bekommen haben

COMPOUND CONDITIONAL	*PAST CONDITIONAL*
ich würde ... bekommen	ich hätte ... bekommen

Wir *bekamen* keine Antwort auf unsere Frage.	We *got* no answer to our question.
Er sagte uns, er *bekomme* eine Jacke zum Geburtstag. Er sagte, er *werde* auch neue Schuhe *bekommen*.	He told us he *was getting* a jacket for his birthday. He said he *would* also *get* new shoes.
Er *ist* der Gefahr *entkommen.* Jetzt aber *ist* er total *verkommen.*	He *escaped* danger. But now he *has gone* completely to *pieces.*
Sie *sind* alle aus dem Lager *entkommen.*	They all *escaped* from the camp.

Class IV separable irregular verb, stress on particle **an-**

PRESENT PARTICIPLE
ankommend

PAST PARTICIPLE
angekommen

PRESENT
ich komme an
du kommst an
er/sie/es kommt an
wir kommen an
ihr kommt an
sie/Sie kommen an

SIMPLE PAST
ich kam an
du kamst an
er/sie/es kam an
wir kamen an
ihr kamt an
sie/Sie kamen an

KONJUNKTIV I
ich komme an

KONJUNKTIV II
ich käme an

Similar verbs

abkommen *(+sein) (von)*	deviate (from)
ankommen *(+sein) (in+dat)*	arrive
auskommen *(+sein)*	get by, manage
davonkommen *(+sein)*	escape, get away
gleichkommen *(+sein) (dat)*	equal, match
herausbekommen *(+sein)*	get out, work out
hereinkommen *(+sein)*	enter, come in
herkommen *(+sein)*	come (here)
herüberkommen *(+sein)*	come across
herunterkommen *(+sein)*	come down
nachkommen *(+sein)*	come later
reinkommen *(+sein)*	come in
umkommen *(+sein)*	perish
vorbeikommen *(+sein)*	come by, call in
vorkommen *(+sein)*	occur
zugutekommen *(+sein) (dat)*	benefit
zurechtkommen *(+sein) (mit)*	cope (with)
zurückkommen *(+sein)*	come back, get back
zusammenkommen *(+sein)*	link up
zuvorkommen *(+sein) (dat)*	anticipate

Kommen Sie bitte **herein!**   Please *come in!*

IMPERATIVE
komme an! (du)   kommen Sie an!   kommt an! (ihr)

PRESENT PERFECT	*PAST PERFECT (PLUPERFECT)*
ich bin ... angekommen	ich war ... angekommen

FUTURE	*FUTURE PERFECT*
ich werde ... ankommen	ich werde ... angekommen sein

COMPOUND CONDITIONAL	*PAST CONDITIONAL*
ich würde ... ankommen	ich wäre ... angekommen

Kommt her, Kinder, Paul *ist* **zurückgekommen**.	*Come here* children, Paul *has come back*.
Unser Nachbar *kommt* seit Jahren alle drei Wochen *vorbei*.	Our neighbor *has been dropping in on us* every three weeks for years.
Als er *hereinkam*, wollten wir ihn nach dem Unfall fragen, aber er *ist* uns *zuvorgekommen*.	When he *came in*, we wanted to ask him about the accident but he *anticipated* us.
Er erzählte uns, er *sei* vor ein paar Tagen aus England *zurückgekommen*.	He told us he *had got back* a few days ago from England.
Sie *werden* ohne uns *auskommen müssen*.	You *will have to do* without us.
Er *ist* öfters vom Thema *abgekommen*, aber wir *haben* endlich *herausbekommen*, was vorgefallen sei.	He frequently *lost the thread*, but we eventually *found out* what had happened.
Viele Menschen *sind* beim Unfall *umgekommen*. Er *ist* mit seinem Leben *davongekommen*.	Many people *died* in the accident. He *escaped* with his life.
Wir *sind* endlich dahinter *gekommen*, wo er *herkommt*. Er *kommt* aus Australien.	We *have* at last *found out* where he *comes from*. He *comes* from Australia.

Class V verb, stress on stem **geb-**

PRESENT PARTICIPLE	PAST PARTICIPLE
gebend	gegeben

PRESENT	SIMPLE PAST
ich gebe	ich gab
du gibst	du gabst
er/sie/es gibt	er/sie/es gab
wir geben	wir gaben
ihr gebt	ihr gabt
sie/Sie geben	sie/Sie gaben

KONJUNKTIV I	KONJUNKTIV II
ich gebe	ich gäbe

Similar verbs

liegen	lie, be located

Wer *gibt* Englisch in der Schule? –Mr. Smith.	Who *teaches* English at school? –Mr. Smith.
***Gib* mir bitte noch etwas Wein. *Gibt es* noch Brot?**	Please *give* me some more wine. *Is there* any bread left?
Ich *habe* mir viel Mühe *gegeben*, euch ein gutes Essen *zu geben*.	I *have taken* a lot of trouble *to give* you a good meal.
Kannst* du mir noch etwas Geld *geben*? –*Das gibt's nicht!	*Can* you *give* me some more money? –That's *incredible/ impossible!*
***Geben Sie sich* Zeit, mir zu antworten.**	*Take* your time answering me.
Wir *werden* eine Party *geben*. Das Wohnzimmer geht auf die Terrasse - wir *werden* den Kaffee draußen *geben*.	We *are going to have* a party. The living room opens onto the terrace - we *will serve* the coffee outside.
Gestern *wurde* 'Galileo' im Theater *gegeben*.	Yesterday 'Galileo' *was performed* at the theater.

IMPERATIVE
gib! (du)   geben Sie!   gebt! (ihr)

PRESENT PERFECT   *PAST PERFECT (PLUPERFECT)*
ich habe ... gegeben   ich hatte ... gegeben

FUTURE   *FUTURE PERFECT*
ich werde ... geben   ich werde ... gegeben haben

COMPOUND CONDITIONAL   *PAST CONDITIONAL*
ich würde ... geben   ich hätte ... gegeben

Was *gibt's* zu Mittag?   What*'s* for lunch?

Es gab keinen Zweifel - sie *hat*   *There was* no doubt - she *gave*
ihm das Geld *gegeben*. Dieter   him the money. Dieter said she
sagte, sie *hätte* es ihrer   *had given* it to her friend.
Freundin *gegeben*.

Ich *gäbe* etwas *darum*, wenn ich   I *would give* a lot to know what he
wüßte, was er für das Auto   *paid* for the car.
gegeben hat.

Hamburg *liegt* an der Elbe.   Hamburg *lies* on the Elbe.

Unsere Mutter *liegt* seit zwei   Our mother *has been sick* in bed
Wochen *krank* im Bett.   for two weeks.

Jetzt *liegt* der Schmutz   Now the dirt *is lying* thick on the
fingerdick auf dem Boden. Es   floor. It really *ought to be up to* my
läge eigentlich *an* meiner   sister to clean it all again.
Schwester alles wieder
sauberzumachen.

Bis Dezember *lag* unsere   Our team *was in the lead* until
Mannschaft ganz *vorn* aber der   December but the snow *lay* for a
Schnee *hat* letztes Jahr lange   long time last year and there was
gelegen und es gab keinen   no more football until March.
Fußball mehr bis März.

Class V inseparable verb, stress on stem **-geb-**

PRESENT PARTICIPLE	PAST PARTICIPLE
vergebend	vergeben

PRESENT	SIMPLE PAST
ich vergebe	ich vergab
du vergibst	du vergabst
er/sie/es vergibt	er/sie/es vergab
wir vergeben	wir vergaben
ihr vergebt	ihr vergabt
sie/Sie vergeben	sie/Sie vergaben

KONJUNKTIV I	KONJUNKTIV II
ich vergebe	ich vergäbe

Similar verbs

sich begeben	make one's way
ergeben	produce, result in
übergeben	hand over
umgeben	surround

Der Wald *umgibt* die Stadt von allen Seiten. Wir *waren* vom Feind *umgeben*.

The forest *surrounds* the town on all sides. We *were surrounded* by the enemy.

Er *hat* uns nie *vergeben*, daß wir dem Feind die Gefangenen *übergeben haben*.

He *has* never *forgiven* us for *handing over* the prisoners to the enemy.

Er *hätte* mir vielleicht *vergeben*, wenn ich ihm das Kind *übergeben hätte*.

He *might have forgiven* me if I *had handed* the child *over* to him.

IMPERATIVE
vergib! (du)   vergeben Sie!   vergebt! (ihr)

PRESENT PERFECT   *PAST PERFECT (PLUPERFECT)*
ich habe ... vergeben   ich hatte ... vergeben

FUTURE   *FUTURE PERFECT*
ich werde ... vergeben   ich werde ... vergeben haben

COMPOUND CONDITIONAL   *PAST CONDITIONAL*
ich würde ... vergeben   ich hätte ... vergeben

Vergib mir! –Du *hast* die Theaterkarten *vergeben*. Das *vergebe* ich dir nie!

Forgive me! –You *gave away* the theater tickets. I *will* never *forgive* you for that.

Wir fuhren öfters nach München. Damals hatte unser Cousin Theaterkarten *zu vergeben*.

We frequently visited Munich. At that time our cousin had theater tickets *to give away.*

Vier mal drei *ergibt* zwölf.

Four times three *makes* 12.

Sie *hatten* freie Plätze *vergeben*. Die Umfrage *hat ergeben*, daß alle Leute dafür sind.

They *had given away* free seats. The poll *showed* that everyone is in favor.

Er *ergab sich* als Kind dem Fußball.

He *devoted himself* to soccer as a child.

Sie *hat sich übergeben*.

She *has been sick.*

Class V separable verb, stress on particle **zurück-**

PRESENT PARTICIPLE	PAST PARTICIPLE
zurückgebend	zurückgegeben

PRESENT	SIMPLE PAST
ich gebe zurück	ich gab zurück
du gibst zurück	du gabst zurück
er/sie/es gibt zurück	er/sie/es gab zurück
wir geben zurück	wir gaben zurück
ihr gebt zurück	ihr gabt zurück
sie/Sie geben zurück	sie/Sie gaben zurück

KONJUNKTIV I	KONJUNKTIV II
ich gebe zurück	ich gäbe zurück

Similar verbs

abgeben	hand in	**bekanntgeben**	disclose
abliegen	be at a distance	**brachliegen**	lie fallow
achtgeben *(auf+acc)*	pay attention (to)	**durchgeben**	radio
		herausgeben	issue, publish
angeben	state, show off	**hergeben**	hand over
		sich hingeben	give up
anliegen	fit closely, be headed for	**nachgeben**	give way
		naheliegen	suggest itself
aufgeben	give up, renounce	**vorliegen**	be available
aufliegen	be on the table	**weggeben**	give away
		wiedergeben	give back, resound
ausgeben	spend, pay out	**zugeben**	admit, concede
ausliegen	be displayed		

Seit Jahren *gibt* er Hunderte von Mark für das Rauchen *aus*. Jetzt *hat* er es *aufgegeben*.	He *has spent* hundreds of Marks on smoking over the years. Now he *has given* it *up*.
Gib nicht so *an*!	Don't *show off*!

IMPERATIVE
gib zurück! (du)   geben Sie zurück!   gebt zurück! (ihr)

PRESENT PERFECT	*PAST PERFECT (PLUPERFECT)*
ich habe ... zurückgegeben	ich hatte ... zurückgegeben
FUTURE	*FUTURE PERFECT*
ich werde ... zurückgeben	ich werde ... zurückgegeben haben
COMPOUND CONDITIONAL	*PAST CONDITIONAL*
ich würde ... zurückgeben	ich hätte ... zurückgegeben

Gib acht! Das Haus **liegt** weit **ab**.

Pay attention! The house *is a long way away.*

Geben Sie darauf **acht** , daß Sie das Gepäck am richtigen Schalter **abgeben.**

Take care to *hand* the luggage *in* at the right counter.

Die Lösung liegt nahe. Der Katalog liegt vor. Gib ihn **her!**

The solution *is obvious.* The catalogue *is available. Hand* it *over.*

Es *wurde* im Radio *durchgegeben*, daß er die Wahrheit *zugegeben hat*. **Näheres** *wird* morgen in der Zeitung *bekanntgegeben*.

It *was announced* on the radio that he *has admitted* the truth. Further details *will be disclosed* in the paper tomorrow.

Der Verlag *gab* die Zeitschrift *heraus.*

The publisher *used to publish* the magazine.

Ich *gebe zu*, wir *würden* nicht soviel Geld *ausgeben*, wenn mein Vater nicht soviel Land *weggegeben hätte*.

I *admit* we *would* not *spend* so much money if my father *had* not *given away* so much land.

Ich *werde* Ihnen morgen das Geld *zurückgeben*, daß Sie mir gestern *gegeben haben.*

Tomorrow I *will give* you *back* the money you *gave* me yesterday.

Class V verb, stress on stem **tret-**

PRESENT PARTICIPLE	PAST PARTICIPLE
tretend	getreten

PRESENT	SIMPLE PAST
ich trete	ich trat
du trittst	du tratst
er/sie/es tritt	er/sie/es trat
wir treten	wir traten
ihr tretet	ihr tratet
sie/Sie treten	sie/Sie traten

KONJUNKTIV I	KONJUNKTIV II
ich trete	ich träte

Notes   **treten** (to kick, pedal) takes **haben.**
treten is the only verb of this type. However, note the compound
verbs ➤**betreten** 64; **hinaustreten** 65.

---

tritt! (du)   treten Sie!   tretet! (ihr)

PRESENT PERFECT
ich bin ... getreten

PAST PERFECT (PLUPERFECT)
ich war ... getreten

FUTURE
ich werde ... treten

FUTURE PERFECT
ich werde ... getreten sein

COMPOUND CONDITIONAL
ich würde ... treten

PAST CONDITIONAL
ich wäre ... getreten

Tritt nach vorn!

Step forward!

Treten Sie näher!

Come closer!

Er trat ans Fenster.

He *went* to the window.

Er trat mich gegen das Schienbein. Die Tränen traten mir vor Schmerz in die Augen. Ich wäre zur Seite getreten, wenn ich ihn hätte kommen sehen.

He *kicked* me on the shin. Tears of pain *came* into my eyes. I *would have stepped* aside if I had seen him coming.

Er hat gegen die Tür getreten.

He *has kicked* the door.

Man berichtet, der Fluß sei über die Ufer getreten.

They say that the river *has burst* its banks.

Er hat stark getreten.

He *pedalled* hard.

Class V irregular verb, stress on stem **bitt-**

PRESENT PARTICIPLE	PAST PARTICIPLE
bittend	gebeten

PRESENT	SIMPLE PAST
ich bitte	ich bat
du bittest	du batst
er/sie/es bittet	er/sie/es bat
wir bitten	wir baten
ihr bittet	ihr batet
sie/Sie bitten	sie/Sie baten

KONJUNKTIV I	KONJUNKTIV II
ich bitte	ich bäte

Similar verbs

sich *(dat)* **verbitten**   refuse to tolerate

IMPERATIVE
bitte! (du)   bitten Sie!   bittet! (ihr)

PRESENT PERFECT
ich habe ... gebeten

PAST PERFECT (PLUPERFECT)
ich hatte ... gebeten

FUTURE
ich werde ... bitten

FUTURE PERFECT
ich werde ... gebeten haben

COMPOUND CONDITIONAL
ich würde ... bitten

PAST CONDITIONAL
ich hätte ... gebeten

Wenn ich *bitten darf*, gehen Sie alle in den Garten.	If you *don't mind*, please will you all go into the garden.
Er *bat* mich ständig um mehr Geld, obwohl ich ihn immer *gebeten hatte* zu warten.	He always *asked* me for more money, although I *had* always *asked* him to wait.
Dieses Benehmen *verbitte* ich *mir!*	I *won't tolerate* this behavior.
Er *hat* tausendmal um Entschuldigung *gebeten.*	He *begged* my pardon a thousand times.
Ich *werde* ihn nächste Woche um Hilfe *bitten*. Ich *hätte* lieber meinen Vater darum *gebeten.*	I *will ask* him for help next week. I *would* rather *have asked* my father for it.

Class V inseparable verb, stress on stem **-tret-**

PRESENT PARTICIPLE	PAST PARTICIPLE
betretend	betreten

PRESENT	SIMPLE PAST
ich betrete	ich betrat
du betrittst	du betratst
er/sie/es betritt	er/sie/es betrat
wir betreten	wir betraten
ihr betretet	ihr betratet
sie/Sie betreten	sie/Sie betraten

KONJUNKTIV I	KONJUNKTIV II
ich betrete	ich beträte

Similar verbs

vertreten	replace, represent
zertreten	trample

IMPERATIVE
betritt! (du)   betreten Sie!   betretet! (ihr)

PRESENT PERFECT   **PAST PERFECT (PLUPERFECT)**
ich habe ... betreten   ich hatte ... betreten

FUTURE   **FUTURE PERFECT**
ich werde ... betreten   ich werde ... betreten haben

COMPOUND CONDITIONAL   **PAST CONDITIONAL**
ich würde ... betreten   ich hätte ... betreten

Das Betreten der Baustelle ist verboten. | It is forbidden *to enter* the building site.

Kaum *hatte* ich das Zimmer *betreten*, als mein Vater eintrat. | I *had* hardly *entered* the room, when my father came in.

Die Kinder *dürfen* den Rasen nicht betreten. Sie *zertreten* alle meine Blumen. | The children *may* not *go* on the lawn. They *trample* all my flowers.

Ich *habe* mir den Fuß *vertreten*. | I *have twisted* my ankle.

Er *vertritt* der Firma. Er *wird* die Interessen seiner Kollegen *vertreten*. | He *represents* the firm. He *will represent* the interests of his colleagues.

Ich *werde* morgen den Geschäftsleiter *vertreten*. | I *will be standing in* for the manager tomorrow.

Class V separable verb, stress on particle **hinaus-**

PRESENT PARTICIPLE	PAST PARTICIPLE
hinaustretend	hinausgetreten

PRESENT	SIMPLE PAST
ich trete hinaus	ich trat hinaus
du trittst hinaus	du tratst hinaus
er/sie/es tritt hinaus	er/sie/es trat hinaus
wir treten hinaus	wir traten hinaus
ihr tretet hinaus	ihr tratet hinaus
sie/Sie treten hinaus	sie/Sie traten hinaus

KONJUNKTIV I	KONJUNKTIV II
ich trete hinaus	ich träte hinaus

Similar verbs

abtreten *(+sein/haben)*	resign
auftreten *(+sein)*	appear, come on
austreten *(+sein/haben)*	come out
beitreten *(+sein) (dat)*	join
eintreten *(+sein)*	enter
herantreten *(+sein)*	approach
hervortreten *(+sein)*	step forward
zurücktreten *(+sein)*	resign, step back

Mein Bruder *trat* **eben** *ein*, **als wir durch die Tür** *hinausgetreten sind.* **Er** *hatte* **seine Schuhe ganz** *ausgetreten.* **Meine Mutter sagte, er** *solle sich* **die Schuhe** *abtreten.*

My brother *was* just *coming in* as we *went out* of the door. He had completely *worn out* his shoes. My mother said he *should wipe* his feet.

Er *ist ausgetreten.*

He *has gone to the cloakroom/bathroom.*

Wir *sind* **vor Jahren der Partei** *beigetreten* **aber gestern** *sind* **wir wieder** *ausgetreten.*

We *joined* the party years ago, but yesterday we *resigned*.

IMPERATIVE

tritt hinaus! (du)   treten Sie hinaus!   tretet hinaus! (ihr)

PRESENT PERFECT
ich bin ... hinausgetreten

PAST PERFECT (PLUPERFECT)
ich war ... hinausgetreten

FUTURE
ich werde ... hinaustreten

FUTURE PERFECT
ich werde ... hinausgetreten sein

COMPOUND CONDITIONAL
ich würde ... hinaustreten

PAST CONDITIONAL
ich wäre ... hinausgetreten

Ich *muß austreten*.	I *must find the cloakroom/ bathroom.*
***Treten Sie* von der Straße *zurück*!**	*Step back* from the road!
***Treten Sie* näher *heran*!**	*Come* closer!
Wenn der Minister (vom Amt) nicht *abgetreten wäre*, *wäre* die ganze Regierung *zurückgetreten*.	If the minister *had* not *stepped down*, the whole government *would have resigned.*
Er *ist* als Zeuge *hervorgetreten* und *tritt* jetzt vor Gericht *auf*.	He *came forward* as a witness and *is* now *appearing* in court as a witness.
Der Schauspieler *trat* als Faust *auf*.	*The actor* appeared as Faust.
Die Sonne *war* aus den Wolken *hervorgetreten*, und der Fluß *trat* allmählich *zurück*.	The sun *had come out* of the clouds and the river gradually *went down* again.

Class V irregular verb, stress on stem **ess-**

PRESENT PARTICIPLE	PAST PARTICIPLE
essend	gegessen

PRESENT	SIMPLE PAST
ich esse	ich aß
du ißt	du aßest
er/sie/es ißt	er/sie/es aß
wir essen	wir aßen
ihr eßt	ihr aßt
sie/Sie essen	sie/Sie aßen

KONJUNKTIV I	KONJUNKTIV II
ich esse	ich äße

Similar verbs

fressen	eat, guzzle
messen	measure

Was *wollen* wir zum Frühstück *essen?*	What *shall* we *have* for breakfast?
Ich *möchte* gern ein gekochtes Ei *essen.*	I *would like* a boiled egg.
Wir *gehen* heute mittag *essen.*	We *are going out for lunch.*
Was *möchten* Sie *essen?* Ich *würde* gern Gulasch *essen.*	What *would* you *like to eat?* I *would like* some goulash.
Wir *werden* abends *kalt essen.*	We *will have a cold meal* in the evening.
Das Baby ist *zum Fressen.*	The baby is *so sweet I could eat him.*

IMPERATIVE
iß! (du)　　　　　　　essen Sie!　　　　　　eßt! (ihr)

PRESENT PERFECT	*PAST PERFECT (PLUPERFECT)*
ich habe ... gegessen	ich hatte ... gegessen

FUTURE	*FUTURE PERFECT*
ich werde ... essen	ich werde ... gegessen haben

COMPOUND CONDITIONAL	*PAST CONDITIONAL*
ich würde ... essen	ich hätte ... gegessen

Was gibt's *zu essen?*	What is there *to eat?*
Gib dem Hund was *zu fressen.*	*Give* the dog something *to eat.*
In England *mißt* man Benzin jetzt nach Litern.	In England gasoline *is now measured* by the liter.
Der Wagen *hat* immer zuviel Benzin *gefressen.*	The car *always consumed* too much gasoline.
Er *maß* sie von oben nach unten, als *wollte* er sie *fressen.*	He *looked* her up and down as if he *wanted to eat* her.
Die Mutter *hätte* seine Temperatur *gemessen,* wenn sie nicht gewußt hätte, daß er zuviel *gefressen hatte.*	His mother *would have taken* his temperature if she had not known that he *had eaten* too much.
Iß nicht so schnell. Er *ißt* nicht, er *frißt.*	*Do*n't *eat* so fast. He doesn't *eat,* he *gobbles.*
Er *hat* immer gut und gern *gegessen.*	He *has* always *been fond of* his food.

Class V irregular verb, stress on stem **sitz-**

PRESENT PARTICIPLE	PAST PARTICIPLE
sitzend	gesessen

PRESENT	SIMPLE PAST
ich sitze	ich saß
du sitzt	du saßest
er/sie/es sitzt	er/sie/es saß
wir sitzen	wir saßen
ihr sitzt	ihr saßt
sie/Sie sitzen	sie/Sie saßen

KONJUNKTIV I	KONJUNKTIV II
ich sitze	ich säße

Similar verbs

[Inseparable verb ➤**vergessen** 68]
besitzen   possess

[Separable verb ➤**aufessen** 69]
absitzen   sit out
nachsitzen   stay in (at school)

Bitte *bleiben Sie sitzen!*	Please *don't get up!*
Wir setzten uns, und dann mußten wir lange *sitzen bleiben.* Wir *haben* alle drei Stunden *abgesessen.* Wenn ich mehr Mut *besessen hätte, hätte* ich noch länger da *gesessen.*	We sat down and then we *had to stay sitting down* for a long time. We *sat out* the full three hours. If I *had had* more courage, I *would have sat* there even longer.
Ich *habe* zu lange an dem Computer *gesessen.*	I *sat* too long at the computer.

IMPERATIVE
sitz(e)! (du)   sitzen Sie!   sitzt! (ihr)

PRESENT PERFECT	*PAST PERFECT (PLUPERFECT)*
ich habe ... gesessen	ich hatte ... gesessen

FUTURE	*FUTURE PERFECT*
ich werde ... sitzen	ich werde ... gesessen haben

COMPOUND CONDITIONAL	*PAST CONDITIONAL*
ich würde ... sitzen	ich hätte ... gesessen

Das Kleid *sitzt* gut!	The dress *fits* well.
Als Studenten *saßen* wir lange Stunden über den Büchern.	As students, we spent long hours *sitting* over our books.
Sie *saßen* beim Frühstück, als wir ankamen.	They *were sitting* at breakfast when we arrived.
Wir *besitzen* ein großes Grundstück.	We *own* a large piece of land.
Wenn wir nur ein größeres Haus *besäßen*!	If only we *owned* a bigger house!
Goethe *besaß* viel Phantasie.	Goethe *had* a lot of imagination.
Wir *haben* alle in der Schule *nachgesessen*.	We all *had to stay in* at school.

Class V inseparable verb, stress on stem **-gess-**

PRESENT PARTICIPLE	PAST PARTICIPLE
vergessend	vergessen

PRESENT	SIMPLE PAST
ich vergesse	ich vergaß
du vergißt	du vergaßest
er/sie/es vergißt	er/sie/es vergaß
wir vergessen	wir vergaßen
ihr vergeßt	ihr vergaßt
sie/Sie vergessen	sie/Sie vergaßen

KONJUNKTIV I	KONJUNKTIV II
ich vergesse	ich vergäße

Similar verbs

vermessen	survey
zerfressen	corrode

IMPERATIVE

vergiß! (du)	vergessen Sie!	vergeßt! (ihr)

PRESENT PERFECT
ich habe ... vergessen

PAST PERFECT (PLUPERFECT)
ich hatte ... vergessen

FUTURE
ich werde ... vergessen

FUTURE PERFECT
ich werde ... vergessen haben

COMPOUND CONDITIONAL
ich würde ... vergessen

PAST CONDITIONAL
ich hätte ... vergessen

Vergiß nicht, rechtzeitig da zu sein.	*Do*n't *forget* to be punctual.
Als Kind *vergaß* er immer seinen Fahrschein.	As a child, he always *forgot* his bus ticket.
Er *hat* seinen Schirm bei uns *vergessen*.	He *has left* his umbrella at our house.
Das Grundstück *wird vermessen*.	The plot of land *is being surveyed*.
Der Rost *hat* das Eisen des Tors *zerfressen*.	Rust *has corroded* the iron of the gate.
Ich *hätte beinahe vergessen*, ihn anzurufen.	I *almost forgot* to phone him up.
Ich *werde* dieses Konzert nie *vergessen*.	I *will* never *forget* this concert.

Class V separable irregular verb, stress on particle **-auf-**

PRESENT PARTICIPLE	PAST PARTICIPLE
aufessend	aufgegessen

PRESENT	SIMPLE PAST
ich esse auf	ich aß auf
du ißt auf	du aßest auf
er/sie/es ißt auf	er/sie/es aß auf
wir essen auf	wir aßen auf
ihr eßt auf	ihr aßt auf
sie/Sie essen auf	sie/Sie aßen auf

KONJUNKTIV I	KONJUNKTIV II
ich esse auf	ich äße auf

Similar verbs

abmessen	measure (off)
ausessen	eat up, finish eating
beimessen	attach value to
nachmessen	measure again, check
zumessen	measure out, apportion

IMPERATIVE

iß auf! (du)   essen Sie auf!   eßt auf! (ihr)

PRESENT PERFECT
ich habe ... aufgegessen

PAST PERFECT (PLUPERFECT)
ich hatte ... aufgegessen

FUTURE
ich werde ... aufessen

FUTURE PERFECT
ich werde ... aufgegessen haben

COMPOUND CONDITIONAL
ich würde ... aufessen

PAST CONDITIONAL
ich hätte ... aufgegessen

Iß das Fleisch *auf!*	*Eat up* your meat!
Essen Sie bitte alles auf!	*Do* please *eat* it all!
Wir *werden* bis morgen all unsere Vorräte *aufgegessen haben.*	We *shall have eaten up* all our supplies by tomorrow.
Die Kinder *haben* das ganze Brot *aufgegessen.* Sie *hätten* auch die Butter *aufgegessen,* wenn das Brot nicht alle gewesen wäre.	The children *have eaten up* the whole loaf. They *would have eaten up* the butter as well if the bread had not all gone.
Ich *werde* ihm seine Temperatur *nachmessen.* Man *darf* der Temperatur aber keine zu große Bedeutung *zumessen.*	I *will check* his temperature. You *must* not *rely* too much on temperature, though.
Der Stoff *wurde* genau *abgemessen.*	The material *was measured off* exactly.

Class V verb, stress on stem **les-**

PRESENT PARTICIPLE	PAST PARTICIPLE
lesend	gelesen

PRESENT	SIMPLE PAST
ich lese	ich las
du liest	du lasest
er/sie/es liest	er/sie/es las
wir lesen	wir lasen
ihr lest	ihr last
sie/Sie lesen	sie/Sie lasen

KONJUNKTIV I	KONJUNKTIV II
ich lese	ich läse

Similar verbs

sehen　　　　　　　　　　see, glance

Notes　**sehen** has an alternative second person imperative form **siehe!** (du)

Das Kind *lernt lesen*. **Die Mutter sagt, es** *lese* **sehr** *gern*.	The child *is learning to read*. Her mother says she *enjoys reading*.
'Faust' *wurde* **später in der Schule** *gelesen*.	'Faust' *was read* later at school.
Ich *habe* **in der Zeitung** *gelesen*, **daß Kinder heutzutage weniger** *lesen*.	I *read* in the paper that children *read* less nowadays.
Der Professor *las* **auf der Uni über deutsche Literatur. Er lud Dichter ein, aus ihren Werken** *zu lesen*.	The professor *taught* German literature at the university. He invited poets *to read* from their own works.

IMPERATIVE

lies! (du)   lesen Sie!   lest! (ihr)

PRESENT PERFECT
ich habe ... gelesen

PAST PERFECT (PLUPERFECT)
ich hatte ... gelesen

FUTURE
ich werde ... lesen

FUTURE PERFECT
ich werde ... gelesen haben

COMPOUND CONDITIONAL
ich würde ... lesen

PAST CONDITIONAL
ich hätte ... gelesen

Als Kind *habe* ich *eifrig gelesen*.	As a child I *loved reading*.
Die Trauben *werden* im Herbst *gelesen*.	The grapes *are gathered* in the fall/autumn.
Sie *sieht* nur auf einem Auge. Sie *sieht* sehr schlecht.	She *can* only *see* with one eye. Her *sight is* very bad.
Die Mutter *sah* immer auf die Uhr, da sie wußte, daß sie rechtzeitig nach dem Kind *sehen mußte*.	The mother *kept looking* at the clock, since she knew she *must attend* to the child punctually.
***Sieh* mal, ob die Maschine läuft.**	*See* if the machine is on.

Class V inseparable verb, stress on stem **-seh-**

PRESENT PARTICIPLE	PAST PARTICIPLE
versehend	versehen

PRESENT	SIMPLE PAST
ich versehe	ich versah
du versiehst	du versahst
er/sie/es versieht	er/sie/es versah
wir versehen	wir versahen
ihr verseht	ihr versaht
sie/Sie versehen	sie/Sie versahen

KONJUNKTIV I	KONJUNKTIV II
ich versehe	ich versähe

Similar verbs

geschehen *(+sein)*	happen
übersehen	overlook, ignore
verlesen	read out
sich verlesen	make a slip

Notes   **sich** (dat) **übersehen** (get tired of seeing) is separable.

Ich *kann* nicht *übersehen*, ob wir alle Arbeitskräfte werden entlassen müssen.	I *am* not *sure* whether we shall have to fire all the staff.
Ich habe es *aus Versehen* getan. Ich *habe mich verlesen*.	I did it *by mistake*. I *made a slip when reading*.
Bitte *übersehen* Sie den Fehler.	Please *overlook* the mistake.
Von hier aus *übersieht* man die ganze Gegend.	From here you *can look out over* the whole area.

IMPERATIVE

versieh(e)! (du)   versehen Sie!   verseht! (ihr)

PRESENT PERFECT

ich habe ... versehen

PAST PERFECT (PLUPERFECT)

ich hatte ... versehen

FUTURE

ich werde ... versehen

FUTURE PERFECT

ich werde ... versehen haben

COMPOUND CONDITIONAL

ich würde ... versehen

PAST CONDITIONAL

ich hätte ... versehen

Was *geschieht*, wenn man hier auf den Knopf drückt?	What *happens* when you press this knob?
Was *wäre geschehen*, wenn ich zu spät gekommen wäre?	What *would have happened* if I had been late?
Was *ist* heute *geschehen?* — Er hat die Namen *verlesen*.	What *happened* today? — He *read out* the names.
Er *hat* mich absichtlich *übersehen*.	He *ignored* me on purpose.

Class V separable verb, stress on particle **an-**

PRESENT PARTICIPLE	PAST PARTICIPLE
ansehend	angesehen

PRESENT	SIMPLE PAST
ich sehe an	ich sah an
du siehst an	du sahst an
er/sie/es sieht an	er/sie/es sah an
wir sehen an	wir sahen an
ihr seht an	ihr saht an
sie/Sie sehen an	sie/Sie sahen an

KONJUNKTIV I	KONJUNKTIV II
ich sehe an	ich sähe an

Similar verbs

absehen *(von)*	foresee, disregard	**hinwegsehen** *(über + acc)*	ignore
aussehen	look like	**nachsehen**	look up
durchlesen	read through	**sich umsehen** *(nach)*	look around (at)
durchsehen	check over		
einsehen	see, realize	**vorhersehen**	foresee
fernsehen	watch TV	**vorlesen**	read aloud
gleichsehen *(dat)*	resemble	**zusehen** *(dat)*	watch, look on

Lies mir bitte etwas *vor.*   Please *read aloud* to me.

Ich *sah* ihm bei der Arbeit *zu.* Er *sah sich* nach mir *um*, aber ich habe nur *zugesehen.*   I *watched* him at work. He *looked around* at me but I only *watched.*

Es *sieht* danach *aus*, als ob er das Problem *vorhergesehen* hätte.   It *looks* as if he *had foreseen* the problem.

IMPERATIVE
sieh(e) an! (du)   sehen Sie an!   seht an! (ihr)

PRESENT PERFECT
ich habe ... angesehen

PAST PERFECT (PLUPERFECT)
ich hatte ... angesehen

FUTURE
ich werde ... ansehen

FUTURE PERFECT
ich werde ... angesehen haben

COMPOUND CONDITIONAL
ich würde ... ansehen

PAST CONDITIONAL
ich hätte ... angesehen

Sie *sieht* jünger *aus*, als sie ist.	She *looks* younger than she is.
Sie *sieht* ihrem Vater *gleich*.	She *looks like* her father.
Sehen Sie im Wörterbuch *nach*, ob es stimmt oder nicht.	*Look* it *up* in the dictionary to see whether it is right or not.
Es *ist* nicht *abzusehen*, wann sie das Problem lösen werden.	You *can* not *foresee* when they will solve the problem.
Abgesehen davon, daß die Kinder den ganzen Tag *fernsehen*, *mußte* ich auch *zusehen*, wie sie sich stritten.	*Apart from the fact* that the children *watch TV* all day, I also *had to watch* them quarrelling.
Ich *werde* diesmal darüber *hinwegsehen*, daß du deine Hausaufgaben nicht gemacht hast.	This time I *will ignore* the fact that you have not done your homework.
Wir *müssen zusehen*, daß wir möglichst schnell nach Hause kommen.	We *must see* that we get home as fast as possible.

Class VI verb, stress on stem **fahr-**

PRESENT PARTICIPLE	PAST PARTICIPLE
fahrend	gefahren

PRESENT	SIMPLE PAST
ich fahre	ich fuhr
du fährst	du fuhrst
er/sie/es fährt	er/sie/es fuhr
wir fahren	wir fuhren
ihr fahrt	ihr fuhrt
sie/Sie fahren	sie/Sie fuhren

KONJUNKTIV I	KONJUNKTIV II
ich fahre	ich führe

Similar verbs

backen	bake, cook	**tragen**	carry
graben	dig, mine	**wachsen** (+sein)	grow
laden	load, charge	**waschen**	wash
schlagen	hit, strike		
(+sein/haben) (auf+acc)			

Notes   **laden** present tense: **du lädst, er/sie/es lädt**.

Der Zug *fährt* nur werktags. Er *fährt* über Frankfurt.	The train only *runs* during the week. It *goes* via Frankfurt.
Wir *werden* erster Klasse *fahren*.	We *will travel* first class.
Kannst du Auto *fahren?* Nein, dann *laß* mich *fahren!*	*Can* you *drive* a car? No, then *let* me *drive.*
Ich *mußte* ein Paket zur Post *tragen*, so *habe* ich ihn auch nach Hause *gefahren*.	I *had to take* a parcel to the post office, so I *drove* him home too.
Wir *sind* sehr langsam *gefahren*, aber es schneite, und ich *bin* gegen einen Baum *gefahren*.	We *drove* very slowly but it was snowing and I *ran* into a tree.
Wer *wird* die Kosten *tragen?*	Who *will cover* the costs?

IMPERATIVE
fahr(e)! (du)   fahren Sie!   fahrt! (ihr)

PRESENT PERFECT	*PAST PERFECT (PLUPERFECT)*
ich bin ... gefahren	ich war ... gefahren

FUTURE	*FUTURE PERFECT*
ich werde ... fahren	ich werde ... gefahren sein

COMPOUND CONDITIONAL	*PAST CONDITIONAL*
ich würde ... fahren	ich wäre ... gefahren

Er *ist* mit dem Kopf gegen die Windschutzscheibe *geschlagen*.	He *hit* his head on the windshield/windscreen.
Wollen wir das nächste Mal lieber *gehen*, anstatt zu *fahren?*	Next time *shall* we *walk* rather than *drive?*
Claudia *ist* jetzt fast *aufgewachsen*. Sie *muß* leider eine Brille *tragen*. Sie *trägt* lieber Jeans als ein Kleid.	Claudia *has* now almost *grown up.* She *has to wear* glasses unfortunately. She *prefers wearing* jeans to a dress.
Wasch dir die Hände! Deine Jeans *müssen gewaschen werden*.	*Wash* your hands! Your jeans *must be washed.*
Ich *habe mich* schon *gewaschen*.	I *have* already *washed.*
Ich *werde* morgen *waschen*.	I *am doing the washing* tomorrow.
Das Kind *ist* um 2 Zentimeter *gewachsen*.	The child *has grown* two centimeters.
Ich *habe* es jahrelang *ertragen*, wie die Kinder *sich geschlagen haben*.	I *put up with* the children *fighting* for years.
Die Waren *sind* auf die Wagen *geladen worden*.	The goods *have been loaded* onto the trucks.

Class VI verb, stress on stem **schaff-**

PRESENT PARTICIPLE	PAST PARTICIPLE
schaffend	geschaffen

PRESENT	SIMPLE PAST
ich schaffe	ich schuf
du schaffst	du schufst
er/sie/es schafft	er/sie/es schuf
wir schaffen	wir schufen
ihr schafft	ihr schuft
sie/Sie schaffen	sie/Sie schufen

KONJUNKTIV I	KONJUNKTIV II
ich schaffe	ich schüfe

Notes   schaffen (do, achieve) is always weak [➤machen 11].

beschaffen and verschaffen (procure) are always weak
[➤verkaufen 14].

IMPERATIVE
schaff(e)! (du)   schaffen Sie!   schafft! (ihr)

PRESENT PERFECT   *PAST PERFECT (PLUPERFECT)*
ich habe ... geschaffen   ich hatte ... geschaffen

FUTURE   *FUTURE PERFECT*
ich werde ... schaffen   ich werde ... geschaffen haben

COMPOUND CONDITIONAL   *PAST CONDITIONAL*
ich würde ... schaffen   ich hätte ... geschaffen

Der Architekt *schafft* hier ein Meisterwerk.	The architect *is creating* a masterpiece here.
Wir *werden* hier eine neue Siedlung *schaffen*.	We *will build* a new estate here.
Am Anfang *schuf* Gott Himmel und Erde.	In the beginning, God *created* heaven and earth.
Dieser Posten *ist* wie für ihn *geschaffen*.	This job *is made* for him.
Mozart *hat* unsterbliche Musik *geschaffen*. Er *hätte* noch weiterere Meisterstücke *geschaffen*, wenn er länger gelebt hätte.	Mozart *created* immortal music. He *would have created* more masterpieces if he had lived longer.

Class VI inseparable verb, stress on stem **-trag-**

PRESENT PARTICIPLE	PAST PARTICIPLE
ertragend	ertragen

PRESENT	SIMPLE PAST
ich ertrage	ich ertrug
du erträgst	du ertrugst
er/sie/es erträgt	er/sie/es ertrug
wir ertragen	wir ertrugen
ihr ertragt	ihr ertrugt
sie/Sie ertragen	sie/Sie ertrugen

KONJUNKTIV I	KONJUNKTIV II
ich ertrage	ich ertrüge

Similar verbs

begraben	bury	**überschlagen**	pass over
beladen	load	**übertragen**	transmit
beschlagen	shoe	**unterschlagen**	embezzle
betragen	amount to	**sich verfahren**	commit crime
erfahren	find out, hear	**vergraben**	bury
erschlagen	murder	**vertragen**	tolerate
überfahren	run over	**zerschlagen**	smash

Notes   **überschlagen** (cross [one's legs]) is separable.

Die Kinder *vertragen sich* **gut.**	The children *get on* well *together*.
Ich *kann* **es nicht länger** *ertragen.*	I *can't stand* it any longer.
Er *überschlug sich* **mehrere Male beim Fallen.**	He *somersaulted* several times when he fell.
Wann *werden* **wir das Ergebnis** *erfahren?*	When *shall* we *find out* the result?

IMPERATIVE

ertrag(e)! (du)   ertragen Sie!   ertragt! (ihr)

PRESENT PERFECT	**PAST PERFECT (PLUPERFECT)**
ich habe ... ertragen	ich hatte ... ertragen

FUTURE	**FUTURE PERFECT**
ich werde ... ertragen	ich werde ... ertragen haben

COMPOUND CONDITIONAL	**PAST CONDITIONAL**
ich würde ... ertragen	ich hätte ... ertragen

Die Miete *beträgt* DM2000.	The rent *comes to* 2000 Marks.
Er *hat* mehrere Seiten des Buchs *überschlagen*.	He *skipped* several pages of the book.
Ich *kann* nicht viel Sonne *vertragen*.	I *can* not *take* much sun.
Wir *erfuhren* gestern durch seinen Brief, daß sein Hund *überfahren worden ist*.	We *found out* yesterday from his letter that his dog *had been run over*.
In seinem Leben *hat* er nur wenig Glück *erfahren*.	He *has experienced* little happiness in his life.
Übertragen Sie das Geld auf mein anderes Konto.	*Transfer* the money to my other account.
Das Theaterstück *ist* aus dem Englischen *übertragen*.	The play *has been translated* from the English.
Es *wird* nächste Woche im Rundfunk *übertragen*.	It *will be broadcast* next week on the radio.

Class VI separable verb, stress on particle **ein-**

PRESENT PARTICIPLE	PAST PARTICIPLE
einladend	eingeladen

PRESENT	SIMPLE PAST
ich lade ein	ich lud ein
du lädst ein	du ludst ein
er/sie/es lädt ein	er/sie/es lud ein
wir laden ein	wir luden ein
ihr ladet ein	ihr ludet ein
sie/Sie laden ein	sie/Sie luden ein

KONJUNKTIV I	KONJUNKTIV II
ich lade ein	ich lüde ein

Similar verbs

abfahren *(+sein)*	depart, leave	**hinauffahren**	go up (climb)
abladen	unload, dump	*(+sein)*	
abtragen	wear out	**losfahren** *(+sein)*	set off,
abwaschen	wash up		get started
anschlagen	nail on, chip	**radfahren** *(+sein)*	bicycle
auffahren	jump up	**schwarzfahren**	travel with
(+sein)		*(+sein)*	no ticket
aufladen	load	**überschlagen**	cross, fold over
aufschlagen	open	**umfahren**	run down
auftragen	apply	**vorbeifahren**	drive past
aufwachsen	grow up	*(+sein) (an+dat)*	
(+sein)		**vorschlagen**	suggest,
ausgraben	dig up, unearth		propose
auswaschen	wash out, erode	**vortragen**	carry forward
beitragen *(zu)*	contribute (to)	**wegtragen**	carry off
einfahren	come in, drive in	**zerschlagen**	smash
(+sein)		**zurückfahren**	drive back
eintragen	register	*(+sein)*	
fortfahren	go away,	**zusammenfahren**	crash
(+sein/haben)	continue	*(+sein)*	
nachschlagen	look up	**zuschlagen**	slam, bang
niederschlagen	knock down		

Notes   **fortfahren** (continue) takes either **haben** or **sein**.

IMPERATIVE
lad(e) ein! (du)   laden Sie ein!   ladet ein! (ihr)

PRESENT PERFECT
ich habe ... eingeladen

PAST PERFECT (PLUPERFECT)
ich hatte ... eingeladen

FUTURE
ich werde ... einladen

FUTURE PERFECT
ich werde ... eingeladen haben

COMPOUND CONDITIONAL
ich würde ... einladen

PAST CONDITIONAL
ich hätte ... eingeladen

Wir *fahren* jetzt *los!*	*Off* we *go* now!
Wir *waren* früh *abgefahren*, da Vater *vorgeschlagen hatte*, daß wir *radfahren sollten*.	We *had set off* early as father *had suggested* that we *should cycle*.
Wir *sind* den Berg *hinauf* und an der Gaststätte *vorbeigefahren*.	We *rode up* the mountain and *past* the restaurant.
Hans *hätte* uns zum Essen *eingeladen*, aber wir *mußten* in 30 Minuten *zurückfahren*. Morgen *sind* wir bei den Nachbarn *eingeladen*.	Hans *would have invited* us to lunch but we *had to go back* in 30 minutes. We *have been invited* to the neighbors tomorrow.
Er *ist* heute *fortgefahren*.	He *went away* today.
Bitte *fahren Sie fort*, zu lesen. Wie heißt das Wort? *Schlagen Sie* im Wörterbuch *nach!*	Please *continue* reading. What does the word mean? *Look* it *up* in the dictionary!
Alle *haben* zum Musikfest *beigetragen*.	Everyone *contributed* to the music festival.
ic*Schlag* die Tür nicht *zu!* Hilf deinem Vater *beim Abwaschen!*	*Don*'t *slam* the door. Help your father *with the dish washing!*
Die Kinder *sind* mehrmals *schwarzgefahren*.	The children *have dodged paying the fare* several times.

Class VII verb, stress on stem **schlaf-**

PRESENT PARTICIPLE	PAST PARTICIPLE
schlafend	schlafen

PRESENT	SIMPLE PAST
ich schlafe	ich schlief
du schläfst	du schliefst
er/sie/es schläft	er/sie/es schlief
wir schlafen	wir schliefen
ihr schlaft	ihr schlieft
sie/Sie schlafen	sie/Sie schliefen

KONJUNKTIV I	KONJUNKTIV II
ich schlafe	ich schliefe

Similar verbs

blasen	blow
braten	fry, cook, roast
fallen *(+sein)*	fall
lassen	let
raten *(dat)*	advise

Notes **lassen** belongs in this group, but is listed with its compounds under the modal auxiliaries [➤10].

Schlaf **gut!**	*Sleep* well!
Rate **mal, wer gestern gekommen ist.**	Just *guess* who came yesterday.
Was *würdest* **du mir** *raten?*	What *would* you *advise* me?
Er *bläst* **Flöte.**	He *plays* the flute.
Der Wind *blies,* **und der Schnee** *fiel* **die ganze Nacht.**	The wind *blew* and snow *fell* all night.

IMPERATIVE
schlaf(e)! (du)　　　　　schlafen Sie!　　　　　schlaft! (ihr)

PRESENT PERFECT	*PAST PERFECT (PLUPERFECT)*
ich habe ... geschlafen	ich hatte ... geschlafen

FUTURE	*FUTURE PERFECT*
ich werde ... schlafen	ich werde ... geschlafen haben

COMPOUND CONDITIONAL	*PAST CONDITIONAL*
ich würde ... schlafen	ich hätte ... geschlafen

Wieviele *sind* im Krieg *gefallen?*	How many *were killed* in the war?
Er *ist* vor Schreck fast vom Stuhl *gefallen.*	He nearly *fell off* his chair with fright.
Ich *habe* meinem Kollegen *geraten*, er soll abwarten. Ich *riet* ihm Geduld zu haben.	I *advised* my colleague to wait and see. I *advised* patience.
Der Fisch *sollte* in Butter *gebraten werden*.	The fish *should be fried* in butter.
Das Fleisch *brät* schon in der Pfanne, und das Hähnchen *haben* wir am Spieß *gebraten*.	The meat *is frying* in the pan and we *have roasted* the chicken on a spit.

Class VII inseparable verb, stress on stem **-halt-**

PRESENT PARTICIPLE	PAST PARTICIPLE
behaltend	behalten

PRESENT	SIMPLE PAST
ich behalte	ich behielt
du behältst	du behieltst
er/sie/es behält	er/sie/es behielt
wir behalten	wir behielten
ihr behaltet	ihr behieltet
sie/Sie behalten	sie/Sie behielten

KONJUNKTIV I	KONJUNKTIV II
ich behalte	ich behielte

Similar verbs

beraten	advise	**überfallen**	attack
enthalten	include, hold	**unterhalten**	support
erhalten	receive, preserve	**verfallen** *(+sein)*	decay, deteriorate
erraten	guess	**sich verhalten**	behave
gefallen *(dat)*	please	**verraten**	betray
geraten *(+sein) (in/an+acc)*	get (into)	**verschlafen**	oversleep
mißfallen *(dat)*	displease	**zerfallen** *(+sein)*	disintegrate

---

Er *hat* das Haus nicht *unterhalten* und das ganze Gebäude *verfällt*.

He *has* not *maintained* the house and the whole building *is deteriorating*.

Hat Ihnen der Abend gut gefallen? –Ja, er unterhielt uns lange mit seinen lustigen Geschichten.

Did you *enjoy* the evening? -Yes, he *entertained* us for a long time with his jokes.

IMPERATIVE
behalt(e)! (du)   behalten Sie!   behaltet! (ihr)

PRESENT PERFECT   *PAST PERFECT (PLUPERFECT)*
ich habe ... behalten   ich hatte ... behalten

FUTURE   *FUTURE PERFECT*
ich werde ... behalten   ich werde ... behalten haben

COMPOUND CONDITIONAL   *PAST CONDITIONAL*
ich würde ... behalten   ich hätte ... behalten

Die Oma *behält* die Kinder über Nacht. Sie besteht darauf, daß sie *sich* gut *verhalten*, aber *es gefällt* ihnen sehr bei ihr, denn sie *erhalten* immer ein Geschenk.

Grandma *is keeping* the children for the night. She insists that they *behave* well, but they *like* staying with her very much as they always *get* a present.

Er *hat* seine Stellung nur bis Oktober *behalten* - er *ist* in große Schwierigkeiten *geraten*.

He only *kept* his job until October - he *got* into great difficulties.

Der Film *hat* mir gut *gefallen*. Wir *haben* uns lange darüber *unterhalten*.

I *liked* the movie a lot. We *talked* about it for a long time.

Ich *bin* aber nie *auf den Gedanken verfallen*, ihn zu *unterhalten*.

It *has* never *entered my head* to *support* him.

Ich *hätte* heute morgen *verschlafen*, aber ich habe den Wecker gestellt.

I *would have overslept* this morning but I set the alarm.

Class VII separable verb, stress on particle **herunter-**

PRESENT PARTICIPLE	*PAST PARTICIPLE*
herunterfallend	heruntergefallen

PRESENT	*SIMPLE PAST*
ich falle herunter	ich fiel herunter
du fällst herunter	du fielst herunter
er/sie/es fällt herunter	er/sie/es fiel herunter
wir fallen herunter	wir fielen herunter
ihr fallt herunter	ihr fielt herunter
sie/Sie fallen herunter	sie/Sie fielen herunter

KONJUNKTIV I	*KONJUNKTIV II*
ich falle herunter	ich fiele herunter

Similar verbs

abhalten	keep away	**einschlafen**	fall asleep
abraten *(dat)*	discourage (someone)	*(+sein)*	
		fernhalten	keep away
anhalten	stop, delay	**festhalten**	grasp, hold on
aufblasen	blow up, inflate	**herunterfallen**	fall down
		(+sein)	
auffallen *(+sein)*	stand out	**hinfallen** *(+sein)*	fall down
aufhalten	stop	**hinunterfallen**	fall down
ausfallen *(+sein)*	turn out	*(+sein)*	
aushalten	endure	**innehalten**	pause
ausschlafen	have a good sleep	**mithalten** *(mit)*	keep up (with)
(+sein/haben)		**stillhalten**	keep still
durchfallen	fall through	**zurückfallen**	fall back
(+sein)		*(+sein)*	
durchhalten	hold out	**zurückhalten**	hold back
einfallen	occur (to)	**zusammenfallen**	collapse,
(+sein) (dat)		*(+sein)*	coincide

Es *ist* mir *aufgefallen*, daß die Termine *zusammenfallen*.	It *struck* me that the dates *coincide*.
Wir *müssen* den Streik *durchhalten*.	We *must hold out* to the end of the strike.

IMPERATIVE
fall(e) herunter! (du)   fallen Sie herunter!   fallt herunter! (ihr)

PRESENT PERFECT	*PAST PERFECT (PLUPERFECT)*
ich bin ... heruntergefallen	ich war ... heruntergefallen

FUTURE	*FUTURE PERFECT*
ich werde ... herunterfallen	ich werde ... heruntergefallen sein

COMPOUND CONDITIONAL	*PAST CONDITIONAL*
ich würde ... herunterfallen	ich wäre ... heruntergefallen

Wir *hatten* bis zum Äußersten *durchgehalten.*	We *had stuck it out* to the bitter end.
Wir *wurden* lange an der Grenze *aufgehalten.* Man *hielt* das Auto *an* und die Kinder *mußten stillhalten.* Als wir ankamen, *waren* sie alle *eingeschlafen.*	We *were delayed* a long time at the border. They *stopped* the car and the children *had to keep quiet.* When we arrived they *had* all *gone to sleep.*
Unser Neffe *hielt* es nicht länger an der Universität *aus.* Er ist *im* Staatsexamen *durchgefallen.*	Our nephew *couldn't stick* it any longer at the university. He *failed* his exam.
Ich *habe* ihm von der Reise *abgeraten.*	I *advised* him *not to take* the journey.
Was *fällt* dir *ein?*	What *are* you *thinking of?*
Der Chef *ist* während des Vortrags zusammengebrochen. Er *hielt* einen Augenblick *inne,* dann *ist* er *hingefallen.*	The boss collapsed during the lecture. He *paused* for a moment, then he *fell down.*
Ich wollte schnell nach unten laufen, aber ich *bin* die Treppe *hinuntergefallen.* Mein Bruder stand unten und sah, wie ich *herunterfiel.*	I wanted to run downstairs quickly, but I *fell down* the stairs. My brother was standing downstairs and saw me *falling down.*

Class VII verb, stress on stem **ruf-**

PRESENT PARTICIPLE	PAST PARTICIPLE
rufend	gerufen

PRESENT	SIMPLE PAST
ich rufe	ich rief
du rufst	du riefst
er/sie/es ruft	er/sie/es rief
wir rufen	wir riefen
ihr ruft	ihr rieft
sie/Sie rufen	sie/Sie riefen

KONJUNKTIV I	KONJUNKTIV II
ich rufe	ich riefe

Similar verbs

hauen	hew, bash
heißen	be called
laufen *(+sein)*	run, go
stoßen *(+sein/haben)*	push, bump

Notes   **hauen** has a past simple stem **hieb.** The verb is also used in a weak form [➤**machen** 11].

Wie *heißen* Sie?	What *are* you *called/what is your name* ?
'Hallo' *rief* er, und *hieb* dem Freund auf die Schulter. Zusammen *stießen* sie das Boot ins Wasser. Leider *sind* sie an einen Stein *gestoßen*.	'Hello,' he *called* and *clapped* his friend on the shoulder. Together they *pushed* the boat out into the water. Unfortunately, they *struck* a rock.
Lauf nicht so schnell!	*Don't run* so fast!

IMPERATIVE

ruf(e)! (du)   rufen Sie!   ruft! (ihr)

PRESENT PERFECT	**PAST PERFECT (PLUPERFECT)**
ich habe ... gerufen	ich hatte ... gerufen

FUTURE	**FUTURE PERFECT**
ich werde ... rufen	ich werde ... gerufen haben

COMPOUND CONDITIONAL	**PAST CONDITIONAL**
ich würde ... rufen	ich hätte ... gerufen

Unser Garten *stößt* an eine Wiese.	Our garden *adjoins* a meadow.
Als sie die Kinder zum Essen *rief*, *liefen* sie ins Haus. Sie *hatten* sich grün und blau *gehauen*.	When she *called* the children to lunch they *ran* into the house. They *had beaten* each other black and blue.
Was *soll* das *heißen?*	What *is the meaning* of this?
Mein Mann *ist* mit dem Auto gegen eine Mauer *gestoßen*. Er *ist* ins nächste Dorf *gelaufen*, um mich *anzurufe*n. Dann *hat* er den Notdienst *gerufen*.	My husband *crashed* his car into a wall. He *ran* into the nearest village *to phone me*. Then he *called* the breakdown service.
Wir *rufen* den Hund Heini.	We *call* the dog Heini.
Wir *haben* lange nach dem Hund *gerufen*. Ich *habe* ihn *gefinden/gesahen*, als er zurücklief.	We *called* the dog for a long time. Then I *came upon* him as he was running back.

Class VII inseparable verb, stress on stem **-stoß-**

PRESENT PARTICIPLE	*PAST PARTICIPLE*
verstoßend	verstoßen

PRESENT	*SIMPLE PAST*
ich verstoße	ich verstieß
du verstößt	du verstießst
er/sie/es verstößt	er/sie/es verstieß
wir verstoßen	wir verstießen
ihr verstoßt	ihr verstieß
sie/Sie verstoßen	sie/Sie verstießen

KONJUNKTIV I	*KONJUNKTIV II*
ich verstoße	ich verstieße

Similar verbs

sich belaufen *(auf+acc)*	amount (to)
entlaufen *(dat) (+sein)*	run away from
überlaufen	seize, overrun
verlaufen *(+sein)*	pass
sich verlaufen	lose one's way
zerstoßen	crush

IMPERATIVE
verstoß(e)! (du)   verstoßen Sie!   verstoßt! (ihr)

PRESENT PERFECT
ich habe ... verstoßen

PAST PERFECT (PLUPERFECT)
ich hatte ... verstoßen

FUTURE
ich werde ... verstoßen

FUTURE PERFECT
ich werde ... verstoßen haben

COMPOUND CONDITIONAL
ich würde ... verstoßen

PAST CONDITIONAL
ich hätte ... verstoßen

Der Täter *hat* gegen das Gesetz *verstoßen* und *ist* aus der Gemeinde *verstoßen worden*.

The criminal *offended* against the law and *was expelled* from the community.

Er *ist* den Wärtern *entlaufen*. Es *überlief mich kalt*, als ich das erfuhr.

He *escaped* the guards. *A shudder went down my spine* when I learned that.

Unsere Reise *ist gut verlaufen*. Der Fluß *verläuft* zwischen schönen Wäldern. Wir *haben* uns einmal im Wald *verlaufen*.

Our journey *went well*. The river *flows* between beautiful forests. We *got lost* once in the woods.

Die Zahl der Tounsten *beläuft sich* auf 100 000 in der Woche. Der ganze Ort *ist überlaufen*, aber die Einnahmen *belaufen sich* auf Millionen von Mark.

The number of tourists *amounts* to 100,000 a week. The whole place *is overrun*, but the income *comes* to millions of Marks.

Class VII separable verb, stress on particle **weg-**

PRESENT PARTICIPLE	PAST PARTICIPLE
weglaufend	weggelaufen

PRESENT	SIMPLE PAST
ich laufe weg	ich lief weg
du läufst weg	du liefst weg
er/sie/es läuft weg	er/sie/es lief weg
wir laufen weg	wir liefen weg
ihr lauft weg	ihr lieft weg
sie/Sie laufen weg	sie/Sie liefen weg

KONJUNKTIV I	KONJUNKTIV II
ich laufe weg	ich liefe weg

Similar verbs

abhauen (+sein)	clear off	**Schlittschuhlaufen**	skate
ablaufen (+sein)	run out	(+sein)	
abrufen	call away	**Skilaufen** (+sein)	ski
anlaufen (+sein)	start	**überlaufen** (+sein)	overflow
anrufen	ring up,	**umstoßen**	upset, turn
	phone, call		upside down
anstoßen (+sein)	bump into,	**zurückrufen**	call back
	drink the	**zurufen**	shout at, hail
	health of	**zusammenlaufen**	merge, run
ausrufen	call out	(+sein)	together
davonlaufen (+sein)	run away	**zusammenrufen**	summon
einlaufen (+sein)	come in	**zusammenstoßen**	crash
hervorrufen	evoke	(+sein)	
hinauslaufen	amount (to)		
(+sein) (auf+acc)			

Notes   **abhauen** has a weak simple past **haute ab** and a past participle **abgehauen**.

Kannst du morgen *zurückrufen*?	*Can* you *phone back* tomorrow?
Wir *wollen* heute *Skilaufen* **gehen**. Du **kannst** ab neun Uhr **anrufen**.	*We want to go skiing* today. You *can call* from 9 o'clock on.

IMPERATIVE
lauf(e) weg! (du)   laufen Sie weg!   lauft weg! (ihr)

PRESENT PERFECT
ich bin ... weggelaufen

PAST PERFECT (PLUPERFECT)
ich war ... weggelaufen

FUTURE
ich werde ... weglaufen

FUTURE PERFECT
ich werde ... weggelaufen sein

COMPOUND CONDITIONAL
ich würde ... weglaufen

PAST CONDITIONAL
ich wäre ... weggelaufen

Wie war es *beim Skilaufen?* - Gut, danke, und wir *sind* später *Schlittschuh gelaufen*.

What was the skiing like? -Good thanks, and we *went skating* later.

Sie *rief aus*: 'Paß auf, du *hast* die Milch *umgestoßen!*'

She *called out:* 'Look out, you *have spilled* the milk.'

Die beiden Autos *sind zusammengestoßen*. Wir *haben* nach dem anderen Fahrer *gerufen*, aber er *war* schon *davongelaufen*.

The two cars *crashed into each other*. We *shouted* to the other driver but he *had* already *run away*.

Wir *wären* auf die Straße *hinausgelaufen* aber es war zu gefährlich.

We *would have run out* onto the road and but it was too dangerous.

Die Konferenz *verlief* sehr langsam, und dann *ist* der Chef aus der Sitzung *abgerufen worden*.

The conference *was passing* very slowly and then the boss *was summoned out* of the meeting.

Es *läuft* auf dasselbe *hinaus*, ob wir alle Kollegen *zusammenrufen* oder nur *anrufen*.

It *comes* to the same thing, whether we *call* all colleagues *together* or simply *telephone* them.

Class VII verb, stress on stem **häng-**

PRESENT PARTICIPLE	PAST PARTICIPLE
hängend	gehangen

PRESENT	SIMPLE PAST
ich hänge	ich hing
du hängst	du hingst
er/sie/es hängt	er/sie/es hing
wir hängen	wir hingen
ihr hängt	ihr hingt
sie/Sie hängen	sie/Sie hingen

KONJUNKTIV I	KONJUNKTIV II
ich hänge	ich hinge

Similar verbs

fangen   capture, catch

Notes   **hangen** also exists, but is now obsolete. **hängen** (transitive) is weak [➤**machen** II].

IMPERATIVE

häng(e)! (du)   hängen Sie!   hängt! (ihr)

PRESENT PERFECT	*PAST PERFECT (PLUPERFECT)*
ich habe ... gehangen	ich hatte ... gehangen
FUTURE	*FUTURE PERFECT*
ich werde ... hängen	ich werde ... gehangen haben
COMPOUND CONDITIONAL	*PAST CONDITIONAL*
ich würde ... hängen	ich hätte ... gehangen

Unsere Tochter *hängt* stundenlang am Telefon. Sie *hängt* sehr an ihrem Freund.	Our daughter *is* on the telephone for hours. She *is very fond* of her boyfriend.
Bisher *hat* das Bild im Flur *gehangen*. Es *sollte* lieber im Wohnzimmer *hängen*.	Until now the picture *has been hanging* in the corridor. It *should* really *hang* in the living room.
Unsere Katze *fängt* viele Mäuse. Sie *hat* gestern eine Ratte *gefangen*.	Our cat *catches* a lot of mice. She *caught* a rat yesterday.
Der Rechtsanwalt *hatte* ihn durch geschickte Fragen *gefangen*. Der Verbrecher war lange im Gefängnis.	The lawyer *had trapped* him with skilful questions. The criminal was in prison a long time.
Ich *hätte* ohne Zweifel den größten Fisch *gefangen*, aber er ist mir entwischt.	I *would* definitely *have caught* the largest fish but it got away.

Class VII inseparable verb, stress on stem **-fang-**

PRESENT PARTICIPLE	PAST PARTICIPLE
empfangend	empfangen

PRESENT	SIMPLE PAST
ich empfange	ich empfing
du empfängst	du empfingst
er/sie/es empfängt	er/sie/es empfing
wir empfangen	wir empfingen
ihr empfangt	ihr empfingt
sie/Sie empfangen	sie/Sie empfingen

KONJUNKTIV I	KONJUNKTIV II
ich empfange	ich empfinge

Notes **empfangen** is the only common inseparable compound of **fangen**.

IMPERATIVE

empfang(e)! (du)   empfangen Sie!   empfangt! (ihr)

PRESENT PERFECT	**PAST PERFECT (PLUPERFECT)**
ich habe ... empfangen	ich hatte ... empfangen
FUTURE	**FUTURE PERFECT**
ich werde ... empfangen	ich werde ... empfangen haben
COMPOUND CONDITIONAL	**PAST CONDITIONAL**
ich würde ... empfangen	ich hätte ... empfangen

Wir *empfangen* den Südwestfunk nur schlecht.

We *get* poor *reception* of South-West radio.

Sie *empfing* das Kind von ihrem zweiten Mann.

She *conceived* the baby by her second husband.

Wir *sind* vom Bürgermeister sehr freundlich *empfangen worden*. Er gibt morgen noch einen Empfang und *hätte* uns auch dann *empfangen*.

We *were* very warmly *received* by the mayor. He is having another reception tomorrow and *would have received* us then too.

Die Kinder *haben* eine Menge Geschenke zu Weihnachten *empfangen*.

The children *received* a lot of presents at Christmas.

Class VII separable verb, stress on particle **an-**

PRESENT PARTICIPLE	PAST PARTICIPLE
anfangend	angefangen

PRESENT	SIMPLE PAST
ich fange an	ich fing an
du fängst an	du fingst an
er/sie/es fängt an	er/sie/es fing an
wir fangen an	wir fingen an
ihr fangt an	ihr fingt an
sie/Sie fangen an	sie/Sie fingen an

KONJUNKTIV I	KONJUNKTIV II
ich fange an	ich finge an

Similar verbs

abhängen *(von)*	depend (on)
anfangen	begin, start
auffangen	catch
zusammenhängen *(mit)*	link, relate (to)

Notes anhängen (append), **aufhängen** (hang up, suspend) and **aushängen** (display) are weak [**▶abstellen** 15].

Ich *hätte lieber* **gestern** *angefangen.*	I *would have liked to start* yesterday.
Alles *hing* **davon** *ab,* **wann wir wieder zu arbeiten** *anfangen würden.*	Everything *depended* on when we *would start* work again.
Er *hat sich aufgehängt.* **Es** *wird* **wohl damit** *zusammenhängen,* **daß die Firma pleitegemacht hat.**	He *hanged himself.* It *is* probably *connected* with the fact that the firm went bankrupt.

IMPERATIVE
fang(e) an! (du) fangen Sie an! fangt an! (ihr)

PRESENT PERFECT
ich habe ... angefangen

PAST PERFECT (PLUPERFECT)
ich hatte ... angefangen

FUTURE
ich werde ... anfangen

FUTURE PERFECT
ich werde ... angefangen haben

COMPOUND CONDITIONAL
ich würde ... anfangen

PAST CONDITIONAL
ich hätte ... angefangen

Häng die Wäsche zum Trocknen *auf!*

Hang up the wash/washing to dry!

Alles *hängt* davon *ab*, ob wir rechtzeitig *anfangen*, die Wohnung aufzuräumen.

Everything *depends* on whether we *start* to clear up the apartment punctually.

Wir *fingen* mit der Arbeit *an*. Alles *hing* von uns *ab*.

We *began* on the work. Everything *depended* on us.

Als wir zu spielen *anfingen*, *hat* er den Ball ohne Schwierigkeiten *aufgefangen*. Ich *konnte* den Stoß aber nicht *auffangen* and fiel hin.

When we *began* to play, he *caught* the ball easily. But I *could* not *cushion* the shock and fell down.

Wir *haben* ein Schild *herausgehängt* und *fingen* gleich *an* zu handeln.

We *hung out* a sign and *began* to trade there and then.

Alles *hat* irgendwie *zusammengehangen*.

Everything *was* somehow *connected*.

86 gehen

Strong irregular verb, stress on stem **geh-**

PRESENT PARTICIPLE	PAST PARTICIPLE
gehend	gegangen

PRESENT	SIMPLE PAST
ich gehe	ich ging
du gehst	du gingst
er/sie/es geht	er/sie/es ging
wir gehen	wir gingen
ihr geht	ihr gingt
sie/Sie gehen	sie/Sie gingen

KONJUNKTIV I	KONJUNKTIV II
ich gehe	ich ginge

Notes   **gehen** is the only verb of this type. However, note the compound verbs ➤**begehen** 87; **ausgehen** 88.

Wie *geht es Ihnen?* -Mir *geht's gut*, danke. Und Ihnen?	How *are you?* -I *am well*, thank you. And you?
Ich *bin* gestern zum Arzt *gegangen*. Wenn alles gut *geht*, *können* wir nächste Woche *in Urlaub gehen*. Mein Mann *wird* schon fünf Mal zum Arzt *gegangen sein*.	I *went* to the doctor yesterday. If all *goes* well, we *can go on vacation* next week. My husband *will have been* to the doctor five times.
Wollen wir *spazierengehen?* Ich *möchte* lieber *schwimmengehen*.	*Shall* we *go for a walk?* I *would* rather *go swimming*.
Gehen wir nach Hause!	*Let's go* home!
Heute *geht's* nach München. Der Zug *geht* über Frankfurt.	*We are off* to Munich today. The train *goes* via Frankfurt.

IMPERATIVE
geh(e)! (du)   gehen Sie!   geht! (ihr)

PRESENT PERFECT
ich bin ... gegangen

PAST PERFECT (PLUPERFECT)
ich war ... gegangen

FUTURE
ich werde ... gehen

FUTURE PERFECT
ich werde ... gegangen sein

COMPOUND CONDITIONAL
ich würde ... gehen

PAST CONDITIONAL
ich wäre ... gegangen

Wenn es nach mir *ginge*, *würden* wir zu Oma *gehen*.

If it *was* up to me, we *would go* to Grandma's.

Wie lange *geht* man bis zum Dorf?

How long does it take *to walk* to the village?

Gehen wir oder fahren wir?

Shall we *walk* or take the car?

Hans *muß schlafengehen*. Er *geht* um 8 Uhr in die Schule.

Hans *must go to bed* - he *goes* to school at 8 o'clock.

Die Firma *ist zugrundegegangen*. Es *geht* mir nicht nur *ums* Geld.

The firm *has collapsed*. It's not only the money *that worries me*.

Alles *wäre* mit einer neuen Leitung vielleicht besser *gegangen*.

Perhaps things *would have gone* better under new management.

Strong irregular inseparable verb, stress on stem **-geh-**

PRESENT PARTICIPLE	PAST PARTICIPLE
begehend	begangen

PRESENT	SIMPLE PAST
ich begehe	ich beging
du begehst	du begingst
er/sie/es begeht	er/sie/es beging
wir begehen	wir begingen
ihr begehet	ihr beging
sie/Sie begehen	sie/Sie begingen

KONJUNKTIV I	KONJUNKTIV II
ich begehe	ich beginge

Similar verbs

entgehen *(+sein) (dat)*	avoid
umgehen	go around
vergehen *(+sein)*	pass, decay

Notes   **umgehen** can also be used as a separable verb [➤**ausgehen** 88].

IMPERATIVE
begeh(e)! (du)   begehen Sie!   begeht! (ihr)

PRESENT PERFECT	*PAST PERFECT (PLUPERFECT)*
ich habe ... begangen	ich hatte ... begangen
FUTURE	*FUTURE PERFECT*
ich werde ... begehen	ich werde ... begangen haben
COMPOUND CONDITIONAL	*PAST CONDITIONAL*
ich würde ... begehen	ich hätte ... begangen

Wir *begehen* (feiern) morgen den 80. Geburtstag meiner Mutter.	We *are celebrating* my mother's 80th birthday tomorrow.
Es *war* mir völlig *entgangen*, daß er Selbstmord *begangen* hat.	I *was* completely *unaware* that he *committed* suicide.
Er *hat* ein Verbrechen *begangen* - er *wird* der Strafe nicht *entgehen können*.	He *has committed* a crime - he *will* not *be able to escape* the punishment.
Mir *ist* keines seiner Worte *entgangen*.	Not one of his words *escaped* me.
Das neue Gesetz *wird* öfters *umgangen*.	The new law *is* frequently *evaded*.
Wir *werden* den Wald *umgehen*.	We *will skirt* the woods.
Die Zeit *vergeht*.	Time *passes*.
Der Appetit *ist* mir *vergangen*.	I *have lost* my appetite.

Strong irregular separable verb, stress on particle **aus-**

PRESENT PARTICIPLE	PAST PARTICIPLE
ausgehend	ausgegangen

PRESENT	SIMPLE PAST
ich gehe aus	ich ging aus
du gehst aus	du gingst aus
er/sie/es geht aus	er/sie/es ging aus
wir gehen aus	wir gingen aus
ihr geht aus	ihr gingt aus
sie/Sie gehen aus	sie/Sie gingen aus

KONJUNKTIV I	KONJUNKTIV II
ich gehe aus	ich ginge aus

Similar verbs

angehen *(+sein)*	concern	**schlafengehen**	go to bed
aufgehen *(+sein)*	rise, dawn	*(+sein)*	
ausgehen *(+sein)*	go out	**spazierengehen**	go for a walk
durchgehen *(+sein)*	go through	*(+sein)*	
eingehen *(+sein)*	shrink	**übergehen** *(+sein)*	go over
entgegengehen	go (towards)	**umgehen**	handle,
(+sein) (dat)		*(mit) (+sein)*	deal with
hinausgehen *(+sein)*	go out	**untergehen**	set, sink
hineingehen *(+sein)*	go in	*(+sein)*	
hinübergehen *(+sein)*	cross over	**vorangehen**	go ahead (of)
hinuntergehen	go down,	*(+sein) (dat)*	
(+sein)	descend	**vorbeigehen**	go past
kaputtgehen *(+sein)*	break, bust	*(+sein) (an+dat)*	
losgehen *(+sein)*	go off, set off	**vorgehen** *(+sein)*	proceed
mitgehen *(+sein)*	go along too	**weggehen** *(+sein)*	go away,
nachgehen	follow		depart
(+sein) (dat)		**weitergehen** *(+sein)*	go on
nahegehen	grieve, affect	**zugehen**	approach
(+sein) (dat)		*(+sein) (auf+acc)*	
schiefgehen *(+sein)*	go wrong	**zurückgehen** *(+sein)*	go back

Wir *sind* auch gestern ausgegangen.	We also *went out* yesterday.

IMPERATIVE
geh(e) aus! (du)   gehen Sie aus!   geht aus! (ihr)

PRESENT PERFECT
ich bin ... ausgegangen

PAST PERFECT (PLUPERFECT)
ich war ... ausgegangen

FUTURE
ich werde ... ausgehen

FUTURE PERFECT
ich werde ... ausgegangen sein

COMPOUND CONDITIONAL
ich würde ... ausgehen

PAST CONDITIONAL
ich wäre ... ausgegangen

Wann *geht* das Kino *los?* Wir müssen *losgehen*, sonst kommen wir zu spät. *Gehen* Sie *mit?*

When *does* the movie *start?* We *must set off* or we will be late. *Are* you *going* too?

Er *ging* aus dem Zimmer *hinaus*, am Badezimmer *vorbei*, die Treppe *hinunter* und in die Küche *hinein*.

He *went out* of the room, *past* the bathroom, *down* the stairs and *into* the kitchen.

Wir *würden* am Fluß *spazierengehen*, wenn wir Zeit hätten. Wir *müssen* jetzt *zurückgehen*. Gerd *wird* uns *vorangehen*.

We *would walk* along the river if we had time. We *must go back* now. Gerd *will lead the way*.

Alles *war schiefgegangen*. Die Waschmaschine *war kaputtgegangen*, und alle Stricksachen *sind eingegangen*.

Everything *had gone wrong*. The washing machine *had broken down* and all the sweaters *shrank*.

Das *geht* mich nichts *an*.

That's got nothing *to do with* me.

Die Sonne *geht* um sieben Uhr *auf* und um sechs *unter*.

The sun *rises* at 7 and *sets* at 6.

Ein Gespenst geht im Haus *um*.

The house is *haunted*.

Er *geht* sehr liebevoll mit den Kindern *um*.

He *handles* the children very gently.

Strong irregular verb, stress on stem **steh-**

PRESENT PARTICIPLE	PAST PARTICIPLE
stehend	gestanden

PRESENT	SIMPLE PAST
ich stehe	ich stand
du stehst	du standst
er/sie/es steht	er/sie/es stand
wir stehen	wir standen
ihr steht	ihr standet
sie/Sie stehen	sie/Sie standen

KONJUNKTIV I	KONJUNKTIV II
ich stehe	ich stünde

Notes **stehen** is the only verb of this type. However, note the compound verbs ➤**verstehen** 90; **aufstehen** 91.

IMPERATIVE
steh(e)! (du)   stehen Sie!   steht! (ihr)

PRESENT PERFECT	**PAST PERFECT (PLUPERFECT)**
ich habe/bin ... gestanden	ich hatte/war ... gestanden

FUTURE	**FUTURE PERFECT**
ich werde ... stehen	ich werde ... gestanden haben/sein

COMPOUND CONDITIONAL	**PAST CONDITIONAL**
ich würde ... stehen	ich hätte/wäre ... gestanden

Die Flasche muß *stehen*, nicht liegen.	The bottle must *stand* upright and not lie on its side.
Die kleine Ute *kann* schon *stehen*. Sieh, wie gut ihr das Kleid *steht*. *Stehen* die beiden Cousins im selben Alter?	Little Ute *can* already *stand*. Look how well the dress *suits* her. *Are* the two cousins the same age?
Sie *stand* am Fenster, um hinauszublicken. Er sagte ihr, der Garten *stehe* schon zwei Wochen unter Wasser.	She *stood* by the window in order to look out. He told her the yard/garden *had been* underwater for two weeks.
Es *stand* in der Zeitung, daß es wieder regnen würde.	It *said* in the paper that it would rain again.
Wie *haben Sie* zu der Sache *gestanden*?	What *was your attitude* to the matter?
Ich *würde stehen*, wenn ich nicht so müde wäre.	I *would stand* if I were not so tired.

Strong inseparable irregular verb, stress on stem **-steh-**

PRESENT PARTICIPLE	PAST PARTICIPLE
verstehend	verstanden

PRESENT	SIMPLE PAST
ich verstehe	ich verstand
du verstehst	du verstandst
er/sie/es versteht	er/sie/es verstand
wir verstehen	wir verstanden
ihr versteht	ihr verstandet
sie/Sie verstehen	sie/Sie verstanden

KONJUNKTIV I	KONJUNKTIV II
ich verstehe	ich verstünde

Similar verbs

bestehen	exist
entstehen *(+sein) (dat)*	arise, emerge (from)
gestehen	confess
mißverstehen	misunderstand

Du *darfst* mich nicht *mißverstehen*.	Don't *misunderstand* me.
Mit so wenig Nahrung *kann* kein Mensch *bestehen*.	No-one *can survive* on so little food.
Der Konflikt *besteht* seit Jahren. Er *ist* im 16 Jahrhundert *entstanden*. Damals *entstand* eine große Unruhe.	The conflict *has existed* for years. It *arose* in the sixteenth century. At that time a great unrest *arose*.
Verstehen Sie etwas französisch? Ich *verstehe* etwas aber jedes Jahr *entstehen* neue Redewendungen. Ich *würde* besser *verstehen*, wenn man langsam sprechen würde. *Offen gestanden*, ist es mir lieber deutsch zu sprechen.	Do you *know* any French? I *understand* some, but every year new expressions *arise*. I *would understand* better if people spoke slowly. *Frankly*, I prefer to talk German.

IMPERATIVE
versteh(e)! (du)   verstehen Sie!   versteht! (ihr)

PRESENT PERFECT	PAST PERFECT (PLUPERFECT)
ich habe ... verstanden	ich hatte ... verstanden

FUTURE	FUTURE PERFECT
ich werde ... verstehen	ich werde ... verstanden haben

COMPOUND CONDITIONAL	PAST CONDITIONAL
ich würde ... verstehen	ich hätte ... verstanden

Die Gründe *habe* ich nie *verstanden*.	I *have* never *understood* the reasons.
Es *versteht sich von selbst*, daß die beiden Völker *sich* nur schwer *verstehen*.	It *goes without saying* that the two nations have difficulty in *getting on with one another*.
Ich *habe* meinen Freund am Telephon nur schwer *verstanden*.	I *only understood* my friend on the phone with difficulty.
Er *hat* die Prüfung glänzend *bestanden*.	He *has passed* the examination with a top mark.
Er *verstand* etwas von Musik.	He *knew* something about music.
Er *hat sich* auf das Kochen *verstanden*.	He *was* an expert cook.
Der Täter *hat* das Verbrechen *gestanden*.	The criminal *confessed* to his crime.

Strong separable irregular verb, stress on particle **auf-**

PRESENT PARTICIPLE	PAST PARTICIPLE
aufstehend	aufgestanden

PRESENT
ich stehe auf
du stehst auf
er/sie/es steht auf
wir stehen auf
ihr steht auf
sie/Sie stehen auf

SIMPLE PAST
ich stand auf
du standst auf
er/sie/es stand auf
wir standen auf
ihr standet auf
sie/Sie standen auf

KONJUNKTIV I
ich stehe auf

KONJUNKTIV II
ich stünde auf

Similar verbs

anstehen	line up, queue
ausstehen	endure, stand
beistehen *(dat)*	help
feststehen	be certain
gegenuberstehen *(dat)*	be opposite, face
hervorstehen	show up
zugestehen	confess

IMPERATIVE
steh(e) auf! (du)   stehen Sie auf!   steht auf! (ihr)

PRESENT PERFECT
ich bin ... aufgestanden

PAST PERFECT (PLUPERFECT)
ich war ... aufgestanden

FUTURE
ich werde ... aufstehen

FUTURE PERFECT
ich werde ... aufgestanden sein

COMPOUND CONDITIONAL
ich würde ... aufstehen

PAST CONDITIONAL
ich ware ... aufgestanden

Sie *müssen* in der Konditorei *anstehen*.

You *have to line up* at the pastry shop/patisserie.

Er *würde aufstehen*, wenn er könnte.

He *would stand up* if he could.

Ich bin ihm sehr dankbar, denn er *hat* mir immer *beigestanden*. Trotzdem *stehe* ich seinem Vorhaben etwas skeptisch *gegenüber*.

I am very grateful to him, for he *has* always *helped* me. Nevertheless I *feel* somewhat doubtful *about* his plan.

Er *hat* hervorstehende Zähne.

He *has* prominent teeth.

Ich *kann* die Schmerzen nicht *ausstehen*.

I *can't* *stand* the pain.

Eines *steht fest*, wir können die Konferenz nicht stornieren.

One thing *is certain*, we cannot cancel the conference.

Das Programm *steht* jetzt *fest*.

The program *is* now *fixed*.

Strong irregular verb, stress on stem **tu-**

PRESENT PARTICIPLE	PAST PARTICIPLE
tuend	getan

PRESENT	SIMPLE PAST
ich tue	ich tat
du tust	du tatst
er/sie/es tut	er/sie/es tat
wir tun	wir taten
ihr tut	ihr tatet
sie/Sie tun	sie/Sie taten

KONJUNKTIV I	KONJUNKTIV II
ich tue	ich täte

Similar verbs

[Separable verbs ➤*aufstehen* 91]

guttun *(dat)*	benefit
leidtun *(dat)*	feel sorry for
wehtun *(dat)*	hurt
zusammentun	get/put together

Was *kann* man jetzt *tun*?	What *can* one *do* now?
***Tut* es *weh*?**	*Does* it *hurt*?
Ja, der Magen *tut* mir *weh*.	Yes, my stomach *hurts*.
Es *tut* mir *leid*.	I *am sorry*.
Dieses Mittel *wird* dir *guttun*.	This medicine *will do* you *good*.
Ich *muß* meine Hausaufgaben *tun*.	I *must do* my homework.
Der Hund *tut* dir nichts.	The dog *will* not *hurt* you.

IMPERATIVE
tu(e)! (du)   tun Sie!   tut! (ihr)

PRESENT PERFECT	*PAST PERFECT (PLUPERFECT)*
ich habe ... getan	ich hatte ... getan

FUTURE	*FUTURE PERFECT*
ich werde ... tun	ich werde ... getan haben

COMPOUND CONDITIONAL	*PAST CONDITIONAL*
ich würde ... tun	ich hätte ... getan

Tu die Bücher in den Schrank.	*Put* the books in the cabinet/ cupboard.
Er *tat*, als ob er nichts gesehen hätte.	He *acted (pretended)* as if he had seen nothing.
Wir haben mit dem Finanzamt *zu tun*.	We must *deal* with the Treasury.
Wir *haben uns zusammengetan*, um rentabel zu bleiben.	We *merged/amalgamated* in order to remain profitable.
Sie *tat* den ganzen Tag nichts anderes als arbeiten.	She *did* nothing other than work all day.
Ich *habe* mein Bestes *getan*, da sie mir immer *leid getan hat*.	I *did* my *best* as I *have* always *felt sorry* for her.
Sie muß ihm etwas *zu tun* geben.	She must give him something *to do*.

C
SUBJECT INDEX

Subject Index

Note Where there is a major section devoted to any item, the reference is shown in bold type.

D
VERB INDEX

Index

Note: for each verb only two or three of the most common meanings are given.

An asterisk * has been used to indicate that a verb is conjugated in the Model verbs section.

ab|legen (tr. & intr.) — put down, file 15
   er legt ab — *he takes his coat off*
   sie legt Daten ab — *she stores data*
ab|lehnen (tr. & intr.) — refuse, reject 15
ab|lenken (tr. & intr.) — divert, distract 15
ab|liegen (intr.) — be at a disance 61
ab|lösen (tr.) — detach 15
   es löst sich ab (refl.) — *it peels off*
ab|machen (tr.) — take off 15
   wir machen den Termin ab — *we agree on the time (of the meeting)*
ab|melden (tr.) — cancel 12, 15
   sie meldet sich ab (refl.) — *she checks out*
ab|messen (tr.) — measure (off) 69
ab|nehmen (tr.) — take off 54
   sie nimmt ab — *she loses weight*
abonnieren (auf+acc.) (tr. & intr.) — subscribe (to) 13
ab|raten (dat.) (tr.) — discourage (so.) 79
   ich rate ihm von ... ab — *I advise him against ...*
ab|räumen (tr. & intr.) — clear away 15
ab|rechnen (tr. & intr.) — cash up 12, 15
   er rechnet mit mir ab — *he settles up with me*
ab|reisen (intr.+s.) — depart 15
ab|reißen (tr.) — tear off, demolish 31
ab|rufen (tr.) — call away 82
ab|runden (tr.) — round down (numbers)12, 15
ab|rüsten (tr. & intr.) — disarm 12, 15
ab|sacken (intr.+s.) — subside 15
ab|sagen (tr. & intr.) — call off, cancel 15
ab|schaffen (tr.) — abolish, do away with 15
ab|schalten (tr. & intr.) — switch off 12, 15
ab|schicken (tr.) — send off 15
ab|schleppen (tr.) — tow away 15
***ab|schließen** (tr. & intr.) — complete 41
   er schließt die Tür ab — *he locks the door*
ab|schmecken (tr. & intr.) — taste, season 15
ab|schminken (refl.) — remove make-up 15
ab|schneiden (tr.) — cut off 29, 31
ab|schrauben (tr.) — unscrew 15
ab|schreiben (tr.) — copy 28
   er schreibt es ab — *he writes it off*
ab|sehen (tr.) — foresee 72
   sie sieht von ... ab — *she disregards ...*
***ab|senden** (tr.) — send off 21
ab|setzen (tr.) — set down 15

alarmieren (tr.)	alarm, alert 13
altern (intr.+s.)	age 11
amputieren (tr.)	amputate 13
amüsieren (tr.)	amuse 13
er amüsiert sich (refl.)	*he enjoys himself*
analysieren (tr.)	analyze 13
an|beten (tr.)	adore, worship 12, 15
*an|bieten (tr.)	offer 35
an|blicken (tr.)	look at 15
an|brechen (tr.)	open, break into 51
der Tag bricht an (intr.+s.)	*the day dawns*
ändern (tr. & refl.)	change, alter 11
an|eignen (dat. refl.)	appropriate 12, 15
an|ekeln (tr.)	disgust 15
an|erkennen (tr.)	acknowledge, respect 17, 18
*an|fangen (tr. & intr.)	begin, start 85
ich fange mit ... an	*I make a start on ...*
an|fassen (tr.)	touch, seize 15
an|flehen (tr.)	beg, implore 15
an|geben (tr. & intr.)	state 61
sie gibt an	*she shows off/boasts*
an|gehen (tr.)	concern 88
es geht an (intr.+s.)	*it goes/switches on*
an|gehören (dat.) (intr.)	belong to 14, 15
angeln (tr. & intr.)	fish (for) 11
*an|greifen (tr. & intr.)	attack 31
an|haben (tr.)	have on, wear 2
an|halten (tr. & intr.)	stop, delay 79
an|hängen (tr.)	append 85
an|hören (tr.)	hear, listen to 15
ich höre es mir an (dat. refl.)	*I listen to it*
animieren (tr.)	encourage, animate 13
ankern (intr.)	anchor 11
an|ketten (tr.)	chain up 12, 15
an|klagen (tr. & intr.)	accuse, protest 15
an|knüpfen (tr.)	tie on 15
*an|kommen (in+dat.) (intr.+s.)	arrive 58
es kommt auf+acc ... an (impers.)	
	it depends on ...
an|kündigen (tr.)	announce, signal 15
an|lassen (tr.)	start 10, 79
an|laufen (intr.+s.)	start 82
an|legen (tr.)	lay out 15
das Boot legt an (intr.)	*the boat moors*
an|lehnen (an+acc.) (tr. & refl.)	lean (against) 15

an|zeigen (tr.)	announce, denounce 15
an|ziehen (tr.)	attract, put on 33, 35
sie zieht sich an (refl.)	*she gets dressed*
an|zünden (tr.)	light, set on fire 12, 15
appellieren (an+acc.) (intr.)	appeal (to) 13
applaudieren (dat.) (intr.)	applaud (so.) 13
***arbeiten** (an+dat.) (intr.)	work, labor (on) 12
ärgern (tr.)	annoy 11
er ärgert sich über+acc ... (refl.)	
	he gets cross about ...
arrangieren (tr. & intr.)	arrange, fix 13
atmen (tr. & intr.)	breathe 12
ätzen (tr. & intr.)	corrode 11
auf|bauen (tr. & intr.)	put up, construct 15
auf|bäumen (refl.)	rear up 15
auf|bewahren (tr.)	store 15
auf|blasen (tr.)	blow up, inflate 79
auf|blicken (intr.)	look up 15
auf|blitzen (intr.)	flash 15
auf|brechen (tr. & intr.+s.)	break open/up/out 51
er bricht auf (intr.+s.)	*he sets off*
auf|decken (tr.)	uncover 15
auf|drehen (tr.)	turn on/up 15
***auf|essen** (tr.)	eat up, consume 69
auf|fahren (intr.+s.)	jump up 76
auf|fallen (intr.+s.)	stand out 79
es fällt mir auf (dat.)	*it strikes me*
auf|fangen (tr.)	catch 85
er fängt den Schock auf	*he cushions the shock*
auf|fassen (tr.)	interpret 15
auf|flackern (intr.+s.)	flare up 15
auf|fordern (tr.)	invite, challenge 15
auf|frischen (tr. & refl.)	freshen up 15
auf|führen (tr.)	perform 15
auf|geben (tr. & intr.)	give up, renounce 61
auf|gehen (intr.+s.)	rise, dawn 88
auf|haben (tr.)	have (sth) on/to do 2
auf|halten (tr.)	stop 79
er hält sich in ... auf (refl.)	*he is staying in ...*
auf|hängen (tr.)	hang up, suspend 85
auf|häufen (tr. & refl.)	pile up 15
***auf|heben** (tr.)	pick up, abolish 38
auf|hören (mit) (intr.)	stop, finish (sth.) 15
ich höre damit auf, ... zu machen	
	I stop doing ...
auf|klären (tr.)	clear up, enlighten 15

auf|knöpfen (tr.)	unbutton 15
auf|laden (tr.)	load 76
er lädt die Batterie auf	*he charges the battery*
auf|lauern (dat.) (intr.)	lie in wait for 15
auf|legen (tr.)	put down 15
er legt auf (intr.)	*he hangs up/he rings off*
auf|liegen (intr.)	be on the table 61
auf|lösen (tr. & refl.)	dissolve, break up 15
auf|machen (tr. & intr.)	open, undo 15
auf|muntern (tr. & refl.)	cheer up 15
auf|nehmen (tr.)	receive, absorb 54
auf|passen (intr.)	watch out, pay attention 15
er paßt auf sie auf	*he keeps an eye on them*
auf|räumen (tr. & intr.)	tidy up, clear up 15
auf|regen (tr.)	annoy 15
er regt sich auf (refl.)	*he gets excited*
auf|richten (tr.)	put up 12, 15
sie richtet sich auf (refl.)	*she sits up*
auf|runden (tr.)	even up, round up 12, 15
auf|saugen (tr.)	absorb 15, 38
auf|schlagen (tr.)	open 76
er schlägt das Zelt auf	*he erects the tent*
auf|schließen (tr. & intr.)	unlock 41
auf|schneiden (tr.)	cut up 31
auf|schreiben (tr.)	list, note down 28
auf|schreien (intr.)	exclaim 28
auf|schürfen (tr.)	graze 15
auf|sein (intr.+s.)	be on 1
die Tür ist auf	*the door is open*
auf|setzen (tr.)	put on 15
das Flugzeug setzt auf (refl.)	*the plane lands*
auf|springen (intr.+s.)	jump up, bounce 44
auf|stehen (intr.+s.)	get up, stand up 91
auf|stellen (tr.)	erect 15
sie stellen sich auf (refl.)	*they line up*
auf|tauchen (intr.+s.)	appear, emerge 15
auf|tauen (tr. & intr.+s.)	defrost, thaw 15
auf|tragen (tr.)	apply 76
auf|treten (intr.+s.)	appear, come on 65
auf|wachen (intr.+s.)	wake up 15
auf|wachsen (intr.+s.)	grow up 76
auf|wärmen (tr.)	warm up 15
auf|wickeln (tr.)	coil, untie 15
auf|zäumen (tr.)	bridle, harness 15
auf|zeichnen (tr.)	draw, record 12, 15
auf|ziehen (tr.)	bring up 33, 35

sie zieht die Uhr auf	*she winds the clock up*
aus|atmen (tr. & intr.)	exhale 12, 15
aus|bauen (tr.)	extend, convert 15
aus|bilden (tr.)	train, develop 12, 15
er bildet sich (als) ... aus (refl.)	*he is studying/training (to be a...)*
aus|blenden (tr. & intr.)	fade out 12, 15
aus|bomben (tr.)	bomb 15
aus|brechen (intr.+s.)	burst out, erupt 51
aus|breiten (tr. & refl.)	spread out 12, 15
aus|dehnen (tr. & refl.)	extend, spread 15
aus|denken (tr.)	think out/up 24
aus|drehen (tr.)	turn off 15
aus|drucken (tr. & intr.)	print out 15
aus|drücken (tr.)	express 15
auseinander|nehmen (tr.)	dismantle 54
aus|essen (tr. & intr.)	eat up, finish eating 69
aus|fallen (intr.+s.)	turn out 79
es fällt aus	*it is cancelled*
aus|fragen (tr.)	question, interrogate 15
aus|führen (tr.)	carry out 15
er führt die Waren aus	*he exports the goods*
aus|füllen (tr.)	fill in, complete 15
aus|geben (tr.)	spend, pay out 61
***aus|*gehen** (intr.+s.)	go out 88
der Wein geht aus	*the wine runs out*
aus|gleichen (tr. & intr. & refl.)	even out, equalize 31
aus|graben (tr.)	dig up, unearth 76
aus|halten (tr. & intr.)	endure 79
aus|hängen (tr. & intr.)	display 15, 85
aus|höhlen (tr.)	hollow out 15
aus|kennen (auf/in+dat.) (refl.)	know a lot about 18
aus|kommen (intr.+s.)	get by, manage 58
aus|lassen (tr.)	omit, leave out 10, 79
aus|leihen (tr.)	lend, borrow 28
aus|liegen (intr.)	be displayed 61
aus|löschen (tr.)	extinguish 15
aus|lösen (tr.)	trigger/set off 15
aus|machen (tr.)	turn out/off 15
es macht nichts aus	*it does not matter*
aus|nehmen (tr.)	make an exception of 54
aus|packen (tr. & intr.)	unpack 15
aus|pressen (tr.)	squeeze out 15
aus|probieren (tr.)	try out 13, 15
aus|radieren (tr.)	erase, rub out 13, 15
aus|räumen (tr.)	clear out 15

aus|wischen (tr.)   wipe off 15
aus|ziehen (tr.)   take off 33, 35
    sie zieht sich aus (refl.)   *she gets undressed*
    sie zieht aus (intr.+s.)   *she moves out*
automatisieren (tr.)   automate 13

B

backen (tr. & intr.)   bake, cook 73
baden (tr. & refl.)   bath, bathe 12, 15
bannen (tr.)   bewitch, charm 11
basieren (auf+acc.) (tr.)   base (on) 13
    es basiert auf+dat ...   *it is based on ...*
basteln (tr.)   make 11
    er bastelt gern (intr.)   *he likes doing handicrafts*
bauen (tr. & intr.)   build, construct 11
beabsichtigen (tr.)   intend 14
beachten (tr.)   observe, keep to 12, 14
beantragen (tr.)   apply for 14
beantworten (tr.)   answer 12, 14
bearbeiten (tr.)   arrange, adapt, edit 12, 14
beaufsichtigen (tr.)   supervize 14
beauftragen (tr.)   commission, appoint 14
bebauen (tr.)   build on (land) 14
    er bebaut das Land   *he cultivates the land*
beben (intr.)   shake, quiver 11
bedanken (refl.)   say thank you 14
bedauern (tr.)   regret, pity 14
bedecken (tr.)   cover 14
    es bedeckt sich (refl.)   *it clouds over*
bedenken (tr. & refl.)   think, consider 23
bedeuten (tr.)   mean 12, 14
bedienen (tr.)   serve, wait on 14
    er bedient (die Maschine)   *he operates (the machine)*
    ich bediene mich (refl.)   *I help myself*
bedrohen (tr.)   threaten 14
bedrücken (tr.)   depress 14
bedürfen (gen.) (intr.)   need 8, 14
beeilen (refl.)   hurry up, make haste 14
beeindrucken (tr.)   impress 14
beeinflussen (tr.)   influence 14
beeinträchtigen (tr.)   spoil 14
beenden (tr.)   finish, end 12, 14
beerdigen (tr.)   bury 14
befassen (mit) (refl.)   deal with 14
befehlen (dat.) (intr.)   order, tell 49, 50

bei|tragen (zu) (tr. & intr.) — contribute (to) 76
bei|treten (dat.) (intr.+s.) — join 65
bei|wohnen (dat.) (intr.) — attend 15
bejahen (tr. & intr.) — affirm, say yes 14
bekannt|geben (tr.) — disclose 61
bekennen (tr.) — confess 17
beklagen (tr.) — lament, regret 14
   sie beklagt sich über+acc ... (refl.) — *she complains about ...*
*bekommen (tr.) — get, receive 57
   das Fleisch bekommt mir (intr.+s.) — *the meat agrees with me*
beladen (tr.) — load 75
belagern (tr.) — besiege 14
belasten (tr.) — debit, weigh down 12, 14
belästigen (tr.) — bother, molest 14
belaufen (auf+acc.) (refl.) — amount (to) 81
beleben (tr.) — liven up, revive 14
belegen (tr.) — occupy, cover 14
belehren (tr.) — teach 14
beleidigen (tr.) — offend, insult 14
beleuchten (tr.) — illuminate, light up 12, 14
bellen (intr.) — bark 11
belohnen (tr.) — reward 14
belustigen (tr.) — amuse 14
bemerken (tr.) — remark, note 14
bemühen (um) (refl.) — take trouble (with) 14
benachrichtigen (tr.) — inform 14
benachteiligen (tr.) — handicap 14
*benehmen (refl.) — behave 53
beneiden (tr.) — envy 12, 14
benoten (tr.) — grade 12, 14
benötigen (tr.) — need, require 14
benutzen (tr.) — use 14
benützen (tr.) — use 14
beobachten (tr.) — observe 12, 14
bepflanzen (tr.) — plant 14
beraten (tr.) — advize 78
   sie berät sich mit mir (refl.) — *she consults with me*
berauben (tr.) — rob 14
berechnen (tr.) — compute, calculate 12, 14
berechtigen (tr.) — authorize, entitle 14
bereichern (tr.) — enrich 14
bereuen (tr. & intr.) — regret 14
bergen (tr.) — rescue, salvage 48
berichten (über+acc.)(tr. & intr.) — report (on), detail 12, 14

es besteht in+dat   *it consists of ...*
er besteht auf+dat   *he insists on ...*
sie besteht die Prüfung (tr.)   *she passes the examination*

bestehlen (tr.)	rob 49, 50
besteigen (tr.)	climb, mount 27
bestellen (tr. & intr.)	order, book 14
besteuern (tr.)	tax 14
bestimmen (tr. & intr.)	determine, decide 14
bestrafen (tr.)	punish 14
bestreichen (tr.)	spread 30
bestreiten (tr.)	dispute 30
bestürzen (tr.)	dismay 14
besuchen (tr.)	visit, attend 14
betätigen (tr.)	operate, work 14
betäuben (tr.)	stupefy, drug 14
beten (intr.)	pray 12
betonen (tr.)	stress, emphasize 14
betonieren (tr.)	pave, concrete over 13
betragen (intr.)	amount to 75
sie beträgt sich gut (refl.)	*she behaves well*
betreffen (tr.)	concern, affect 56, 57
***betreten** (tr.)	enter 64
betrinken (refl.)	get drunk 43
betrüben (tr.)	sadden 14
betrügen (tr.)	deceive, cheat 37
betteln (intr.)	beg 11
beugen (tr. & refl.)	bend, stoop 11
beunruhigen (tr. & refl.)	worry 14
beurlauben (tr.)	grant leave 14
beurteilen (tr.)	judge, assess 14
bevorzugen (tr.)	favor 14
bewachen (tr.)	guard 14
bewaffnen (tr.)	arm 12, 14
bewahren (tr.)	preserve, store 14
bewähren (refl.)	prove one's worth 14
bewältigen (tr.)	manage 14
bewässern (tr.)	irrigate 14
bewegen (tr. & refl.)	move 14, 37
beweisen (tr.)	prove, show 27
bewerben (um) (refl.)	apply (for) 50
bewerten (tr.)	evaluate 12, 14
bewilligen (tr.)	authorize 14
bewohnen (tr.)	live in 14
bewölken (refl.)	cloud over 14
bewundern (tr.)	admire 14

brummen (tr. & intr.)	growl, hum, buzz 11
brüllen (tr. & intr.)	roar, blare, bellow 11
buchen (tr.)	book 11
buchstabieren (tr.)	spell 13
bummeln (intr.+s.)	stroll, dawdle 11
bumsen (tr.& intr.)	bang 11
sie bumsen (intr.)	*they bang/have it off*
bücken (refl.)	bend 11
büffeln (tr. & intr.)	swot (study too much) 11
bügeln (tr. & intr.)	iron 11
bürgen (für) (intr.)	guarantee 11
bürsten (tr.)	brush 12

C
charakterisieren (tr.)	characterize 13
chartern (tr.)	charter 11

D
dämmern (impers.)	dawn 11
dampfen (intr.)	steam 11
dämpfen (tr.)	muffle, steam 11
danken (dat.) (intr.)	thank 11
dar|stellen (tr.)	represent, depict 15
dauern (intr.)	last, take 11
davon|kommen (intr.+s.)	escape, get away 58
davon|laufen (intr.+s.)	run away 82
dazu|rechnen (tr.)	add on 12, 15
debattieren (tr. & intr.)	debate 13
decken (tr.)	cover 11
ich decke den Tisch	*I set the table*
definieren (tr.)	define 13
dehnen (tr. & refl.)	stretch 11
dekodieren (tr.)	decode 13
demonstrieren (tr. & intr.)	demonstrate 13
demütigen (tr.)	humiliate 11
***denken** (tr. & intr.)	think 22
ich denke an ihn (intr.)	*I think of him*
was denken Sie von ihm?	*what is your opinion of him?*
ich denke mir (dat. refl.) (tr.)	*I imagine*
deponieren (tr.)	deposit 13
deprimieren (tr.)	depress 13
desinfizieren (tr.)	disinfect 13
destillieren (tr.)	distil 13
deuten (auf+acc.) (tr. & intr.)	point (to) 12
er deutet den Text	*he interprets the text*

durch|geben (tr.)	radio 61
durch|gehen (tr. & intr.+s.)	go through 88
durch|halten (tr. & intr.)	hold out 79
durch|lassen (tr.)	let in, leak 10, 79
durch|lesen (tr.)	read through 72
durchleuchten (tr.)	X-ray 12, 14
durchlöchern (tr.)	riddle with 14
durch|machen (tr.)	undergo, experience 15
durchnässen (tr.)	soak 14
durchqueren (tr.)	cross 14
durch|sagen (tr.)	announce 15
durchschauen (tr.)	catch, catch out 14
durch|sehen (tr. & intr.)	look through, check over 72
durch|setzen (tr.)	carry through 15
sie setzt sich durch (refl.)	*she asserts herself*
durchstechen (tr. & intr.)	pierce 50
durchsuchen (tr.)	search through 14
durch|wählen (intr.)	dial direct 15
*dürfen (intr.)	be allowed, may 8
duschen (intr. & refl.)	shower 11
duzen (tr.)	address as 'du' 11

E

ebnen (tr.)	flatten 12
eignen (für/zu) (tr. & refl.)	be suitable (for) 12
eilen (intr.)	rush, hurry 11
ein|äschern (tr.)	cremate 15
ein|atmen (tr. & intr.)	breathe in, inhale 12, 15
ein|bauen (tr.)	build in, install 15
ein|berufen (tr.)	call up 14, 15
ein|biegen (in+acc.) (tr. & intr.+s.)	
	bend in, turn in 35
ein|bilden (dat. refl.) (tr.)	imagine 12, 15
ein|blenden (tr.)	fade in 12, 15
ein|brechen (bei/in+acc./dat.)(intr.+s.)	
	burglarize, burgle, break into 51
ein|dämmen (tr.)	dam 15
ein|ebnen (tr.)	level 12, 15
ein|fahren (intr.+s.)	come in, drive in 76
ein|fallen (dat.) (intr.+s.)	occur (to) 79
ein|färben (tr.)	color in 15
ein|frieren (tr. & intr.+s.)	freeze, deepfreeze 35
ein|fügen (tr.)	insert 15
ein|führen (tr.)	introduce, import 15
ein|gehen (intr.+s.)	shrink 88

die Firma geht ein	*the firm fails*
ein|gravieren (tr.)	engrave 13, 15
ein|hämmern (tr.)	hammer in 15
ein|holen (tr.)	catch up with 15
einigen (tr.)	unite 11
sie einigen sich auf+acc ... (refl.)	
	they agree to ...
ein|kaufen (tr. & intr.)	shop, buy 15
ein|klemmen (tr.)	pin down, box in 15
*ein|laden (zu) (tr.)	invite (to), entertain 76
ein|laufen (in+acc.) (intr.+s.)	come in, arrive (at) 82
ein|leiten (tr.)	initiate, introduce 12, 15
ein|lösen (tr.)	cash 15
ein|machen (tr.)	preserve 15
ein|mischen (in+acc.) (refl.)	interfere (in) 15
ein|nehmen (tr.)	earn 54
er nimmt die Stadt ein	*he captures the town*
er nimmt viel Platz ein	*he takes up much space*
ein|nicken (intr.+s.)	nod off, doze 15
ein|ordnen (tr. & refl.)	class, fit in 12, 15
ein|packen (in+acc.)(tr. & intr.)	wrap up, pack (in) 15
ein|pflanzen (tr.)	graft 15
ein|planen (tr.)	allow for, budget 15
ein|prägen (tr.)	make an impression 15
ich präge es mir ein (dat. refl.)	*I commit it to memory*
ein|rechnen (tr.)	allow for 12, 15
ein|reichen (tr.)	hand in 15
ein|richten (tr.)	furnish, equip 12, 15
ein|sammeln (tr.)	collect 15
ein|schalten (tr.)	switch on, tune in 12, 15
ein|schätzen (tr.)	estimate 15
ein|schenken (tr.)	pour out 15
ein|schicken (tr.)	send in 15
ein|schiffen (tr.)	ship, embark 15
er schifft sich nach ... ein (refl.)	*he embarks for ...*
ein|schlafen (intr.+s.)	fall asleep 79
ein|schließen (tr.)	enclose, include 41
ein|schneiden (in+acc.) (tr.)	cut, carve into 31
ein|schränken (tr. & refl.)	cut back, economize 15
ein|schreiben (tr.)	enter 28
er schreibt sich in+acc ... ein (refl.)	
	he enrols in ...
ein|schreiten (intr.+s.)	intervene 31
ein|sehen (tr. & intr.)	see, realize 72
ein|seifen (tr.)	soap 15
er seift mich ein	*he cons me*

ein|setzen (tr.)	put in 15
sie setzt sich dafür ein (refl.)	*she is committed to it*
ein|sperren (tr.)	imprison 15
ein|springen (für) (intr.+s.)	stand in (for) 44
ein|steigen (intr.+s.)	get in/on, board 28
ein|stellen (tr.)	appoint, adjust 15
wir stellen die Arbeit ein	*we stop the work*
er stellt sich auf+acc ... ein (refl.)	*he adapts to ...*
ein|stufen (tr.)	grade, classify 15
ein|stürzen (intr.+s.)	collapse 15
ein|teilen (tr.)	divide up 15
ein|tragen (tr.)	register 76
sie trägt sich ein (refl.)	*she enters her name*
ein|treffen (intr.+s.)	arrive 56, 58
ein|treten (intr.+s.)	enter 65
ein|wandern (intr.+s.)	immigrate 15
ein|weihen (tr.)	initiate 15
ein|wenden (tr.)	object 21
ein|werfen (tr.)	post, mail 51
ein|willigen (in+acc.) (intr.)	consent (to) 15
ein|zahlen (tr.)	pay in, bank 15
ein|ziehen (tr.)	draft, enlist 33, 35
er zieht ein (intr.+s.)	*he moves in (to a house)*
ekeln (tr.)	disgust 11
es ekelt mich vor+dat ... (impers.)	
	I find ... disgusting
elekrifizieren (tr.)	electrify 13
***empfangen** (tr. & intr.)	receive 84
sie empfängt	*she conceives*
empfehlen (tr.)	recommend 49, 50
empfinden (tr.)	feel 46
empören (tr.)	outrage 14
sie empört sich über+acc ... (refl.)	
	she gets angry about ...
emulgieren (tr. & intr.)	emulsify 13
enden (intr.)	conclude, end 12
engagieren (tr.)	involve 13
er engagiert sich (refl.)	*he gets involved*
entbehren (tr.) (& gen. intr.)	spare, lack 14
entblößen (tr.)	bare 14
entdecken (tr.)	discover, reveal 14
enteisen (tr.)	de-ice 14
enterben (tr.)	disinherit 14
entfernen (tr.)	remove, go away 14
er entfernt sich (refl.)	*he goes away*
entfliehen (dat.) (intr.+s.)	escape (from) 34

entzünden (tr.) ignite 12, 14
   es entzündet sich (refl.) *it gets inflamed*
erben (tr. & intr.) inherit 11
erblassen (intr.+s.) turn pale 14
erblicken (tr.) catch sight of 14
erbrechen (tr. & intr.) break open 50
   er erbricht sich (refl.) *he vomits*
ereignen (refl.) occur, happen 12, 14
erfahren (tr.) find out, hear 75
erfassen (tr.) seize, comprehend 14
erfinden (tr.) invent, make up 46
erfreuen (tr.) please, delight 14
   sie erfreut sich an+dat ... (refl.) *she enjoys ...*
erfrischen (tr.) refresh 14
erfüllen (tr.) fulfill 14
   es erfüllt sich (refl.) *it is fulfilled*
ergänzen (tr.) complete, amend 14
ergeben (tr.) produce, result in 60
   er ergibt sich (refl.) *he surrenders*
ergrauen (intr.+s.) go gray 14
ergreifen (tr.) grasp, seize 30
erhalten (tr.) receive, preserve 78
erheben (tr.) raise 37
   er erhebt sich (refl.) *he rises up*
erhitzen (refl.) heat up 14
erhöhen (tr. & refl.) raise, increase 14
erholen (von) (refl.) get well, recover (from) 14
erinnern (an+acc.) (tr.) remind (of) 14
   sie erinnert sich an+acc etw. (refl.)
      she remembers sth.
erkälten (refl.) catch a cold 12, 14
***erkennen** (tr.) (an+dat.) recognize (from) 17
erklären (tr. & intr.) explain, declare 14
erklimmen (tr.) climb 40
erkranken (intr.+s.) fall ill 14
erkundigen (nach) (refl.) inquire, ask (about) 14
erlassen (tr.) pass (law) 10, 78
   ich erlasse ihm seine Schulden
      I release him from his debts
erlauben (tr.) allow 14
erleben (tr.) experience 14
erledigen (tr.) deal with, dispose of 14
erleichtern (tr.) make easier, lighten 14
erleuchten (tr.) illumine 12, 14
erlöschen (intr.+s.) die out 40
erlösen (tr.) save, deliver 14

erwischen (tr.)	catch 14
erzählen (tr. & intr.)	tell 14
erzeugen (tr.)	produce, generate 14
erziehen (tr.)	bring up 33, 34
erzielen (tr.)	achieve, score 14
***essen** (tr. & intr.)	eat 66
existieren (intr.)	exist 13
experimentieren (intr.)	experiment 13
explodieren (intr.+s.)	explode 13
exportieren (tr. & intr.)	export 13

F

***fahren** (tr. & intr.+s.)	drive, ride, go 73
fallen (intr.+s.)	fall 77
fällen (tr.)	fell 11
sie fällt das Urteil	*she gives judgment*
fallen|lassen (tr.)	drop 10, 79
fälschen (tr.)	forge, fake 11
falten (tr.)	fold 12
fangen (tr. & intr.)	capture, catch 83
färben (tr.)	color 11
fassen (tr. & intr.)	grasp 11
er faßt es	*he understands it*
fasten (intr.)	fast 12
faulen (intr.+s.)	rot 11
faxen (tr.)	fax 11
fechten (intr.)	fence 39
fegen (tr. & intr.)	sweep 11
fehlen (intr.)	be lacking 11
es fehlt mir an+dat ... (impers.+dat.)	
	I lack ...
feiern (tr. & intr.)	celebrate 11
feilen (tr. & intr.)	file 11
feilschen (intr.)	haggle 11
fern|halten (tr. & refl.)	keep away 79
fern|sehen (intr.)	watch TV 72
fertig|machen (tr.)	finish 15
fertig|werden (intr.+s.)	cope 3
fertig|kriegen (tr.)	get done 15
fesseln (tr.)	tie, grip 11
fest|binden (tr.)	tie up 47
fest|halten (tr. & intr.)	grasp, hold on 79
er hält sich an+dat ... fest (refl.)	*he holds on to ...*
fest|klammern (tr.)	fix 15
er klammert sich an+dat ... fest (refl.)	
	he clings to ...

fest|legen (tr.)	determine, fix 15
fest|machen (tr.)	fasten 15
fest|nehmen (tr.)	arrest 54
fest|setzen (tr.)	arrange, fix 15
fest|stehen (intr.)	be certain 91
fest|stellen (tr.)	find out, establish 15
feuern (tr. & intr.)	fire, fling 11
filtern (tr. & intr.)	filter 11
finanzieren (tr.)	finance 13
finden (tr. & intr.)	find 45
fischen (tr. & intr.)	fish 11
flackern (intr.)	flicker 11
flattern (intr.)	flutter 11
flechten (tr.)	twine 39
flehen (um) (intr.)	plead (for) 11
flicken (tr.)	mend, darn 11
fliegen (tr. & intr.+s.)	fly 32
fliehen (intr.+s.)	flee 32
fließen (intr.+s.)	flow 39
flimmern (intr.)	flicker 11
flirten (intr.)	flirt 12
flitzen (intr.+s.)	dart out 11
florieren (intr.)	flourish 13
fluchen (intr.)	curse 11
flüchten (intr.+s.)	escape, flee 12
flüstern (tr. & intr.)	whisper 11
folgen (dat.) (intr.+s.)	follow 11
es folgt auf+acc ...	*it comes after ...*
folgern (auf +acc.) (aus) (tr. & intr.)	
	come after, conclude (from) 11
fordern (tr. & intr.)	ask for, demand 11
fördern (tr.)	support 11
er fördert mich	*he promotes me*
formatieren (tr. & intr.)	format 13
formen (tr.)	form, shape 11
forschen (nach) (intr.)	search (for) 11
ich forsche (tr.) *über + acc ...*	*I research (into) ...*
fort|bilden (tr. & refl.)	train 12, 15
fort|fahren (intr.+s.)	go away 76
er fährt mit ... fort	*he continues with ...*
fort|führen (tr. & intr.)	lead away 15
sie führt den Plan fort	*she continues the plan*
fort|setzen (tr.)	continue 15
fotografieren (tr. & intr.)	photograph 13
fotokopieren (tr.)	photocopy 13

fragen (nach) (tr. & intr.)   ask (about) 11
frankieren (tr.)   stamp, frank 13
frei|sprechen (tr.)   acquit 51
frei|lassen (tr.)   free, release 10, 79
frequentieren (tr.)   frequent 13
fressen (tr. & intr.)   eat, guzzle 66
freuen (tr.)   please 11
   es freut mich (impers.)   *I am glad*
   ich freue mich auf+acc ... (refl.) *I look forward to ...*
   ich freue mich über+acc ...   *I am pleased about ...*
   ich freue mich an+dat ...   *I take pleasure in ...*
frieren (intr.+s.)   freeze 32
   mich friert (impers.)   *I am cold*
frönen (dat.) (intr.)   be a slave to 11
frühstücken (intr.)   have breakfast 11
fühlen (tr. & intr.)   feel 11
   er fühlt sich (krank) (refl.)   *he feels (ill)*
führen (tr. & intr.)   take, lead 11
füllen (tr.)   fill 11
funkeln (intr.)   sparkle 11
funken (tr. & intr.)   radio 11
funktionieren (intr.)   work, function 13
fürchten (tr.)   fear 12
   er fürchtet sich vor+dat ... (refl.) *he is afraid of ...*
fusionieren (tr. & intr.)   merge, amalgamate 13
füttern (tr.)   feed 11

G

gaffen (intr.)   gape 11
gähnen (intr.)   yawn 11
garantieren (tr. & intr.)   guarantee 13
gären (intr+s./h.)   ferment 36
gebären (tr. & intr.)   give birth (to) 49, 50
*geben (tr.)   give 59
   es gibt (impers.)(+acc.) ...   *there is ...*
gebrauchen (tr.)   use 14
gedeihen (intr.+s.)   flourish 27
gedenken (gen.) (intr.)   commemorate 23
gedulden (refl.)   be patient 12, 14
gefallen (dat.) (intr.)   please 78
gefangen|nehmen (tr.)   take prisoner 54
gegenüber|stehen (dat.) (intr.)   be opposite, face 91
gegenüber|stellen (dat.) (refl.)   confront 15
   (tr.) *er stellt es* (dat.) *... gegenüber*
      he compares it (with) ...
*gehen (intr.+s.)   go 86

groß|ziehen (tr.)   bring up, rear 33,35
grunzen (tr. & intr.)   grunt 11
gründen (tr.)   found 12
     es gründet sich auf+dat ... (refl.)
                      it is based on
grüßen (tr. & intr.)   greet 11
gucken (intr.)   look, peep 11
gut|schreiben (dat.) (tr.)   credit (to) 28
gut|tun (dat.) (intr.)   benefit 92, 91

H   ***haben** (tr.)   have 2
     ich habe Angst vor+dat ...   *I am afraid of ...*
hacken (tr. & intr.)   hack, chop 11
haften (für) (intr.)   be liable (for) 12
haken (tr. & intr.)   hook 11
halten (tr.)   hold 77
     er hält mich für einen Idioten   *he thinks I am an idiot*
     er hält (intr.)   *he stops*
halt|machen (intr.)   stop 15
hämmern (tr. & intr.)   hammer, beat 11
hamstern (tr. & intr.)   hoard 11
handeln (mit) (intr.)   trade (in) 11
     er handelt (intr.)   *he acts*
     es handelt sich um ... (refl.)   *it concerns/is a matter of ...*
handhaben (tr.)   handle 11
*hängen (tr. intr. & refl.)   hang, suspend 83
harken (tr. & intr.)   rake 11
harmonieren (intr.)   blend 13
harmonisieren (tr.)   harmonize 13
hassen (tr. & intr.)   hate, detest 11
hauen (tr. & intr.)   hew, bash 80
häufen (tr. & refl.)   heap, pile up 11
*heben (tr.)   lift, raise 36
     er hebt sich (refl.)   *he gets up*
heften (tr.)   staple, fix 12
hegen (tr.)   cherish 11
heilen (tr. & intr.)   heal 11
heim|kehren (intr.+s.)   return home 15
heim|suchen (tr.)   afflict 15
heim|zahlen (tr.)   pay back 15
heiraten (tr.)   marry 12
     sie heiraten (sich) (intr. & refl.)   *they get married*
heißen (intr.)   be called 80
     das heißt auf Deutsch   *that means in German*
heizen (tr. & intr.)   heat 11

heulen (intr.)   howl, cry 11
hinab|blicken (intr.)   look down 15
hinauf|fahren (intr.+s.)   go up (climb) 76
hinaus|blicken (intr.)   look out 15
hinaus|gehen (intr.+s.)   go out 88
hinaus|laufen (auf.+acc.)(intr.+s.)

                                                 amount (to) 82
hinaus|stehlen (intr.+s.)   steal out 49, 51
*hinaus|treten (intr.+s.)   step out 65
hinaus|ziehen (tr.)   draw out 33, 35
    er zieht hinaus (intr.+s.)   *he moves out*
hindern (tr. & intr.)   hinder 11
    er hindert   *he is in the way*
    er hindert mich an+dat ...   *he keeps me from ...*
    er hindert mich daran, ... zu tun

                                                 he prevents me from doing ...
hinein|gehen (intr.+s.)   go in 88
hin|fallen (intr.+s.)   fall down 79
hin|geben (tr.)   give up 61
    sie gibt sich hin (dat.)(refl.)   *she surrenders (to)*
hinken (intr.)   limp 11
hin|knien (intr. & refl.)   kneel down 15
hin|legen (tr.)   lay down 15
    er legt sich hin (refl.)   *he lies down*
hin|reichen (tr.)   hand over 15
    es reicht hin   *it is enough*
hin|richten (tr.)   execute 12, 15
hin|scheiden (intr.+s.)   pass away 28
hin|setzen (tr.)   set down 15
    sie setzt sich hin (refl.)   *she sits down*
hin|stellen (intr.)   put down 15
    sie stellt sich hin (refl.)   *she goes and*
                                                 stands (there)

hinter|lassen (tr.)   bequeath, leave 10, 78
hinüber|gehen (intr.+s.)   cross over 88
hinunter|fallen (intr.+s.)   fall down 79
hinunter|gehen (intr.+s.)   go down, descend 88
hinweg|sehen (von) (intr.)   ignore 72
hin|weisen (auf+acc.) (intr.)   point (out) 28
    er weist auf+acc ... hin   *he refers to ...*
hinzu|fügen (tr.)   add 15
hoch|heben (tr.)   hoist 38
hocken (intr. & refl.)   squat 11
hoffen (auf+acc.) (tr. & intr.)   hope (for) 11
holen (tr.)   fetch, get 11
horchen (auf+acc.) (intr.)   listen (to) 11

hören (tr. & intr.)   hear, listen 11
hungern (intr.)   starve 11
hupen (intr.)   hoot 11
hüpfen (intr.+s.)   hop 11
husten (intr.)   cough 12
hüten (tr.)   look after 12
    sie hütet sich vor+dat ... (refl.)   *she is on her guard against ...*

_I_   **illustrieren** (tr.)   illustrate 13
impfen (tr.)   innoculate 11
imponieren (dat) (intr.)   impress 13
importieren (tr.)   import 13
infizieren (tr.)   infect 13
informieren (über+acc.) (tr.)   inform 13
    sie informiert sich über+acc ... (refl.)   *she finds out about ...*
inhaftieren (tr.)   imprison 13
innehalten (intr.)   pause 79
inserieren (tr. & intr.)   advertize 13
installieren (tr.)   install 13
inszenieren (tr.)   stage 13
integrieren (tr.)   integrate 13
interessieren (tr.)   interest 13
    ich interessiere mich für ... (refl.)   *I am interested in ...*
interviewen (tr.)   interview 14
intrigieren (intr.)   scheme 13
investieren (tr. & intr.)   invest 13
ionisieren (tr.)   ionize 13
irren (intr. & refl.)   be mistaken 11
    er irrt   *he is wrong*
irre|führen (tr)(intr.+s.)   mislead 15

_J_   **jagen** (tr. & intr.)   hunt, chase 11
jammern (intr.)   moan, wail 11
joggen (intr.)   jog 11
jubeln (intr.)   rejoice 11
jucken (tr. & intr.)   itch 11

_K_   **kalkulieren** (tr.)   calculate 13
kämmen (tr. & refl.)   comb 11
kämpfen (um) (tr. & intr.)   fight (for) 11

kapieren (intr.)	understand 13
kapitulieren (intr.)	capitulate 13
kaputt|gehen (intr.+s.)	break, bust 88
karikieren (tr.)	caricature 13
katalogisieren (tr.)	catalogue 13
kauen (tr. & intr.)	chew, gnaw 11
kauern (intr. & refl.)	cower 11
kaufen (tr. & intr.)	buy 11
kehren (tr. & refl.)	turn, return 11
***kennen** (tr.)	know 16
kennen|lernen (tr.)	get to know, meet 15
kennzeichnen (tr.)	mark, characterize 12, 15
kentern (intr.+s.)	capsize 11
keuchen (intr.)	gasp, pant 11
kichern (intr.)	giggle 11
kitzeln (tr. & intr.)	tickle 11
klagen (tr. & intr.)	moan, complain 11
klappen (tr.)	fold 11
es klappt (intr.)	*it's working out (well)*
klären (tr. & refl.)	clear up, clarify 11
klassifizieren (tr.)	classify 13
klatschen (tr. & intr.)	applaud, clap 11
klauen (tr. & intr.)	nick, steal 11
kleben (tr. & intr.)	stick, bond 11
kleiden (tr. & refl.)	dress, clothe 12
klettern (auf+acc.) (intr.+s.)	climb (up) 11
klingeln (intr.)	ring 11
klingen (intr.)	sound 42
klirren (intr.)	chink, rattle 11
klönen (intr.)	gossip 11
klopfen (tr. & intr.)	knock 11
knabbern (tr. & intr.)	nibble 11
knacken (tr. & intr.)	crack 11
knallen (tr. & intr.)	bang, explode 11
knarren (intr.)	creak 11
kneifen (tr. & intr.)	pinch 29
knien (intr. & refl.)	kneel 11
knipsen (tr. & intr.)	snap, photograph 11
knirschen (intr.)	crunch 11
knistern (intr.)	crackle 11
knittern (tr. & intr.)	crush, crease 11
knurren (tr. & intr.)	growl 11
kochen (tr. & intr.)	cook, boil 11
koexistieren (intr.)	coexist 13
kolorieren (tr.)	color in 13
***kommen** (intr.+s.)	come 55

er kommt um etw.	*he loses sth.*
kommunizieren (intr.)	communicate 13
er kommuniziert	*he takes communion*
komplizieren (tr.)	complicate 13
komponieren (tr. & intr.)	compose 13
kompromittieren (tr.)	compromise 13
kondensieren (tr. & intr.)	condense 13
konkurrieren (intr.)	compete 13
***können** (tr. & intr.)	be able to, can 4
konstruieren (tr.)	construct, design 13
kontrollieren (tr.)	control, check, inspect 13
konzentrieren (tr. & refl.)	concentrate 13
kooperieren (intr.)	co-operate 13
koordinieren (tr.)	coordinate 13
kopieren (tr. & intr.)	copy 13
korrespondieren (tr.)	correspond 13
der Winkel korrespondiert mit ...	*the angle corresponds to/with ...*
korrigieren (tr.)	correct 13
kosten (tr. & intr.)	cost, taste 12
kotzen (intr.)	be sick 11
krachen (intr.)	bang, crash 11
krächzen (intr.)	croak 11
kramen (intr.)	rummage 11
kränken (tr.)	hurt, offend 11
kratzen (tr. & intr.)	scratch 11
kräuseln (tr. & intr.)	ruffle, curl 11
kreisen (intr+s./h.)	circle, orbit 11
kreuzen (tr. & refl.)	cross 11
kreuzigen (tr.)	crucify 11
kriechen (intr.+s.)	crawl 39
kriegen (tr.)	get 11
kristallisieren (intr. & refl.)	crystallize 13
kritisieren (tr. & intr.)	criticize 13
kritzeln (tr. & intr.)	scribble 11
krönen (tr.)	crown 11
krümmen (tr. & refl.)	bend 11
kühlen (tr. & intr.)	cool, ice 11
kultivieren (tr.)	cultivate 13
kümmern (um) (refl.)	take care (of), worry (about) 11
kümmere dich nicht um ...	*don't worry about ...*
das kümmert mich nicht (tr.)	*that is no concern of mine*
kündigen (tr. & intr.)	cancel, give notice 11
sie kündigt mir (intr.+dat.)	*she dismisses me*

kürzen (tr.)	cut 11
kurz|schließen (tr. & refl.)	short-circuit 41
küssen (tr. & intr. & refl.)	kiss 11

L

lächeln (intr.)	smile 11
lachen (intr.)	laugh 11
laden (tr. & intr.)	load, charge 73
lagern (tr.)	store 11
lähmen (tr.)	cripple, paralyze 11
landen (tr. & intr.+s.)	land 12
langweilen (tr.)	bore 11
er langweilt sich (refl.)	*he is bored*
***lassen** (tr.)	leave, let, stop 10, 77
laufen (intr.+s.)	run, go 80
laufen|lassen (tr.)	let go 10, 79
läuten (tr. & intr.)	chime, ring 12
leben (intr.)	live, exist 11
lecken (tr. & intr.)	lick, lap 11
leeren (tr.)	empty 11
legalisieren (tr.)	legalize 13
legen (tr.)	lay down, put 11
er legt sich (refl.)	*he lies down*
der Wind legt sich	*the wind abates*
lehnen (an+acc.) (tr. & intr. & refl.)	lean (up against) 11
er lehnt sich an die Wand	*he leans on the wall*
lehren (tr. & intr.)	teach 11
***leiden** (tr.)	bear 29
sie leidet an+dat ... (intr.)	*she suffers from ...*
leid|tun (dat.) (impers)	feel sorry 92
er tut mir leid (intr.)	*I am sorry for him*
leihen (tr.)	lend, borrow 26
leisten (tr.)	accomplish 12
ich leiste es mir (dat. refl.)	*I can afford it/I treat myself*
leiten (tr.)	lead, manage 12
lenken (tr.)	direct, steer 11
lernen (tr. & intr.)	learn, study 11
***lesen** (tr. & intr.)	read 70
leuchten (intr.)	glow, shine 12
leugnen (tr. & intr.)	deny 12
lieben (tr. & intr.)	love 11
sie lieben sich (refl.)	*they are in love/they make love*
liebkosen (tr.)	caress 11
liefern (tr. & intr.)	supply, deliver 11

mimen (tr. & intr.)	mime 11
mindern (tr.)	diminish 11
mischen (tr. & refl.)	mix 11
mißbilligen (tr.)	disapprove of 11
mißbrauchen (tr.)	misuse 11
mißfallen (dat.) (intr.)	displease 78
mißglücken (dat.) (intr.+s.)	fail (of so.) 14
mißhandeln (tr.)	mistreat 14
mißlingen (dat.) (impers.+s)	fail 43
es mißlingt ihm	*he fails*
mißtrauen (dat.) (intr.)	distrust 14
mißverstehen (tr. & intr.)	misunderstand 90
mit|bringen (tr.)	bring along 24
mit|erleben (tr.)	live through 15, 14
mit|fühlen (tr.)	sympathize 15
mit|gehen (intr.+s.)	go along too 88
mit|halten (mit) (intr.)	keep up (with) 79
mit|machen (tr. & intr.)	join in, co-operate 15
mit|nehmen (tr.)	take along 54
mit|rechnen (tr.)	count in 12, 15
mit|teilen (dat.) (tr.)	advize, inform (so.) 15
mit|wirken (intr.)	collaborate 15
mixen (tr.)	blend, mix 11
möblieren (tr.)	furnish 13
modernisieren (tr.)	modernize 13
mogeln (intr.)	cheat 11
*mögen (tr. & intr.)	like, want 6
montieren (tr.)	assemble, fit 13
motivieren (tr.)	motivate 13
multiplizieren (tr. & intr.)	multiply 13
murmeln (tr. & intr.)	murmur 11
murren (intr.)	grumble 11
münden (in+acc.) (intr.+s.)	flow (into) 12
*müssen (tr. & intr.)	must 7
mustern (tr.)	survey 11

N

nach|ahmen (tr.)	imitate, copy 15
*nach|denken (über+acc.) (intr.)	think (about) 24
nach|geben (intr.)	give way 61
nach|gehen (dat.) (intr.+s.)	follow 88
die Uhr geht nach	*the clock is slow*
nach|grübeln (über+acc.) (intr.)	ponder over 15
nach|holen (tr.)	catch up 15
nach|jagen (dat.) (intr.+s.)	pursue 15

O   **öffnen** (tr., intr. & refl.)   open 12
            operieren (tr. & intr.)   operate (on) 13
            opfern (tr. & intr.)   sacrifice 11
            ordnen (tr.)   arrange, sort 12
            organisieren (tr.)   organize 13
            orientieren (tr. & intr.)   orientate 13
                er orientiert sich über+acc ... (refl.)
                                     he finds out about ...
            oxydieren (tr. & intr.+s.)   oxydize 13

P   **paaren** (tr. & refl.)   couple, mate 11
            packen (tr.)   pack, grip 11
            paddeln (tr. & intr.+s./h.)   paddle 11
            parken (tr. & intr.)   park 11
            passen (dat.) (intr.)   fit 11
                es paßt zu ...   *it matches ...*
            passieren (tr.)   pass 13
                es passiert ihm (mit ihm) (intr.+s.)
                                     it happens to him
            patentieren (tr.)   patent 13
            pauken (tr. & intr.)   swot, drill 11
            pendeln (intr.+s.)   swing 11
                er pendelt   *he commutes*
            pennen (intr.)   doze, kip 11
            pensionieren (tr.)   pension off 13
            pfeffern (tr.)   pepper 11
            pfeifen (tr. & intr.)   whistle 29
            pflanzen (tr.)   plant 11
            pflegen (tr.)   look after 11
                er pflegt, ... (zu tun)   *he is in the habit of*
                                     (doing) ...
            pflücken (tr.)   pick 11
            pflügen (tr. & intr.)   plow/plough 11
            pfuschen (intr.)   bungle 11
            picken (tr. & intr.)   peck 11
            pinkeln (intr.)   urinate 11
            pissen (intr.)   urinate 11
            plagen (tr.)   torment 11
            planen (tr. & intr.)   plan, organize 11
            plätschern (intr.)   splash, patter 11
            platzen (intr.+s.)   blow up, burst 11
            plaudern (intr.)   gossip, chat 11
            pleite|machen (intr.)   bankrupt 15
            plombieren (tr.)   fill (tooth) 13
            plumpsen (tr. & intr.+s.)   tumble 11

plündern (tr. & intr.)	rob 11
pochen (intr.)	knock 11
pochieren (tr.)	poach 13
polieren (tr.)	polish 13
poltern (tr.)	crash about 11
potenzieren (mit) (tr.)	raise to the power (of) 13
prägen (tr.)	punch, stamp 11
prahlen (intr.)	boast 11
praktizieren (tr. & intr.)	practice 13
predigen (tr. & intr.)	preach 11
preisen (tr.)	praise 26
pressen (tr.)	press 11
privatisieren (tr.)	privatize 13
proben (tr. & intr.)	rehearse 11
***probieren** (tr. & intr.)	try, have a go 13
produzieren (tr.)	produce 13
profitieren (tr. & intr.)	benefit, profit 13
programmieren (tr. & intr.)	program 13
prostituieren (refl.)	prostitute oneself 13
protestieren (intr.)	protest, object 13
protokollieren (tr. & intr.)	record, minute 13
prüfen (tr.)	examine, check 11
prügeln (tr. & intr.)	beat 11
sie prügeln sich (refl.)	*they fight*
pudern (tr.)	powder 11
pumpen (tr. & intr.)	pump 11
ich pumpe (mir) Geld bei ihm	*I borrow money from him*
putzen (tr.)	clean 11

Q	**quadrieren** (tr.)	square 13
	quälen (tr.)	torment 11
	er quält sich (refl.)	*he struggles*
	qualifizieren (tr.)	qualify 13
	er qualifiziert sich (refl.)	*he gets qualified*
	quantifizieren (tr.)	quantify 13
	quatschen (tr. & intr.)	talk nonsense 11
	quellen (intr.+s.)	well up 39
	quetschen (tr.)	crush 11
	quittieren (tr. & intr.)	give a receipt 13

R	**rächen** (tr.)	avenge 11
	er rächt sich (refl.)	*he takes revenge*
	radeln (intr.+s.)	bike 11
	rad|fahren/Rad|fahren (intr.+s.)	bicycle 76

radieren (tr.)	erase 13
raffen (tr.)	gather 11
raffinieren (tr.)	refine 13
ragen (intr.)	project 11
rahmen (tr.)	frame 11
randalieren (intr.)	rampage about 13
rascheln (intr.)	crackle, rustle 11
rasieren (tr. & refl.)	shave 13
rasten (intr.)	rest 12
raten (dat.) (intr.)	advize 77
sie rät (tr.)	*she guesses*
rationieren (tr.)	ration 13
rauben (dat.) (tr. & intr.)	steal (from) 11
rauchen (tr. & intr.)	smoke 11
räuchern (tr.)	cure, smoke 11
räumen (tr. & intr.)	clear (up) 11
rauschen (intr.)	roar, rustle 11
raus|schmeißen (tr.)	chuck out 31
reagieren (intr.)	react 13
rebellieren (intr.)	revolt 13
rechnen (tr. & intr.)	calculate, count 12
er rechnet auf mich	*he relies on me*
er rechnet mit ihr	*he reckons on/with her*
rechtfertigen (tr.)	explain, justify 11
er rechtfertigt sich (refl.)	*he justifies himself*
reden (tr. & intr.)	speak 12
regeln (tr.)	regulate, direct 11
regieren (tr. & intr.)	rule, govern 13
regnen (impers.)	rain 12
regulieren (tr.)	regulate, adjust 13
reiben (tr. & intr.)	rub, grate 26
reichen (tr.)	hand, reach 11
es reicht bis ... (intr.)	*it stretches as far as ...*
es reicht	*it is enough*
reifen (tr. & intr.+s.)	ripen, age 11
reinigen (tr.)	clean, purify 11
rein|kommen (intr.+s.)	come in 58
reisen (intr.+s.)	travel 11
reißen (tr. & intr.+s.)	tear 29
reiten (tr. & intr.+s.)	ride 29
reizen (tr. & intr.)	irritate, annoy 11
rennen (intr.+s.)	run 16
rentieren (refl.)	be profitable 13
reparieren (tr.)	repair, mend 13
reproduzieren (tr.)	reproduce 13
reservieren (tr.)	reserve, book 13

schämen (gen./über+acc.) (refl.) be ashamed (of) 11
schätzen (tr.) estimate, value 11
schauen (intr.) look, glance 11
schaufeln (tr. & intr.) scoop, shovel 11
schaukeln (tr. & intr.) rock, swing 11
schäumen (intr.) foam 11
scheiden (tr. & intr.+s.) separate, part 26
   sie läßt sich scheiden (refl.) *she gets divorced*
scheinen (intr.) shine 26
   er scheint *he seems*
scheißen (intr.) defecate, excrete 29
scheitern (intr.+s.) fail, collapse 11
schellen (intr.) ring 11
schenken (tr.) give away 11
scheren (tr.) shear, clip 36
scherzen (intr.) joke 11
scheuen (vor+dat.) (refl.) be frightened (of) 11
schicken (nach) (tr. & intr.) send (for) 11
schieben (tr.) push, shove 32
schief|gehen (intr.+s.) go wrong 88
schielen (intr.) squint 11
*schießen (auf+acc.) (tr. & intr.) shoot, fire (at) 39
schildern (tr.) describe, portray 11
schimmern (intr.) gleam 11
schimpfen (auf+acc.) (intr.) grumble, curse (at) 11
schirmen (tr.) shield 11
schlachten (tr. & intr.) slaughter 12
*schlafen (intr.) sleep 77
schlafen|gehen (intr.+s.) go to bed 88
schlafen|legen (tr.) put to bed 15
schlagen (tr. & intr.) hit, strike 73
   er schlägt gegen/auf+acc ... (intr.+s.)
      he crashes against/onto ...
   sie schlagen sich (refl.) *they fight*
schlängeln (refl.) curl, coil 11
schleichen (intr.+s.) creep, slip, steal 29
schleifen (tr. & intr.+s.) sharpen, drag 29
schlendern (intr.+s.) stroll 11
schleppen (tr. & intr.) drag, haul 11
schleudern (tr.) hurl 11
   es schleudert (intr.) *it spins*
   das Auto schleudert (intr.+s.) *the car skids*
schlichten (tr. & intr.) arbitrate 12
schließen (tr. & intr.) close, conclude 39
   er schließt aus ... *he concludes from ...*
schlittschuh|laufen (intr.+s.) skate 82

schluchzen (tr. & intr.)	sob 11
schlucken (tr. & intr.)	swallow, sip 11
schlüpfen (intr.+s.)	slip 11
schmecken (nach) (tr. & intr.)	taste (of) 11
es schmeckt (mir gut) (impers.)	*it tastes good/I like it*
schmeicheln (dat.) (intr.)	flatter 11
schmeißen (tr. & intr.)	throw, chuck 29
schmelzen (tr. & intr.+s.)	melt 39
schmerzen (tr. & intr.)	pain, ache 11
schmieren (tr. & intr.)	grease, smear 11
schminken (refl.)	put on make-up 11
schmökern (tr. & intr.)	browse in a book 11
schmollen (intr.)	sulk 11
schmücken (tr.)	decorate 11
schmuggeln (tr. & intr.)	smuggle 11
schmusen (intr.)	cuddle 11
schnappen (tr. & intr.)	snap 11
schnarchen (intr.)	snore 11
schneiden (tr. & intr.)	cut, slice 29
schneidern (tr. & intr.)	dressmake 11
schneien (impers.)	snow 11
schnitzen (tr. & intr.)	carve 11
schnüffeln (intr.)	sniff 11
schnüren (tr.)	tie up 11
schnurren (intr.)	purr 11
schocken (tr.)	shock 11
schockieren (tr.)	shock 13
schonen (tr.)	spare, save 11
er schont sich (refl.)	*he takes things gently*
schöpfen (tr.)	scoop, draw 11
schrauben (tr. & intr.)	screw (as in screwdriver) 11
*schreiben (tr. & intr.)	write 26
schreien (tr. & intr.)	scream, call out 26
schreiten (intr.+s.)	stride 29
schrubben (tr. & intr.)	scrub 11
schrumpfen (intr.+s.)	shrink, contract 11
schuften (intr.)	slave, slog 12
schulden (tr.)	owe 12
schütteln (tr.)	shake 11
schütten (tr.)	pour 12
schützen (vor+dat.) (tr.)	shelter (from) 11
schwächen (tr.)	weaken 11
schwanken (intr.)	sway, oscillate 11
schwänzen (tr. & intr.)	play truant 11
schwärmen (für) (intr.)	rave (about) 11
schwarz|arbeiten (intr.)	moonlight 12, 15

schwärzen (tr.)	blacken 11
schwarz|fahren (intr.+s.)	travel with no ticket 76
schwatzen (tr. & intr.)	gossip 11
schweben (intr.+s./h.)	hover, glide 11
schweigen (intr.+s./h.)	be silent 26
schweißen (tr. & intr.)	weld 11
schwellen (intr.+s.)	swell 39, 11
schwimmen (tr. & intr.+s./h.)	swim, float 48
schwindeln (intr.)	lie, cheat 11
mir schwindelt (es) (impers.)	*I feel dizzy*
schwinden (intr.+s.)	dwindle, fade 45
schwingen (tr.& intr. & refl.)	swing, oscillate 42
schwirren (intr.+s.)	whizz, buzz 11
schwitzen (intr.)	sweat 11
schwören (tr. & intr.)	swear 36
scrollen (tr. & intr.)	scroll 11
segeln (tr & intr.+s./h.)	sail 11
segnen (tr.)	bless 12
sehen (tr. & intr.)	see, glance 70
sehnen (nach) (refl.)	long (for) 11
***sein** (intr.+s.)	be 1
senden (nach) (tr. & intr.)	send (for) 19
sie sendet das Signal	*she broadcasts the signal*
senken (tr. & refl.)	lower, sink 11
setzen (tr.)	put, place 11
er setzt sich (refl.)	*he sits down*
seufzen (tr. & intr.)	sigh 11
sichern (tr.)	secure 11
sicher|stellen (tr.)	make safe 15
sichten (tr.)	sight 12
sickern (intr.+s.)	seep 11
sieben (tr.)	sieve 11
siedeln (intr.)	settle (down) 11
sieden (tr. & intr.)	simmer 12
siegen (intr.)	overcome 11
siezen (tr.)	address as 'Sie' 11
singen (tr. & intr.)	sing 42
sinken (intr.+s.)	sink, fall 42
sinnen (intr.)	ponder 48
***sitzen** (intr.)	sit 67
sitzen|lassen (tr.)	abandon 10, 79
ski|laufen (intr.+s.)	ski 82
skizzieren (tr.)	sketch out 13
***sollen** (tr. & intr.)	shall, be obliged to 9
sonnen (refl.)	sunbathe 11
sorgen (für) (intr.)	look (after) 11

stauen (tr.)	dam 11
es staut sich (refl.)	*it piles up*
staunen (über+acc.) (intr.)	be amazed (at) 11
stechen (tr. & intr.)	sting, stab, bite 48
stecken (tr. & intr.)	put, be stuck 11
stecken|bleiben (intr.+s.)	get stuck 28
***stehen** (intr.)	stand 89
stehen|bleiben (intr.+s.)	stop, pause 28
***stehlen** (dat.) (tr. & intr.)	steal (from) 49
er stiehlt sich davon (refl.)	*he creeps away*
steigen (intr.+s.)	climb, go up 26
steigern (tr. & refl.)	increase 11
stellen (tr.)	place, put 11
er stellt eine Frage	*he asks a question*
er stellt es auf den Kopf	*he turns it upside down*
er stellt sich (refl.)	*he goes and stands*
stempeln (tr.)	stamp, frank 11
sterben (an+dat.) (intr.+s.)	die (of) 48
sticken (tr. & intr.)	embroider 11
stiften (tr.)	found, donate 12
stillen (tr.)	ease, suckle 11
still|halten (intr.)	keep still 79
stimmen (tr. & intr.)	tune 11
ich stimme für ihn	*I vote for him*
das stimmt	*that's right*
stinken (intr.)	stink 42
stocken (intr.)	falter 11
stöhnen (intr.)	moan, groan 11
stolpern (intr.+s.)	stumble, trip 11
stopfen (tr. & intr.)	stuff, darn 11
stoppen (tr. & intr.)	stop, block 11
stören (tr. & intr.)	disturb, bother 11
er stört (mich)	*he interrupts (me)*
stornieren (tr. & intr.)	cancel 13
stoßen (tr. & intr.+s.)	push, bump 80
er stößt auf+acc ...(intr.+s.)	*he comes upon ...*
stottern (tr. & intr.)	stammer 11
strafen (tr. & intr.)	punish 11
strahlen (intr.)	shine, glow 11
strapazieren (tr.)	strain 13
sträuben (gegen) (refl.)	resist 11
streben (nach) (intr.)	strive (for) 11
strecken (tr. & refl.)	stretch 11
es streckt sich	*it sticks out*
streicheln (tr.)	stroke 11
streichen (tr.)	stroke, paint 29

tippen (tr. & intr.)	type 11
tönen (intr.)	resound 11
töten (tr. & intr.)	kill 12
trachten (nach) (intr.)	yearn (for) 12
tragen (tr.)	carry 73
er trägt einen Anzug	*he wears a suit*
trainieren (tr. & intr.)	train, exercise 13
trampen (intr.+s.)	hitch-hike 11
tränken (tr.)	water 11
trauen (dat.) (tr. & intr.)	trust 11
wir lassen uns trauen (refl.)	*we get married*
ich traue mich, zu ...	*I dare to ...*
trauern (um) (intr.)	mourn (for) 11
träumen (von) (tr. & intr.)	dream (about) 11
***treffen** (tr. & intr.)	hit 56
er trifft mich (tr. & refl.)	*he meets me*
sie treffen sich	*they meet*
treiben (tr.)	drive 26
er treibt Sport	*he goes in for sport*
wir treiben Werbung	*we advertize*
er treibt (intr.+s.)	*he drifts*
trennen (tr. & refl.)	separate, divide 11
***treten** (intr.+s.)	tread, step 62
er tritt gegen die Tür	*he kicks the door*
er tritt ihn ans Bein (tr.)	*he kicks him on the leg*
triefen (intr.)	drip 11, 39
trimmen (refl.)	train, get fit 11
***trinken** (tr. & intr.)	drink 42
er trinkt auf mich/auf mein Wohl	
	he toasts me
trocknen (tr. & intr.+s.)	dry 12
trödeln (intr.)	dawdle 11
trommeln (tr. & intr.)	drum, beat 11
tropfen (tr. & intr.)	drip 11
trösten (tr.)	comfort, console 12
trotzen (dat.) (intr.)	defy 11
trüben (tr.)	make dull 11
es trübt sich (refl.)	*it goes cloudy*
trügen (tr. & intr.)	deceive 36
***tun** (tr. & intr.)	do, pretend 92
er tut, (als ob)	*he pretends (to be)*
turnen (tr. & intr.)	do gymnastics 11
tyrannieren (tr.)	bully 13

U   **übel|nehmen** (tr.)   take amiss 54

überwiegen (tr. & intr.)   outweigh, predominate 34
überwinden (tr.)   overcome 46
überzeugen (tr.)   persuade, convince 14
umarmen (tr.)   embrace 14
um|bauen (tr. & intr.)   adapt, convert 15
um|bringen (tr.)   kill 24
um|drehen (tr. & refl.)   turn around, turn over 15
um|fahren (tr.)   run down 76
umfassen (tr.)   comprise, encircle 14
umgeben (tr.)   surround 60
um|gehen (intr.+s.)   go around 88

     ein Gespenst geht im Haus um   a ghost haunts the house
     er weiß mit Kindern umzugehen
                       he knows how to handle children

umgehen (tr.)   avoid, bypass 87
um|kehren (tr. & refl.)   turn back 15
um|kippen (tr.)   tip over 15
     er kippt um (intr.+s.)   *he passes out*
um|kommen (intr.+s.)   perish 58
um|leiten (tr.)   bypass, divert 15
um|rahmen (tr.)   frame 15
umreißen (tr.)   outline 30
um|schalten (tr. & intr.)   switch over, change 15
umschließen (tr.)   border, enclose 40
um|sehen (nach) (refl.)   look around (at) 72
um|steigen (intr.+s.)   change (trains) 28
um|stellen (tr. & intr.)   rearrange, retune 15
     sie stellt sich auf+acc ... um (refl.)
                       she adapts to ...
um|stoßen (tr.)   upset, turn upside down 82
um|tauschen (tr.)   exchange 15
um|wandeln (in+acc.) (tr. & refl.) change (into) 15
um|werfen (tr.)   knock over, down 51
um|ziehen (intr.)   move house 33, 35
     er zieht sich um (refl.)   *he changes his clothes*
unterbrechen (tr.)   break off, interrupt 50
unter|bringen (tr.)   house, accommodate 24
unterdrücken (tr.)   suppress 14
unter|gehen (intr.+s.)   set, sink 88
unterhalten (tr.)   support 78
     er unterhält mich   *he entertains me*
     sie unterhält sich mit ... (refl.)   *she talks with ...*
unterrichten (tr. & intr.)   teach, instruct 12, 14
untersagen (tr.)   forbid 14
unterscheiden (tr. & intr.)   distinguish 27
     sie unterscheiden sich (refl.)   *they differ*

verdampfen (tr. & intr.+s.)	evaporate 14
verdanken (dat.) (tr.)	owe, be indebted (to) 14
verdauen (tr.)	digest 14
verderben (tr. & intr.+s.)	spoil 50
verdeutlichen (tr.)	make clear 14
verdichten (tr. & refl.)	compress 12, 14
verdienen (tr. & intr.)	deserve, earn 14
verdoppeln (tr. & refl.)	double 14
verdrängen (tr.)	displace 14
verdrehen (tr.)	distort 14
verdrießen (tr.)	annoy 40
verdunkeln (tr. & refl.)	darken 14
verdünnen (tr.)	dilute 14
verehren (tr.)	respect 14
vereinbaren (tr.)	arrange, agree 14
vereinen (tr. & refl.)	unite 14
vereinfachen (tr.)	simplify 14
vereinigen (tr. & refl.)	reunite, combine 14
verengen (tr. & refl.)	narrow 14
verfahren (refl.)	lose one's way 75
verfallen (intr.+s.)	decay, deteriorate 78
verfassen (tr.)	compile, write 14
verfilmen (tr.)	film 14
verflüssigen (tr. & refl.)	liquify 14
verfolgen (tr.)	pursue 14
verformen (tr. & refl.)	deform 14
verfrachten (tr.)	transport 12, 14
verfremden (tr.)	alienate 12, 14
verfügen (über+acc.) (intr.)	have at one's disposal 14
verführen (tr.)	seduce 14
*****vergeben** (tr.)	forgive, give away 60
vergehen (intr.+s.)	pass, decay 87
*****vergessen** (tr. & intr.)	forget 68
vergewaltigen (tr.)	rape 14
vergießen (tr.)	spill 40
vergiften (tr.)	poison, contaminate 12, 14
vergleichen (tr.)	compare 30
vergnügen (tr.)	satisfy 14
sie vergnügt sich mit ... (refl.)	*she amuses herself with ...*
vergraben (tr.)	bury 75
vergrößern (tr. & refl.)	enlarge 14
verhaften (tr.)	arrest 12, 14
verhalten (refl.)	behave 78
verhandeln (über+acc.) (tr. & intr.)	
	negotiate (about) 14
verhauen (tr.)	bash 14

vermitteln (tr. & intr.)	arrange, arbitrate 14
vermögen (tr.)	be capable of 6
vernachläßigen (tr.)	neglect 14
vernehmen (tr.)	hear, perceive 53
er vernimmt die Zeugen	*he interrogates the witnesses*
verneigen (refl.)	bow 14
verneinen (tr. & intr.)	answer with 'no' 14
vernichten (tr.)	destroy 12, 14
veröffentlichen (tr. & intr.)	publish 14
verordnen (tr.)	prescribe, decree 12, 14
verpacken (tr.)	wrap up, package 14
verpassen (tr.)	miss 14
verpflegen (tr.)	feed 14
verpflichten (tr.)	oblige 12, 14
er verpflichtet sich (refl.)	*he commits himself*
verprügeln (tr.)	beat, thrash 14
verraten (tr.)	betray 78
verreisen (intr.+s.)	go away 14
verrenken (tr.)	dislocate 14
verrichten (tr.)	carry out 12, 14
verriegeln (tr.)	bar, bolt down 14
verringern (tr.)	reduce 14
verrühren (tr.)	mix 14
versagen (intr.)	fail, break down 14
versammeln (tr. & refl.)	assemble 14
versäumen (tr.)	miss 14
verschärfen (tr.)	intensify 14
verschieben (auf+acc.) (tr.)	postpone (until) 34
verschiffen (tr.)	ship 14
verschimmeln (intr.+s.)	go moldy 14
verschlafen (intr. & refl.)	oversleep 78
verschlechtern (tr. & refl.)	worsen 14
verschleiern (tr.)	veil 14
verschließen (tr.)	lock, seal 40
verschlingen (tr.)	devour, gobble 43
verschmutzen (tr.)	pollute 14
verschonen (tr.)	spare 14
verschöne(r)n (tr.)	brighten up 14
verschrauben (tr.)	screw together 14
verschreiben (tr.)	prescribe 27
verschrotten (tr.)	scrap 12, 14
verschweigen (tr.)	keep quiet about 27
verschwenden (tr.)	waste 12, 14
verschwimmen (intr.+s.)	become blurred 50
***verschwinden** (intr.+s.)	disappear 46

verunglücken (intr.+s.)	have an accident 14
verunstalten (tr.)	disfigure 12, 14
verursachen (tr.)	cause 14
verurteilen (tr.)	condemn 14
verüben (tr.)	commit 14
vervielfältigen (tr.)	duplicate 14
vervollkommnen (tr.)	perfect 12, 14
vervollständigen (tr.)	complete 14
verwalten (tr.)	manage 12, 14
verwandeln (in+acc.) (tr. & refl.)	transform, change (into) 14
verwanzen (tr.)	bug 14
verwechseln (tr.)	confuse, mix up 14
verweigern (tr.)	refuse 14
verweisen (tr.)	expel 27
er verweist auf+acc ... (intr.)	*he refers to ...*
verwenden (tr.)	use 20
verwickeln (tr.)	tangle up, involve 14
er verwickelt sich in+acc ... (refl.)	
	he gets involved in ...
verwirklichen (tr.)	fulfil 14
verwirren (tr.)	confuse 14
verwischen (tr.)	blur 14
verwöhnen (tr.)	spoil 14
verwunden (tr.)	wound 12, 14
verwundern (tr.)	astonish 14
verwüsten (tr.)	devastate 12, 14
verzehren (tr.)	consume 14
verzeichnen (tr.)	record, note 12, 14
verzeihen (dat.) (tr. & intr.)	forgive (so) 27
verzerren (tr.)	distort 14
verzichten (auf+acc.) (intr.)	do without 12, 14
verzieren (tr.)	decorate 14
verzögern (tr.)	delay 14
verzollen (tr.)	pay duty on 14
verzweifeln (an+dat.) (intr.+s.)	despair (of) 14
vibrieren (intr.)	vibrate 13
vollbringen (tr.)	accomplish 23
vollenden (tr.)	complete 12, 14
voll|stopfen (tr.)	stuff, cram 15
vollstrecken (tr.)	execute 14
vollziehen (tr.)	carry out 33, 34
voran|gehen (dat.) (intr.+s.)	go ahead (of) 88
voraus|sagen (tr.)	forecast 15
voraus|setzen (tr.)	presuppose 15
vorbei|fahren (an+dat.) (intr.+s.)	drive past 76
vorbei|gehen (an+dat.) (intr.+s.)	go past 88

vorbei|kommen (intr.+s.)	come by, call in 58
vorbei|schauen (intr.)	call in 15
vor|bereiten (tr.)	prepare, get ready 12, 15
vor|beugen (dat.) (intr.)	forestall 15
vor|führen (tr.)	present 15
vor|gehen (intr.+s.)	proceed 88
die Uhr geht vor	*the clock is fast*
vor|haben (tr.)	intend 2
vorher|sehen (tr.)	foresee 72
vor|kommen (intr.+s.)	occur 58
vor|lesen (tr. & intr.)	read aloud 72
vor|liegen (intr.)	be available 61
vor|merken (tr.)	note down, reserve 15
vor|nehmen (tr.) (dat. refl.)	intend to do sth. 54
vor|rücken (tr. & intr.+s.)	advance, move forward 15
vor|schlagen (tr.)	suggest, propose 76
vor|schreiben (tr.)	specify 28
vor|spielen (tr. & intr.)	play, audition 15
vor|stellen (tr.)	introduce 15
sie stellt sich vor (refl.)	*she introduces herself*
ich stelle es mir vor (dat. refl.)	*I imagine it*
vor|täuschen (tr.)	fake 15
vor|tragen (tr.)	carry forward 76
vor|werfen (dat.) (tr.)	reproach (so.) with 51
vor|zeigen (tr.)	show 15
vor|ziehen (dat.) (tr.)	prefer (to) 33, 35

W

wachen (intr.)	be awake 11
wachsen (intr.+s.)	grow 73
wagen (tr.)	dare 11
er wagt sich (refl.)	*he ventures*
wägen (tr.)	weigh 36
wählen (tr. & intr.)	choose, vote for 11
er wählt die Nummer	*he dials the number*
wir wählen (intr.)	*we vote/hold an election*
wahren (tr.)	protect 11
wahr|nehmen (tr.)	perceive 54
wandeln (tr. & refl.)	change 11
wandern (intr.+s.)	walk, hike 11
wärmen (tr.)	warm 11
warnen (vor+dat.) (tr. & intr.)	warn (of), alert 11
warten (auf+acc.) (intr.)	wait (for) 12
waschen (tr. & refl.)	wash 73
weben (tr. & intr.)	weave 36
wechseln (intr.)	change 11

wecken (tr.)	wake 11
wedeln (mit) (intr.)	wag 11
weg|geben (tr.)	give away 61
weg|gehen (intr.+s.)	go away, depart 88
*weg|laufen** (intr.+s.)	run away 82
weg|nehmen (dat.) (tr.)	take away (from) 54
weg|räumen (tr. & intr.)	clear away 15
weg|tragen (tr.)	carry off 76
weg|werfen (tr.)	throw away 51
wehen (tr. & intr.+s/h)	blow 11
wehren (refl.)	resist 11
weh|tun (dat.) (intr.)	hurt 92
weichen (dat.) (intr.+s.)	yield (to) 29
weiden (intr.)	browse 12
weigern (refl.)	refuse 11
weihen (tr.)	dedicate 11
weinen (intr.)	weep 11
weisen (auf+acc.) (tr. & intr.)	point (to) 26
weiter|gehen (intr.+s.)	go on 88
weiter|machen (tr. & intr.)	carry on 15
welken (intr.+s.)	wilt 11
*wenden** (tr. & refl.)	turn 19
ich wende mich an ihn	*I consult him*
werben (intr.)	recruit, advertize 48
*werden** (intr.+s.)	become 3
werfen (tr. & intr.)	throw, cast 48
wetten (tr. & intr.)	bet, gamble 12
wickeln (tr.)	bind, wrap 11
widerlegen (tr.)	refute 14
widersetzen (dat.) (refl.)	oppose 14
widersprechen (dat.) (intr.)	contradict 50
wider|hallen (tr.)	resound, echo 15
wider|spiegeln (tr.)	reflect 15
widmen (tr.)	dedicate 12
sie widmet sich (dat.) (refl.)	*she devotes herself (to)*
wieder|finden (tr.)	find again 47
er findet sich wieder (refl.)	*he recovers, finds himself*
wieder|geben (tr.)	give back, resound 61
wiederholen (tr. & intr.)	repeat 14
wieder|verwerten (tr.)	recycle 12, 14, 15
wieder|herstellen (tr.)	restore 15
wiegen (tr. & intr.)	weigh 11, 32
sie wiegt das Kind	*she rocks the child*
er wiegt sich	*he sways*
wiehern (intr.)	neigh 11
wimmeln (von) (impers.)	teem (with) 11

zerstören (tr. & intr.)	ruin, destroy 14
zerstoßen (tr.)	crush 81
zerstreuen (tr. & refl.)	scatter, disperse 14
zertreten (tr.)	trample 64
zeugen (tr. & intr.)	generate, testify 11
***ziehen** (tr.)	pull 33
er zieht nach ... (intr.+s.)	*he moves to ...*
zielen (auf+acc.) (intr.)	aim (at) 11
zieren (tr.)	adorn 11
zirkulieren (intr.)	circulate 13
zischen (tr. & intr.)	hiss 11
zitieren (tr.)	quote 13
zittern (intr.)	tremble, shiver 11
zögern (intr.)	hesitate 11
zoomen (tr. & intr.)	zoom 11
zucken (tr. & intr.)	twitch 11
er zuckt die/mit den Schultern	
	he shrugs his shoulders
zu|decken (tr.)	cover up 15
zu|drehen (tr.)	turn off 15
zufrieden|stellen (tr.)	satisfy 15
zu|geben (tr.)	admit, concede 61
zu|gehen (auf+acc.) (intr.+s.)	approach (so., sth.) 88
zu|greifen (intr.)	help oneself 31
zugute|kommen (dat.) (intr.+s.)	benefit 58
zu|haken (tr.)	hook up/on 15
zu|hören (dat.) (intr.)	listen (to) 15
zu|knöpfen (tr.)	button 15
zu|korken (tr.)	cork up 15
zu|lassen (tr.)	allow, authorize 10, 79
zu|machen (tr. & intr.)	shut, close down 15
zu|messen (tr.)	measure out, apportion, 69
zu|muten (dat.) (tr.)	expect (of so.) 12, 15
zunichte|machen (tr.)	wreck, shatter 15
zurecht|finden (refl.)	cope, find one's way 47
zurecht|kommen (mit) (intr.+s.)	cope (with) 58
zurück|bringen (tr.)	bring back 24
zurück|fahren (tr. & intr.+s.)	drive back 76
zurück|fallen (intr.+s.)	fall back 79
***zurück|geben** (tr.)	give back 61
zurück|gehen (intr.+s.)	go back 88
das Meer geht zurück	*the sea ebbs*
zurück|halten (tr. & refl.)	hold back 79
zurück|kehren (intr.+s.)	return 15
zurück|kommen (intr.+s.)	come back, get back 58
zurück|lassen (tr.)	leave behind 10, 79

es zieht sich zusammen (refl.) *it contracts*
zusammen|arbeiten (intr.)   co-operate 12, 15
zu|schauen (dat.) (intr.)   watch 15
zu|schlagen (tr. & intr.)   slam, bang 76
zu|schreiben (dat.) (tr.)   credit, ascribe (to) 28
zu|sehen (dat.) (intr.)   watch, look on 72
zu|sprechen (tr.)   award 51
zu|stimmen (dat.) (intr.)   agree (to) 15
zu|teilen (dat.) (tr.)   allocate (to) 15
zu|trauen (dat.) (tr.)   credit (so.) with 15
    ich traue mir nichts zu (dat. refl.)
        I have no confidence in myself
zu|treffen (intr.)   apply 56, 58
zuvor|kommen (dat.) (intr.+s.)   anticipate 58
zu|weisen (tr.)   assign 28
zu|ziehen (tr. & intr.)   close 33, 35
    ich ziehe mir ... zu (dat. refl.)   *I incur ...*
zu|bereiten (tr.)   prepare 12, 15
zu|gestehen (tr.)   confess 91, 90
zu|nehmen (tr. & intr.)   increase, grow 54
zu|trinken (dat.) (intr.)   toast 44
züchten (tr.)   rear 12
zünden (tr.)   light 12
zweifeln (an+dat.) (intr.)   doubt 11
zwingen (zu) (tr.)   force (into), compel 42
zwitschern (tr. & intr.)   twitter 11